MASTERS OF ROCK

PAUL GAMBACCINI

BRITISH BROADCASTING CORPORATION

OMNIBUS PRESS

To my parents and grandparents

First Published in 1982 by the
British Broadcasting Corporation
35 Marylebone High Street
London W1M 4AA
and Omnibus Press
(a division of Book Sales Limited)
78 Newman Street
London W1

© Paul Gambaccini 1982

ISBN 0 563 20068 5 (BBC)

ISBN 0 711 90081 7 (Omnibus Press)
UK Order No. OP 41821

Filmset by August Filmsetting,
Warrington, Cheshire
printed and bound
in Great Britain by
Thomson Litho Ltd,
East Kilbride,
Scotland

MASTERS OF ROCK

CONTENTS

INTRODUCTION

This is a book of scripts of a radio series about artists who made hit records, and you asked for it. To be more precise, it is, chapter-for-chapter, the slightly edited transcripts of hour-long appreciations I delivered on BBC Radio 1 twenty-five Thursday evenings in the second half of 1981, many of which have been repeated in 1982.

The reason for the book, as for the repeated broadcasts, is listener demand. Devotees of particular artists wanted word-for-word printed copies of the programmes, and generalists who missed the occasional show, either because they succumbed to the siren songs of *Top of the Pops* or had to cook dinner, sought to catch up on what had eluded them.

There was far more interest in this type of radio than any of us had anticipated. Usually pop radio takes the form of a disc jockey show or an interview, the latter being either an objective history or the presentation of a new release. Producer Teddy Warrick fancied a series of subjective evaluations of leading rock heroes, illustrated only by the records of the artists in question. We anticipated a thirteen-week run, so my initial choice of subjects was confined to acts I thought well-suited to this format. This meant their own music contained a good deal of variety or that other artists had covered their compositions, offering an occasional change of pace within the hour.

Someone like Isaac Hayes, who had both vocal and instrumental successes and who wrote major hits for several stars, was perfect for this style, while a Little Richard was not. In no way was my selection of subjects an attempt to choose a thirteen-member all-star team. I was not implying, for example, that Isaac Hayes was more important to the development of rock and roll than Little Richard, though I suppose some upstart at the Cambridge Union might wish to make a case on Ike's behalf.

The first few programmes were startlingly well-received and the series immediately extended to twenty-five weeks. Aubrey Singer, the then

Managing Director of Radio, made the observation that enough time had now elapsed since the rock and roll revolution of the mid-fifties to allow one to identify those artists who had played historic roles in the development of the music. One could, free of the confusing hurly-burly of weekly charts, see the trees from the forest.

Here are twenty-five trees. The words I delivered are printed as I wrote them, with two exceptions. Since we cannot include in this book the musical selections we aired in the transmissions (that would be value for money but also grounds for legal action by the record companies), the actual introductions and back announcements of specific songs have been removed. We have also slightly altered many phrases which are not sentences. They are great for verbal effect but make little sense when read.

Otherwise the chapters are exactly as delivered, and I would remind everyone that they were written to be broadcast. Had I undertaken a prose project for publication, I would have written quite differently. There is a lot of alliterative fooling around, for example, that I put in to keep the spoken portions from being too dry. I doubt I would have dared try to slip them past a magazine sub-editor. The fanatasists among you, and I imagine there are quite a few, may wish to lie back and pretend that either they or I are presenting the programme at the very moment. If you wish to try this out and find yourself doing a good job at it, for heaven's sake tell Teddy Warrick. I can't go on doing this sort of thing for ever.

You see, it was hard, the most difficult series I have ever undertaken at Radio 1. For half a year I spent two and a half days a week researching, writing and delivering an hour-long programme on a particular subject. I couldn't not do it one week, I couldn't decide that I wanted a rest. The details of the upcoming Thursday night were always there in *Radio Times* threatening me with unspeakable censure if I didn't come through with the goods.

I have often been asked how my Oxford education could possibly be of relevance to my career, and here is one case where I can affirm it was of great importance. Having to generate an essay a week on an assigned topic proved to be direct training for this series. I therefore wish to acknowledge my debt to all my tutors, though I doubt that any of the material herein will be suitable for publication in *Proceedings of the Aristotelian Society*. Thanks must certainly go to Pauline Smith, who retyped my copy into formal radio scripts, a gruelling task if ever there was one.

I must also acknowledge my sources but do not need to go into great depth here, since those books and articles which were of most value were mentioned in the programmes themselves. Some pieces were of great use for only one show, such as Dave Marsh's *Born to Run* and Malka's interview with Joni Mitchell. Those books which proved valuable on many occasions included the *New Musical Express Book of Rock*, always best on details, the *Rolling Stone Illustrated History of Rock and Roll*, sometimes good for facts and always worthwhile for opinions, and the two chart Bibles, *Record Research* by Joel Whitburn of the US and the *Guinness Book of British Hit Singles* from the UK.

This is an exciting book for me because it weds my two greatest interests, broadcasting and writing. I can't imagine doing anything quite like it for some time. You have to be a Daley Thompson of the brain to go through so many events in so short a time. I think that, secretly, I will probably do what I hope some of you might want to do – listen to a few repeats following along with the text. After all, I'll be hearing them for the first time.

Paul Gambaccini
January 1982

SMOKEY ROBINSON

I have a letter from a Mr Tybertt of Solihull, who writes 'I was pleased to hear you'll be introducing a tribute to Smokey Robinson, although disappointed that only an hour has been allocated. A series would be more than justified. Perhaps you'd do me a favour by not starting with that Bob Dylan quote about Smokey being "America's greatest living poet" that everyone else wheels out when writing about Smokey. The man's music speaks for itself.'

It is difficult to fit into one hour the music of a man who has written over sixty hit songs and is celebrating his twenty-fifth year in show business, but I have a feeling you won't be disappointed.

By the way, I wouldn't worry about that Dylan quote 'America's greatest living poet'. How about Marvin Gaye's quote: 'Smokey Robinson is probably the greatest living poet?'

The group that would become the Miracles met in high school in Detroit in 1955 and went professional in 1957. They met an independent songwriter/producer named Berry Gordy who was originally attracted to the female vocalist of the group, Claudette. But Gordy quickly realised the great talent of the group was the lead singer and composer, William 'Smokey' Robinson, and under Gordy's supervision the Miracles recorded 'Got a Job', an answer record to the 1958 number one by the Silhouettes, 'Get a Job'. Berry Gordy liked Robinson's falsetto, which had been cultivated in admiration of Clyde McPhatter, but wasn't crazy about his early songs, most of which he rejected. One number that was recorded, 'Bad Girl', became the Miracles' first hit, making it all the way to number ninety-three.

'Bad Girl' appeared on the Chess label. 'Got a Job' had come out on End Records. What Berry Gordy was doing was leasing his Miracles productions to establish companies – just as he was doing with his hit artists, Jackie Wilson and Marv Johnson. But no matter how big a hit he had, the big company got most of the royalties, and Smokey Robinson

Opposite: Smokey Robinson (on the skateboard) with the Miracles

thought something should be done about that. He convinced Gordy that he should cut out the middle man – form his own independent record company – and keep the lion's share of the profits for himself and his artists. Gordy was convinced, borrowed eight hundred dollars, and started his own operation. The first group to sign with Tamla Records was the Miracles. Their first single on Tamla, 'Way Over There', sold sixty thousand copies, a good total for a local hit.

Smokey and Gordy then collaborated on a song that the executive believed in . . . but he didn't think much of the recorded version. Then it came to him in the middle of the night . . . cut the same song with a faster tempo. He called the Miracles and had them come into the studio at three in the morning, when they made a new version of 'Shop Around' . . . the version that became Tamla's first million seller.

'Shop Around' was number one on the rhythm and blues charts for eight weeks in 1961. Just as importantly, it reached number two in the Hot 100. Right from the beginning, the Miracles were establishing the Tamla Motown priority: make a hit record, not just for the Negro population, as it was then called, but one for the broad pop audience as well, because that's where the money is.

After 'Shop Around', the Tamla Motown string of hits began in earnest with artists like the Marvelettes and Contours. But Gordy never forgot his important friendship with Smokey Robinson. In 1963 he named him a Vice-President of the company, though his duties were primarily artistic rather than executive, and ten years later Gordy gave Robinson 235 shares of Motown worth approximately a million dollars. Previously Gordy had owned all the shares himself. The relationship was personal as well as professional. Smokey named his son Berry, and when Gordy's daughter Hazel married Jermaine Jackson years later, Robinson wrote and sang a song called 'From This Time and Place' specially for the wedding. It was probably more appropriate than the Miracles' second top ten hit, 'You've Really Got A Hold On Me'.

'You've Really Got A Hold On Me' was Smokey's 1962 top ten hit as an artist. As a songwriter/producer, he had three others that year, all for Mary Wells. The girl was not yet twenty-one, but she was a perfect vehicle for the Robinson songs 'The One Who Really Loves You', 'You Beat Me To The Punch', and 'Two Lovers'. 'Vehicle' is an appropriate word. Smokey said about the early days at Motown that 'the artists . . . don't really have anything to do with it. The producer is doing the tune so they just go and they sing it and fortunately for us we have artists who do not bitch about their songs.' It was for the company as a whole that Smokey Robinson wrote one of his weaker lyrics. Berry Gordy ordered his employees to sing it at the beginning of every staff meeting. Someone would have to sing 'We are a very swinging company, working hard from day to day/Nowhere will you find more unity than at Hitsville, USA'. According to Motown historian Peter Benjaminson, 'Gordy invariably chose people who were trying to hide, (so) some employees would jump up and down and wave and yell "Pick me! Pick me!" to avoid being chosen.'

It may not have been Robinson's most popular song with the staff, but Gordy certainly remembered it. When Smokey headlined in Los Angeles this June to begin his twenty-fifth anniversary year, Gordy joined him on stage, and they sang, 'we are a very swinging company. . . .'

The Miracles – Ronnie White, Pete Moore, Bobby Rogers and the woman who would soon drop out to become Smokey's wife, Claudette – were not averse to singing another writer's material. In 1963, shortly after Major Lance had scored with 'Monkey Time', Smokey heard Lamont Dozier playing a repetitious sequence at the piano and singing 'Dum de dum de lie'. It may not sound commercial but Smokey thought so – and he was right. It gave the Miracles the first and biggest of their three Holland-Dozier-Holland hits: 'Mickey's Monkey'.

It came in 1963 – a year when the group first came to British attention courtesy of the Beatles.

'You Really Got A Hold On Me' was included on the LP *With The Beatles* and in the American re-package *The Beatles' Second Album*. It came out in the States in 1964, the year when Smokey began a two-year period writing and producing for the Temptations. Theirs was a short but glorious relationship. Robinson brilliantly balanced the raw guttural voice of David Ruffin with a string section on beautiful ballads, while he gave the falsetto tenor Eddie Kendricks gutsy up-tempo numbers. The album *The Temptations Sing Smokey* remains one of the best in the Motown catalogue. It begins with the first big hit the Temptations ever had, 'The Way You Do The Things You Do'.

'The Way You Do The Things You Do', 'Since I Lost My Baby', 'Don't Look Back' and 'Get Ready' were just some of the classics that resulted from The Temptations-Smokey Robinson partnership. The greatest of all came out in 1965, less than a year after Mary Wells had recorded her last single for Motown. Together they made one of the most impressive couplings in pop history. Smokey wrote and produced

'My Guy' and it was Mary Wells' first number one. Then Smokey wrote and produced 'My Girl' . . . and it was the Temptations' first number one.

The Temptations would have others. Mary Wells was not so lucky. She was lured away to another company – Smokey called it 'misled' – and never had another big hit. She also missed out on a Holland-Dozier-Holland song she was scheduled to record: 'Where Did Our Love Go'. That one went instead to a struggling young trio Smokey had worked with called the Supremes.

In 1965, the year 'My Girl' was number one in America, the Miracles recorded their greatest LP, *Going To A Go Go*. It contained four top twenty hits, all of them a brilliant showcase for Robinson's talents. The first was 'Ooh Baby, Baby', probably the best example of Smokey's controlled use of his falsetto voice. The effect it has was best summed up by Nik Cohn, who wrote: 'He pleads, he sobs, he keens. Torments of one teenage girl-child, operatic agonies, and his voice breaks, bends and trembles on every last note. Sometimes it's a cry of pure pain and sometimes it's only a sigh. Either way, it would like to break your heart. So high and soft and busted. Such fractured sound: "Ooh Baby Baby" is likely the most lung-pumping ballad in pop.'

Cohn concluded, 'How can I criticise him. He only has to open his mouth and I'm melted.'

It was another English writer – and notice that the best analyses of Motown music have been written by Englishmen – who identified the key element of Smokey's songwriting. Charlie Gillett pointed out his use of apparent contradiction: in 'My Girl', the line 'I've got sunshine on a cloudy day/When it's cold outside I've even got the month of May'. There's the title of the song 'The Love I Saw In You Was Just A Mirage', and then there's the entire predicament in the Miracles' finest single. You see, there's this man who's a big success at parties, everybody thinks he's happy as can be, but if you look closely at his face, you know what you'll see?

'The Tracks Of My Tears' was one of the all-time great singles. It scored in the States in 1965 and in Britain in 1969, and become one of Robinson's most recorded tunes. 'My Girl' probably has the honour of being the most covered Smokey song, with versions by a wild selection of artists including the Rolling Stones, the New Christy Minstrels, Stevie Wonder and Little Jimmy Osmond. But Smokey's personal favourite group of covers is that of 'Tracks Of My Tears'. It's not surprising when you consider some of the talents who have spent time on it, including

Bryan Ferry, Linda Ronstadt, Gladys Knight and the Pips, Johnny Rivers (a US top ten single) and Aretha Franklin. Incredibly enough, the Miracles' original was not the last hit found on the *Going To A Go Go*, album. There was 'My Girl Has Gone', another top-notch ballad, and one of the top dance numbers of the mid-sixties, the title track, 'Going To A Go Go'.

So much of Smokey Robinson's talent is defined by what he did on the *Going To A Go Go* album. Classy ballads that would come later, like 'More Love' or the top ten single 'Baby Baby Don't Cry', or hit up-tempo songs like 'Yester Love' and 'If You Can Want,' are wonderful, but they don't quite define styles as those 1965 songs did. 'Going To A Go Go' itself was a success in early 1966 . . . by which time Britain had awakened and made Smokey Robinson's 'My Girl' a top twenty hit for the first time. Ironically, it was a version that was never a single in the United States, because the Temptations had already made 'My Girl' their song. But in the UK, it was Otis Redding's first hit.

'My Girl' by Otis Redding enjoyed two runs in the British charts, one before and one after the soul singer's death. It wasn't the only Smokey song to be a hit by other artists in 1965. Marvin Gaye had come to an impasse in his life, and, as he put it 'Smokey pulled me out of my depression'. He co-wrote and produced two big hits for Marvin: 'I'll Be Doggone' and 'Ain't That Peculiar'.

With the Marvelettes, Smokey had three major hits – records that were more sophisticated than much of the pop-oriented Motown product. Indeed, 'The Hunter Gets Captured by The Game' has been covered by Ella Fitzgerald and Grace Jones.

The vivid imagery and poetic quality of Smokey's lyrics suggested that songs must have been profoundly considered. But sometimes they just happened. 'The Tracks Of My Tears' was born when Robinson heard guitarist Marv Tarplin play the introductory riff. He liked it so much he sat down with Tarplin and wrote out a song. One day he went shopping with Al Cleveland. In reply to a shop assistant, Cleveland said 'I second that emotion' when he meant to say 'I second that motion'. When leaving the store, the two men discussed the possibilities of making the blooper the title of a song. 'I Second That Emotion' was the Miracles' second biggest hit to date.

'I Second That Emotion' became a hit in Britain by Diana Ross and the Supremes and the Temptations in 1969, meaning that Smokey scored a hit with the Supremes six years after he had stopped trying. By now the

Miracles were officially billed as Smokey Robinson and the Miracles, in recognition of his dominant role. It changed with the release of 'The Love I Saw In You Was Just A Mirage' in 1967, when Smokey first started thinking about leaving the group. That move was four years off. Another marvellous album emerged, this one called *Make It Happen*. A track on it would give the group their only British number one, but not for three years. First, came 1968, and the American top ten success of 'Baby Baby Don't Cry', then 1969 and the British breakthrough with 'Tracks Of My Tears' going to number nine on re-release. A London-based Tamla Motown executive named John Marshall decided the following year that Robinson and the Miracles needed a stronger single than their American release, so went back to the *Make It Happen* LP. He lifted out the last track on the album which, incidentally, was co-written by Stevie Wonder. In September, 1970, Smokey Robinson and the Miracles went to number one in Britain with 'Tears Of A Clown'.

The British success of 'Tears Of A Clown', was not lost on Berry Gordy, who ordered its release in America. It became number one there, too, but with a heavier drum beat added.

Smokey Robinson had finally gone to number one with one of his songs performed by his own group. But most of the big hits he wrote in the early seventies were performed by others. The Four Tops scored a top ten success on both sides of the Atlantic with Smokey's beautiful two-sided composition 'Still Water (Love)' and 'Still Water (Peace)'. The Supremes had two UK top ten hits with 'Floy Joy' and 'Automatically Sunshine'. Rare Earth sold millions of copies of their version of 'Get Ready'. But the Miracles wound down and, in late 1971, simply expired. They and Smokey started separate careers, careers that, for the most part, did not excite white America. Smokey's ballads seemed more laid back now that he had passed thirty, and his up-tempo numbers had a more freely flowing, jazz-influenced backing. *Billboard* called the seventies Smokey's 'missing decade', and the artist replied 'that's true with white radio, but not with concerts or black radio. We're back into a time period where the white stations don't readily programme black music.'

As a matter of fact, Smokey had a secret million seller in 1973, almost totally ignored by white radio and so passed over in Britain it is now deleted. His 'unknown' gold disc was 'Baby Come Close'.

During the seventies Robinson continued to make music, writing the score for the film *Big Time* and building a relationship with his Quiet Storm group. He had a minor hit in Britain with the vocalist from

Motown's Indian group, Xit. The song was 'Just My Soul Responding'. But the revival of his fortunes didn't really start until late 1979. In Britain, the Beat made the top ten with a ska version of 'Tears Of A Clown', and in America, Smokey made a very slow climb to the top ten with 'Cruisin'' which spent about half a year on the American Hot 100 and marked Smokey Robinson's return to the heart of the music business. Producer George Tobin chose one of his songs for Kim Carnes, and the result was a top ten success in a very different style from the original.

Smokey Robinson was so impressed with Carnes' reading of 'More Love' that he wrote two songs for her and presented them to producer Tobin. Smokey was unaware that Tobin was no longer working with Carnes, but when the producer suggested they cut the songs themselves, he agreed. It was a crazy way to get a hit, but what a hit: 'Being With You' went to number one in Britain and number two in the States, where it spent six weeks in the top three and was only kept out of number one by Kim Carnes' 'Bette Davis Eyes'.

The topic of 'Being With You' is the same subject as almost all of Smokey's hit songs: love. 'People got discoed out, they got messaged out,' he said recently, 'but love is everlasting. There are so many variations of it and so many things it does and causes, it's always a good subject.'

Love *is* a good subject. The American songwriter who has had the most success writing about it during the last twenty years is the man who writes about it best: Smokey Robinson.

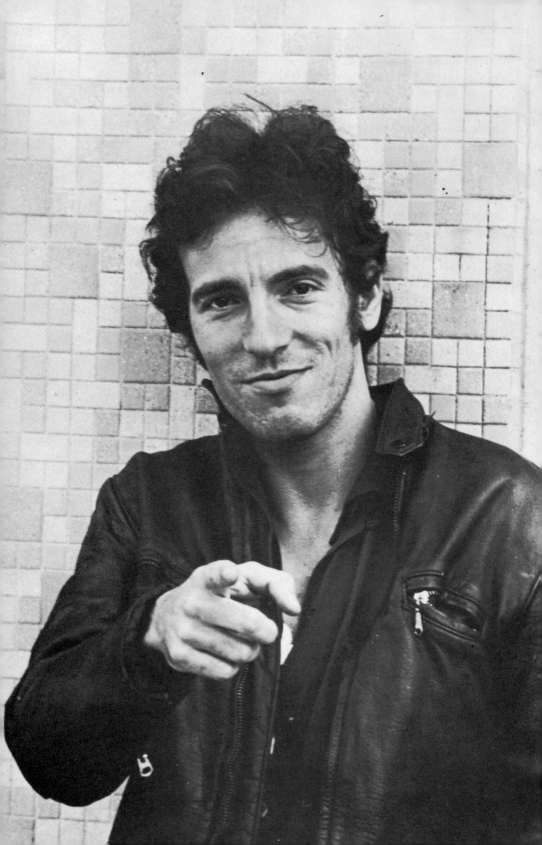

BRUCE SPRINGSTEEN

When I was at Oxford in the early seventies I used to go home to the States a couple of times a year. One of the places I'd usually go was Boston, the only town in New England that deserves to be called a city. And one friend I'd always visit was Jon Landau, the record reviews editor of *Rolling Stone* magazine. Jon was married and had a beautiful house in Concord, where the author Thoreau spent a year at Walden Pond.

But one day in 1974 Jon was talking as if that didn't matter. 'I've just seen an artist,' he said at a deliberate word-for-word pace. 'I'd throw it all in if I could just get to produce this guy.' Throw in a secure, well-paying job and a house in the country? 'The only thing I really want to do now is produce this artist. I've got a contact and I'm working on it.' I thought, to affect the life of a successful editor who's seen it all this profoundly, this guy had to be good! Who is he?

Landau looked at me with a steadfast gaze. 'His name is Bruce Springsteen.'

The impact Bruce Springsteen had on Jon Landau is typical of the effect he has on concert-goers every time he performs. It is personal and it is powerful. The great gift of Bruce Springsteen is that he is able to pass on to his listeners how much rock and roll means to him. He is a musical medium. He couldn't be unless the music had a fundamental and all-consuming importance to him when he was a boy. It did.

Springsteen was brought up in Freehold, New Jersey. As he recently told the *New Musical Express*, 'If you said you came from New Jersey, everyone'd go "Arrrrghhhh".' To outsiders, New Jersey meant the motorway that connected New York and Washington and an almost endless procession of obnoxious-smelling refineries and marshland. To holidaymakers, it meant tacky seaside towns like Atlantic City, deteriorating from its former splendour into a kind of unmaintained living museum. Asbury Park was definitely a minor league Atlantic City.

What New Jersey did have was New York City radio stations beaming their signals down the Atlantic coast. And in the early and mid-sixties, New York's top 40 radio stations played the most exciting music in the world, twenty-four hours a day.

'That music on the radio gave me my first real reason for being alive 'cos it made me *feel* alive,' Springsteen says. 'OK, I'm surrounded by all this drabness . . . but there are things in this music – real emotions, *real* joy, *real* passion, hope – that I *know* are out *there*. Rock and roll gave me that sense of wonderment and it provided both dream and a direct channel through which I could fulfil that dream.'

Born in 1949, Springsteen was introduced to rock and roll when he saw Elvis Presley on the *Ed Sullivan Show*. 'When I was nine, I couldn't imagine anyone *not* wanting to be Elvis,' he later recalled. From the age of fifteen Springsteen played in a succession of local groups, beginning with the Castiles, named after another guitarist's favourite soap. He played at a supermarket opening, a roller derby, a drive-in movie theatre. Most importantly, he played at Asbury Park, fifteen miles from home, where a club called The Upstage attracted local musicians with its late hours and open music policy. The bonds between the musicians who met in the beach town carried on into their careers and Springsteen acknowledged his roots in the title of his first album, *Greetings From Asbury Park, New Jersey*.

Greetings appeared on the CBS label. Springsteen had been signed by the legendary talent scout, John Hammond, but Hammond hadn't been looking for him. Bruce was taken to Hammond by his manager, Mike Appel, with whom he had a rapport many associates couldn't understand. Bruce didn't realise he had one of the least favourable long-term management contracts any major talent had ever signed. He didn't care. He signed it on the bonnet of a car in an unlit parking lot.

As Dave Marsh recalls in his Springsteen biography, *Born To Run*, manager Appel steamed in to his appointment with John Hammond and said 'You're the guy who discovered Bob Dylan, huh? Well we want to find out if that was just luck or if you really have ears.' Hammond, a gentleman, was insulted. 'Stop!' he cried. 'You're making me hate you!'

Whatever he felt for Appel, it was quite different from his first impression of Bruce. Springsteen sang 'It's Hard To Be A Saint In The City', accompanied only by his own guitar, and Hammond got the feeling. 'I couldn't believe it,' he remembered. 'I reacted with a force I've felt maybe three times in my life. I knew at once he would last a generation.'

But Springsteen, a rock and roll artist, had given the impression of being a voice-and-guitar folk artist, and the confusion was evident on the *Greetings* album, which was also poorly produced, recorded too quickly, and lyrically long-winded. Springsteen hadn't yet learned to edit his extremely wordy verses. It took another artist to see the potential of the songs on the LP. Manfred Mann's Earth Band released three of them as singles and one of them became a British top ten hit and an American number one in 1976.

'Blinded By The Light' was full of vivid descriptions and images. It was natural that rock critics, for whom prose is a profession, were drawn to this aspect of Springsteen's work. *Crawdaddy* Magazine compared 'Blinded By The Light' to Bob Dylan's 'Like A Rolling Stone', and CBS made the mistake of using this quote in the ads for *Greetings From Asbury Park*. Combined with the obvious fact that John Hammond had signed both Dylan and Springsteen, it had the effect of labelling Bruce the latest 'new Bob Dylan'. A succession of worthy artists had been attracting this title for half a decade, and it was invariably the kiss of death.

Things were worsened by having Springsteen appear on the bill with wildly different artists. On one tour, he supported Chicago. Without a sound check, he flopped in Madison Square Garden.

It was a formative experience. From there on in, Springsteen would almost always do his own show, or, if he was supporting, a lengthy set. This prohibited him from appearing in parts of the country where he was not yet well known. In other words, he was confined to the northeast. The second album, *The Wild, The Innocent & The E Street Shuffle*, therefore had a limited audience on its release in 1974. And radio was not going to spread the Springsteen story because none of the tracks were under four minutes. Besides, Mike Appel alienated many programmers by sending them bags of coal for Christmas because they weren't playing his client.

What saved Springsteen from being a complete wash-out was that he was developing a first-rate live act. One number, 'Rosalita', became a killer concert closer and its fine sax work by Clarence Clemmons attracted critical attention as did '4th of July, Asbury Park'. The Hollies did a more popular version of that under its subtitle, 'Sandy'.

An important new ally was Jon Landau. In the spring of 1974, he wrote a column in the Boston weekly *The Real Paper* in which he called Springsteen's second LP 'the most under-rated album so far this year'. He then went to see Bruce perform, and loved him. A month later, the group was back in town. Landau went bananas. He went home and at four in the morning, typed out his piece for the week. He listed in emotional fashion the artists who had previously touched him greatly: the Righteous Brothers, the Four Tops, the Rolling Stones.

'Last Thursday,' he wrote, 'I saw my rock and roll past flash before my eyes. And I saw something else: I saw rock and roll future and its name is Bruce Springsteen.'

A quote like that comes along once a decade, and the record company jumped on it. They even changed it around a bit: instead of 'rock and roll future', they made it 'the future of rock and roll'. But the main point is, it had the effect Landau and editor Dave Marsh had hoped: it re-kindled CBS' interest in Bruce Springsteen at a time the label was rumoured to be close to dropping him. Landau and Springsteen became friends, a relationship that was safe because they were completely different and didn't threaten each other. They found they were complementary, Springsteen with his raw talent and Landau with his critical ear for what makes a hit record and how to make a written passage less wordy.

Springsteen and Appel had only been able to finish one track for the third album. It was called *Born To Run*. Bruce brought Jon Landau in on the project, and even though the critic had only had minor experience as a producer, it was a stroke of genius. Landau helped clean up the instrumental sound on the album – there had always been an unorganised clutter in the background – and made the production perfect for radio play. Every sound and lyric line on the album had a reason for being there.

Miami Steve Van Zandt joined the band during the course of recording the album one of whose tracks showed off the group like a showcase. Springsteen, more than ever before, focused his energies and talent for maximum effect. One track better than any other shows his ability to convey the tension and challenge of contemporary urban life . . . or at least, as it is lived in the American northeast. It may be the best thing he's ever recorded: 'Jungleland'.

'Jungleland' was the last track on *Born To Run*, and if anybody wasn't already convinced, it was proof positive that here was an all-time classic album. Indeed, when I polled the world's leading rock critics in 1977 asking them to pick the all-time top LPs, *Born To Run* came in number ten.

Suddenly CBS had a major artist on their hands, and they vowed to promote him. *Newsweek*, sensing an opportunity to indict excessive music business praise and publicity, better known as 'hype', planned a cover story on Springsteen. *Time, Newsweek*'s major competitor, did not want to be caught out. Anyway, they actually liked Springsteen! The result was that for the first time a rock star was on the cover of both major American news magazines in the same week. This was in itself a media event which won further publicity. A senior *Time* executive called it the most embarrassing incident of his career . . . but Springsteen's father saw it in its proper perspective. 'Why not you on the cover of *Time?*' he told his son. 'Better you than another picture of the president.' Springsteen and The E Street Band, now a potential international act, came to London for two shows at London's Hammersmith Odeon . . . and a more disastrous campaign could not be conceived.

CBS took poster space all over London proclaiming, 'Finally London is ready for Bruce Springsteen'. The Landau quote, or shall we say mis-quote, was trotted out again and badges prepared saying 'I have seen the future of rock and roll at Hammersmith Odeon'. The hall itself had the 'Finally London Is Ready' line on the front of the building, and the foyer was decorated with the offending quotes. Springsteen went spare. He personally ripped down the posters, he ordered the badges destroyed, he went missing for a while in the afternoon. When the concert began, he interpreted the English audience's traditional reserve as a sign of failure, and retreated into himself. The finest live rock attraction in the world was not on view that night, and the pop press made full notice that, after all the hype, Bruce Springsteen had not delivered. His career was halted in its tracks in Britain, but the whole episode had even greater meaning to the man himself.

He has since called the disastrous London visit the turning point in his career, the time when he realised that by letting decisions be made for him by others, he had let control of his career slip out of his hands. He vowed the fiasco would not happen again. He began with a tortured legal proceeding to dispense with Mike Appel. The world waited three years for another Bruce Springsteen album. During much of that time bitter litigation kept Springsteen from the studio: Appel was insisting that Jon Landau be barred from producing his artist.

What kept Springsteen going was his live work. In Detroit to promote *Born To Run*, he arranged a medley of Mitch Ryder hits in honour of the Motor City star 'Devil With A Blue Dress/Good Golly Miss Molly/See See Rider/Jenny Take A Ride'. It became his traditional encore, and absolutely stole the show at the 'No Nukes' concerts for safe energy in New York in 1979.

Concerts continued to sustain Bruce Springsteen during his legal fight with management. As critic Langdon Winner observed, it was almost appropriate that in the decade when the sixties children had turned their energy towards making it in the professions, the nation's top rock and roller had become a case study for law students. On 28 May 1977, a settlement was signed. Springsteen was free of Appel, he had better terms on his CBS contract, and he could work with Landau. Four days later, the two went into the studio with the E Street Band.

It took time – it always does now with the notoriously perfectionist Springsteen – but the new album came out the following year. *Darkness On The Edge Of Town* conveyed a sense of threat evident in the title, and perhaps reacting to the traumas of the last few years, Springsteen came across as a strong but frightened animal caught in a corner. On one track, 'Candy's Room', he showed that he could capture the tension and pressure of his up-tempo numbers on quieter songs.

Darkness On The Edge Of Town was another top ten album, but it didn't produce the hit single Jon Landau, now manager Landau, was hoping for. Part of the reason was because Springsteen refused to record his most commercial material. He didn't want to be labelled a crass pop-oriented artist. He gave a song called 'The Fever' to his Asbury Park mate Southside Johnny, even though, as evidenced from live performances, he could have had a smash with his own version. Another Springsteen song he has never recorded became a hit in Britain and then America for Patti Smith. Also a New Jersey artist, Patti was once recording in the studio next door. Bruce let her finish the lyric of 'Because The Night'.

That was an international success for the Patti Smith Group in 1978, but an even greater smash came from the pen of Bruce Springsteen the following year. Bruce had written a song called 'Fire' for Robert Gordon, and the ever-shrewd producer Richard Perry picked it up for the Pointer Sisters. Their version went to number two in America, even though it was the height of the disco craze and at one point their record comes to a dead stop.

It seemed Bruce Springsteen would never have a major hit single of his own . . . especially if he kept giving his most commercial songs away. He must have made a mistake on his next album, because he kept one for himself. The album was the double LP *The River*, his most ambitious project to date. It spawned his first big 45: 'Hungry Heart'.

'Hungry Heart' proved so popular with Springsteen fans that he found it unnecessary in concert to start singing the song – audiences would do it for him, note and word perfect. Bruce would begin it himself when the point had been made, the point being that a Springsteen concert is a true communal event shared by artist and audience. Both are celebrating the range of emotional experiences rock and roll can provide. Springsteen takes his listeners on a roller coaster ride that lasts from three to four hours, plus interval. The second half is joyous celebration, an almost non-stop party featuring Springsteen's most successful up-tempo numbers and a variety of rock classics – the Mitch Ryder songs, some John Fogerty, maybe some Gary US Bonds, an old hero whom Springsteen recently co-produced and for whom he wrote a hit single.

The second half of a Bruce Springsteen concert is as good as live rock gets. It is not the future of rock and roll, it is the spirit of rock and roll's past in the present, the medium through whom and with whom we share the great highs the music allows.

The first part of the show is always different, alternating fast and slow songs. Recently Springsteen has been writing more lengthy and thoughtful ballads, reflections on the struggles of everyday people like the family and friends he grew up with. These are major lyrical pieces, and they can bring you to the verge of tears. 'Wreck On The Highway', 'The River', 'Independence Day', 'Point Blank' all these songs from *The River* are brilliantly phrased stories of people who fight against and sometimes lose to the problems of real life. Forced to pick only one, I find myself choosing 'Independence Day', perhaps because, knowing of Bruce's relationship with his dad and his bitterness over the bad jobs that kept his father from self-fulfilment, it seems the most personal.

Bruce Springsteen's reflective epics carry as much feeling as the best soul music. They are sprinkled throughout the first half of his concerts because, as he says, 'If you aren't given the whole picture, you aren't gonna get the whole picture. Without that foundation of the hard things, and the struggling things, the work things, the second half' – the rock and roll celebration – 'couldn't happen.' Bruce Springsteen is the leading live attraction in rock and roll and is at last selling records in great quantities. And yet when asked what goals can possibly be left, he recently replied 'Doing it is the goal. It's not to play some big place, or for a record to be Number One. Doing it is the end, not the means. So the point is: What's next? More of this.'

For Springsteen, this is the chance to achieve heroism every night on stage, by performing flat out for maximum effect. Those who compared him to Bob Dylan made at least one big mistake. In his early work Dylan was hoping to change society. Springsteen hopes to change the individual life: to tell the tale of one who risks everything to live to the fullest, and to be that person on stage. It is a sense of mission which is as great as the assertive mission of early rock and roll, and it is perfectly summed up in the title and the substance of Bruce Springsteen's best-known song: 'Born To Run'.

SAM COOKE

I can still remember the billboard: a gigantic poster of Sam Cooke in
New York's Times Square with the caption 'The Biggest Cooke in Town'.
He was starring at the Copacabana, America's leading cabaret, and there
he was in Times Square, his arms spread open, his white shirt unbuttoned
at the top, a smile on his face, the black man made good in the white
man's supper clubs. But then there's the scene I couldn't have witnessed:
thousands of distraught fans, pushing, shoving, screaming at the doors of
the funeral home where Sam Cooke's glass-covered coffin lay. People were
crushed, women were weeping, and the plate glass in one of the front
doors gave way. There he was, back home in Chicago, a national hero for
America's black people.

He wound up having forty-three entries in the American Hot 100 and
his songs recorded by many of Britain's greatest rock stars, but Sam
Cooke started as a gospel singer. The son of a minister, he grew up in
Chicago, and while a teenager sang in the gospel group the Highway QCs.
In 1951 R.H. Harris stepped down as lead singer of the Soul Stirrers,
perhaps America's top gospel group. He was getting disillusioned with
what he considered the vulgarising of gospel concerts, and, besides, he
thought the Soul Stirrers needed a younger member. The veteran star's
replacement was the twenty-year-old Sam Cooke. For six years the
handsome young man sang the gospel so purely and so attractively that he
became the nation's top gospel singer. There was something about the
Stirrers that was different from most gospel groups: they wrote a good
deal of their own material. Sam Cooke got his chance, and on one of the
gospel numbers he composed you can clearly hear the foundation of his
pop style. His uncanny talent for conveying great emotion in a controlled
delivery is perhaps first heard on 'Touch The Hem Of His Garment'.

It was obvious from this number that all the musical ingredients for
writing and recording pop material were present in the young Sam
Cooke. And it was clear from the enthusiastic response the star Soul

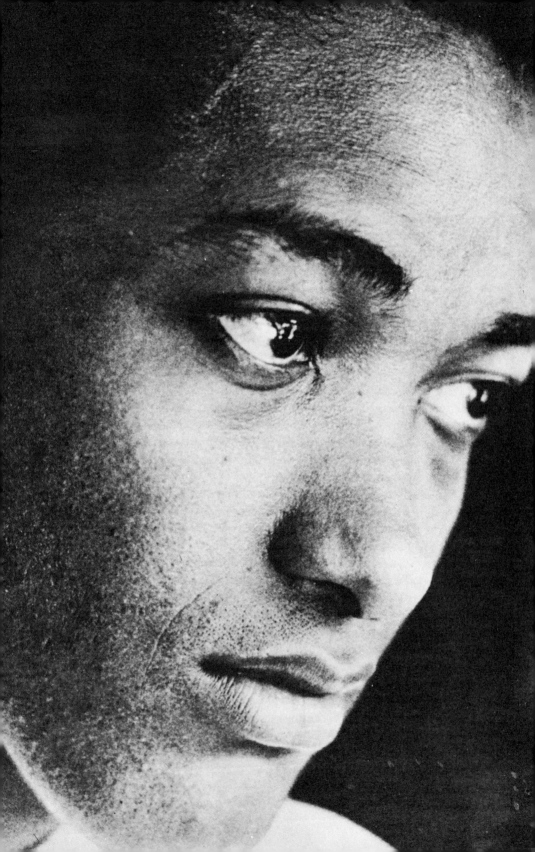

Stirrer was getting from teenage girls that the audience was there, too.

Aware of the sudden progress being made by several black artists in the rock and roll explosion of the mid-50s, Sam Cooke decided he had to try it. In 1956 he re-wrote a Soul Stirrers song called 'Wonderful' and made it 'Loveable'. But just to make sure his gospel fans wouldn't get upset, he released it under the pseudonym Dale Cooke.

'Loveable' wasn't a hit. But Cooke was encouraged to try again by his manager, J.W. Alexander, who was convinced his client could be a mass market idol, and by producer Bumps Blackwell, who enthused that Sam could be 'as big as the Platters'. They tried a number called 'I'll Come Running Back To You' and then they tried again. This time Specialty Records' white owner Art Rupe happened to visit the studio, and when he saw the white female backing group Sam was using, he drew the line. He said he would never put the record out on his label. So producer Blackwell made an agreement: if he could buy Sam's contract and his own, he'd forfeit royalties Rupe owed him from previous recordings. This suited everyone. Blackwell went down the street and made a deal with Bob Keen, who released the offending song on Keen Records. It sold 1.7 million copies and suddenly the young man who had only recently been a gospel hero was number one with his first pop hit, 'You Send Me'.

It was a sensational result. With his first single on a minor label, Sam Cooke had gone number one for three weeks in the Hot 100 and six weeks in the soul chart. The new star got the ultimate mass audience tribute, the closing slot on the *Ed Sullivan Show*, though since it was a live show and overran, he was cut off in mid-number. The only problem was it had happened so fast that no one had any idea of how to follow through. Yes, Specialty Records re-promoted 'I'll Come Running Back To You' and it was a minor hit, but the Keen Records team were at an artistic loss. They took the winning ingredients of 'You Send Me', especially what sounded like wandering improvisation on Sam's part, and applied them to other ballads. There were no great successes. Then in 1959 Cooke reached number two on the rhythm and blues chart with a song about a contemporary dance craze, 'Everybody Likes to Cha Cha Cha'. It was an important record for Sam, and not just because it was his first up-tempo success. It was co-written with two men under the unlikely pseudonym of Barbara Campbell, the high school sweetheart who became Sam's wife. Those two partners were Herb Alpert and Lou Adler, and the next single they wrote with Sam became a pop classic. At one point in August, 1959, there were three recordings of the song in the British top thirty (Craig Douglas went to number one with it), and in 1976 Dr Hook revived it and enjoyed a top ten placing in the States.

'Only Sixteen' showed a gospel influence in pop by having the vocal group pose the lead singer questions he would answer as if enlightened. It was all subdued, of course – in fact the backing singers sounded disinterested – but it showed how shrewd Cooke was in mixing the elements of various styles for maximum audience approval.

The next big song written by the Cooke–Alpert–Adler triumvirate was an even more valuable copyright. But despite the popular versions by Johnny Nash, Bryan Ferry, Herman's Hermits, and Art Garfunkel with Paul Simon and James Taylor, Sam Cooke's is still the definitive performance of 'Wonderful World'.

Once again, Cooke had scored with a pop classic. He managed to reach number two on the r & b chart as well. He was holding both audiences. The next time he reached the runner-up soul spot, in 1960, he had made an even bolder advance into the pop field. Leaving Keen Records, he turned down all offers from independent labels and signed with RCA, one of the giant labels in popular music. RCA only had one other Negro star, Harry Belafonte, and the business waited breathlessly to see if Cooke could crack it with a white record company. His first release, 'Teenage Sonata', didn't make it, but the next one did in a big way. This one reached number two not just on the r & b chart but in the Hot 100. It gives further evidence of Sam Cooke's amazing artistic juggling act. 'Chain Gang' was an out-and-out pop novelty, complete with clever grunts and groans and balls and chains that would have sounded insufferably corny with a lesser artist. But the follow-up, the moderate hit 'Sad Mood', was a straight blues ballad, genuinely touching in its understated emotion. 'Chain Gang' and 'Sad Mood' perfectly illustrate how Sam Cooke successfully fed both the pop and the r & b markets.

'Chain Gang' finally brought him to the British top ten. He returned there a year later, in 1961, with 'Cupid'. It is one of his most recorded songs. Johnny Nash and the Detroit Spinners also have had top ten versions. 'Cupid' was an international smash and hence grossed a lot of money. In an era when a great number of artists were exploited contractually, Cooke had his own publishing company, his own management company, and two small record labels. One can more fully understand Cooke's status in the r & b field when one considers his extraordinary protégés: Billy Preston, who appeared later on one of Sam's great hits; Johnnie Taylor, who replaced Sam in the Soul Stirrers and also became a million-selling hitmaker as a soloist; Bobby Womack, one of the Womack Brothers, later called the Valentinos; Mel Carter, who scored with Sam's beautiful song 'When A Boy Falls In Love'; the Sims Twins, who had a soul smash with 'Soothe Me', later a hit for Sam and Dave; and one of the greatest black music stars, Lou Rawls.

Rawls was also originally a gospel singer. Sam and his manager signed him to Alpert and Adler's Shardee record label, thinking he would eventually go pop as Cooke himself had done. We now know he did, becoming one of the major artists of the late sixties and seventies. But Rawls made his first hit appearance on one side of one of the greatest two-sided hits in history. He sang the memorable replies, in true gospel call-and-response fashion, on Sam Cooke's 'Bring It On Home To Me'. On the other side was a song of which Herb Alpert said 'One thing about Sam was that he would bring the written lyrics into the studio and you would think "This is the worst song ever": "The Cokes are in the icebox/ Popcorn's on the table"? Then he'd sing it and you'd realise it was great.' It was. It was 'Having A Party'.

'Having A Party' and 'Bring It On Home To Me' were both major hits in the same year that Sam had an international top ten record, 'Twistin' The Night Away'. In both the twist hit and 'Having A Party', Cooke showed a lyrical ability he'd first demonstrated in 'Everybody Likes To Cha Cha Cha'. He could insert references to specific records, venues and lifestyles that do not date the records as much as set a mood that survives the particulars. Proof of this came when Southside Johnny and the Asbury Jukes adopted 'Having A Party' as a virtual signature tune, nearly two decades after all the records mentioned in Sam's original had fallen out of the chart.

In the early sixties, top artists released singles with a far greater frequency than they do today. Sam Cooke was no exception. Every three months he had a new title. This partly explains why he was able to accumulate forty-three hits in only seven years of recording. Another was that the B-sides of Cooke singles often charted as well as the A-side. With the wide range of material he cut, there was something for every programmer. His 1963 titles really touched all bases: a Little Richard ballad, 'Send Me Some Lovin'', a nightclub treatment of the evergreen 'Frankie and Johnny', the blues classic 'Little Red Rooster', and a delightful out-and-out pop number, Sam's own song, 'Another Saturday Night'.

In 1963 the British beat boom was under way, but Sam Cooke could have no idea of the influence he had on one emerging group in particular. The Rolling Stones would owe both their first two number ones to Sam. Their first, 'It's All Over Now', was a cover of the Valentinos, Cooke protégés who had recorded on his Sar label. The Stones' second number one was a treatment of a song Sam had an American hit with one year earlier, 'Little Red Rooster'. Sam's version featured an organ solo by Billy Preston.

The Rolling Stones were clearly Sam Cooke fans, and they proved it again in 1965 when they recorded Sam's 1964 hit, 'Good Times'. This number later attracted a fine cover by Phoebe Snow on her million-selling debut album. It would be wonderful to play all the successful recordings of Sam Cooke's material, but it is also impossible, not just in one hour, but in all of a two-hour programme. Sam Cooke and Chuck Berry were the two most successful singer-songwriters in the early years of the rock era. Along with Fats Domino, who co-wrote many of his hits, they were true pioneers. That they were all black is eloquent testimony to the extent rock and roll was a fusion of existing American musical styles.

Sam Cooke's output in 1964 was further evidence of that. His three biggest hits that year were a gospel-flavoured piece of rejoicing, 'Good News', the party song 'Good Times', and the cabaret chestnut, 'Tennessee Waltz'. That Sam Cooke should not only record but have a top twenty hit with the latter, an old Patti Page hit, was evidence of how deeply he had penetrated the pop market. He was at the Copacabana now, the final evidence that he had completely infiltrated the white man's world. His white admirers were not confined to the United States. In Britain a succession of rock stars have had hits with Cooke songs, beginning with the Animals and going through Herman's Hermits and Cat Stevens. But the most fervent Cooke devotee is Rod Stewart, who has often spoken of his worship of the man. It's clear enough from the fact that Rod has re-recorded three of Sam's hits, but it's also obvious from Stewart's ballad singing, which is, minus the throaty quality, a near copy of Cooke.

'Tonight's The Night' sounds like a Sam Cooke record, without Sam Cooke. That is a great tribute, especially considering that it is, in itself, a great record. A few moments ago I said that Sam Cooke's Copacabana engagement was 'final evidence' of his infiltration of the pop field. The word 'final' was unfortunately a deliberate choice. Sam Cooke was shot three times when his sex drive got the better of him one night in Los Angeles. It was 10 December 1964, when Cooke tried to force himself upon a young woman in a local motel. She fled with his clothes, upon which Cooke allegedly assaulted the manageress, demanding to know the young woman's whereabouts. The manageress shot him and, when he charged her, clubbed him. He died before police got to the scene.

It was a terrible and tawdry end. Musically, it wasn't quite the end. There was one incredible single left. On the A-side was a song which became a soul classic.

'Shake' was a top ten hit in early 1965, mere weeks after Sam Cooke's death. It was ironic beyond words that the B-side of the single also became a hit and has lasted through the years as a classic. Sam Cooke may have disappointed some black people by leaving the Soul Stirrers, but he earned near hero-worship from his race by being his own man, by owning his own music companies in the days before Motown and by keeping at least some of his recordings faithful to the finest rhythm and blues. In 'A Change Is Gonna Come', Sam Cooke spoke of the improvement that would soon come to the life of the American black man. It was an eerily perceptive observation, coming mere months before some of the greatest successes of the civil rights movement. But the song is as much autobiographical testimony as it is racial commentary. If I may quote myself for a change, 'A highly expressive instrumental phrase in the second verse and the gritty texture of Sam's last chorus help to maintain a combination of grief and hope. None of the many cover versions of this song have so powerfully developed these twin themes.' I still feel that way. I know Sam Cooke's songs are standards with new hit versions every few months, but for emotional impact I always go back to this one. I like to think that 'A Change Is Gonna Come' is Sam Cooke's very personal goodbye.

ROD STEWART

He had a voice that could tear your head off, a man with a sandpaper throat gargling with acid and still managing to get the words out. If it was a rock track, that voice would take you by both ears and shake you till you were at its mercy. If it was a ballad, the voice was as soulful and expressive as that of a first-class blues singer.

The voice made him an international superstar. Then something strange happened. With wine and women, as well as song, at his disposal, Rod Stewart became the Casanova of pop, publicly lusting after every beautiful woman that crossed his path. At least, that was the image, and he worked hard to cultivate it. You had to marvel at how quickly a tacky show business image can obscure great talent. During the last half-dozen years, Britons have become accustomed to seeing Rod Stewart in their daily papers for some non-musical reason: attending a football match, changing women yet again, or, more recently, fathering two children. The first time he ever made the front page was also for a non-musical reason. He was one of twenty squatters driven out of a derelict houseboat by police using water hoses. The police sank the houseboat, and the *Daily Mirror* ran the story on its front page.

The first crowds Stewart ever led in song were on four Aldermaston Marches. He would play guitar and encourage the demonstrators to sing along. But he was too shy to sing on his own, and when he did join his first band, Jimmy Powell and the Dimensions, he concentrated on harmonica and backing vocals. 'I think Powell was a little bit jealous,' he told *Melody Maker* years later. 'He knew I could sing.' To compensate for being ignored Rod would shout as loud as he could on the backing vocals.

Don't underestimate the harmonica, though. His first appearance on a hit record was playing the mouth organ on Millie's 1964 smash 'My Boy Lollipop'. Millie was a long way from Maggie May, and Rod Stewart still had a lot of stops to make along the way. A break came when Long John Baldry heard him singing at a railway station in Twickenham. Baldry had been in the Cyril Davies All-Stars. When Davies died, the group needed a new vocalist. 'There he was sitting on the platform, singing the blues,' Baldry recalled of Rod. 'He rather impressed me; so I asked him how he'd fancy a gig.' Baldry hired Stewart, reorganised the group, and called it the Hoochie Coochie Men. Rod and John sang a duet, 'Up Above My Head', released on the B-side of a 1964 Baldry single. It was Stewart's first vocal appearance on record.

It gave neither man commercial success, but at least Rod did move up a notch in the world a few months later when Decca released his first solo single. Stewart was a blues and folk man, and picked both tracks from a Sonny Boy Williamson album he liked. The A-side was 'Good Morning Little Schoolgirl'. It was not an outstanding single. It is a sobering comment on the few tracks Rod Stewart did record with various groups in the mid-sixties that none of them enjoyed appreciable sales when reissued after his success. Many old recordings, such as the Beatles' 'My Bonnie' or Elton John's *Empty Sky*, have a considerable sale after the artist's emergence, but old Rod Stewart tracks have not earned even that distinction.

The Steam Packet and Shotgun Express didn't make it, despite having future stars like Brian Auger, Julie Driscoll, Mick Fleetwood and Peter Green. It was the Jeff Beck Group that gave Stewart his first taste of success. Beck had already scored with his out of character singalong, 'Hi Ho Silver Lining', but when he matched his frantic guitar playing against Stewart's gritty voice, the result was exciting hard rock, in evidence on the very first track of the first album, *Shapes Of Things* .

The remake of an old Yardbirds hit by a former Yardbirds guitarist won great airplay in the United States, and the Jeff Beck Group could have been major stars. But internal difficulties and Beck's reluctance to be a public hero doomed the group. In 1969 Beck sacked Ron Wood and invited two members of Vanilla Fudge to join up. 'It sounded like a good idea – but when I met them later I was completely turned off by them,' Stewart explained. 'So I split.' The strange thing about this explanation is that when he formed his own group in 1976, Rod asked one of those very same Vanilla Fudgers to play drums. It wasn't the last time he would do a turnaround on a publicly expressed opinion about a colleague.

One day in the Spaniard's pub on Hampstead Heath, Kenny Jones asked Stewart if he'd like to join the Faces, who had been the Small Faces before singer Steve Marriott departed. Between the break-up of the Beck Group and this time, Rod had already signed a recording contract as a solo artist, but there was nothing to keep him from joining a group as well. He and Wood went in with the Faces, and for a period of six years albums by Rod Stewart the individual alternated with LPs by the Faces. The solo jobs were unquestionably superior. Even on the first two, *An Old Raincoat Won't Ever Let You Down* and *Gasoline Alley*, one could see signs of a major artist in incubation. One particularly outstanding number was a Mike d'Abo song with which Chris Farlowe had scored a minor hit – 'Handbags and Gladrags'. It exemplified a virtue that was uniquely Stewart's. He had been a great blues fan, as we've said, but he had also loved folk artists like Ramblin' Jack Elliot and Woody Guthrie. He managed to synthesise the styles in his delivery, singing tales of the everyday white man with the emotion of the black man. It was a combination which served him perfectly on his third solo LP.

There is very little one can say about *Every Picture Tells A Story*. It is more appropriate to just fall on one's back and throw confetti into the air. This is a classic LP, where Stewart the lyricist, Stewart the vocalist and yes, Stewart the producer all came into their prime simultaneously. There are no fewer than four classic tracks on the album. One, 'Reason To Believe', was a Tim Hardin song chosen as the A-side of the first single. Another beautiful ballad, this one written by Rod himself, was 'Mandolin Wind', one of the most unusual songs in rock music. It's about an extremely cold winter in the American plains. A frontier settler is trying to explain his love for the woman who has stayed beside him while the land freezes and buffalo die around them. With keen perception, Stewart writes in the stumbling style of someone not accustomed to speaking the romantic, and who ironically finds his greatest eloquence when he shouts the liberating words 'I love you' over and over and over.

The characters Rod Stewart created on *Every Picture Tells A Story* seem real, no matter how odd their circumstances: the plainsman in 'Mandolin Wind', the boy already regretting his first affair with 'Maggie May', the unruly youth who goes on a sexual odyssey in 'Every Picture Tells A Story'. This title track shows another aspect of Stewart's talent. Musically, it is actually a shambles. It isn't mixed very well, someone shouts out 'hey' in the middle of a line, and the band sound as if they're playing the song for the first time. But the energy level is so high and the commitment from all the performers so complete that it works, and we are left struggling for breath as we try to take the time to appreciate the individual players and, particularly, Maggie Bell's desperate duet with Stewart.

Every Picture Tells A Story was the rarest of LPs: a work that both establishes an artist as a superstar and makes any other statement not only unnecessary but a seeming comedown. That year, 1971, it also happened with Carole King and *Tapestry* and Don McLean with *American Pie*, although McLean's British success came in '72. *Every Picture Tells A Story* was the number one album and 'Maggie May' the number one single in both Britain and America at the same time. *Rolling Stone* chose Rod as 'Rock Star Of The Year'.

As if to prove it, he closed the year with one of the most torrid rock singles of all-time, 'Stay With Me'. It is also just about the most sexually chauvinistic song ever released. On this one track the band managed to express in music what it was in life – a group of fun-loving, drink-loving lads. Attending a Faces concert in the early seventies was like going to a floating party. You could sometimes see the bottles on stage. Rod wore tartan scarves which became a craze amongst Faces audiences before the Bay City Rollers were big stars. Footballs were sometimes kicked into the audience at the end of the show and, on the tour to promote the *Ooh La La* album, cancan girls appeared. Rod's praise for his musical mates was unrestrained. 'They're a really great bunch of guys,' he said in 1972, 'so understanding. None of them have got egos . . . It's the last band I'll ever be in.' Years later, he slagged them off for all thinking they were stars. What made good mates didn't necessarily make good music. The gigs were sometimes chaotic, and in the studio the Faces never made anything to rate with 'Stay With Me'.

As the mid-70s began, some friends of the Faces thought Rod Stewart was saving his best material for his own LPs. If so, it doesn't say much for what he gave the Faces. *Never A Dull Moment*, released in the summer of '72, was not special. 'You Wear It Well', the first single from the album, was clearly derivative of 'Maggie May'. It was enough to make it number one for one week, but it broke no new ground. Indeed, for four years it suddenly appeared that Rod had dried up.

One reason was the burden of maintaining two different outputs of albums. Another was contractual arguments between the two acts' labels. But another factor was that the rooster-haired rocker put out a series of cover versions as singles. 'Angel' came from Jimi Hendrix, 'What Made Milwaukee Famous' from Jerry Lee Lewis. 'Oh No Not My Baby' had come from Maxine Brown via Manfred Mann, and 'Bring It On Home To Me' and 'You Send Me' from Rod's acknowledged hero, Sam Cooke. A 1972 hit with Rod's voice on it, 'In A Broken Dream' by Python Lee

Jackson, was two years old, and that was someone else's song that Rod had done as a session singer at John Peel's suggestion.

There was one glimmer of vintage Stewart amidst the mass of average material he was releasing. 'Farewell' was a song about a boy leaving home to try to make it in the world. Although sung from the lad's perspective, it took into account the feelings of each member of his family. It was written with such astute observation and sung with such warmth that it is one of the very best songs on the subject. 'Farewell' from the 1974 album *Smiler* was evidence that Stewart could still do it if he wanted to . . . but he seemed less inclined to. The image of the party person he had portrayed with the Faces seemed to take over, and, after the departure of Ronnie Lane in 1974, everything about that group seemed a shambles. Stewart made a courageous career move: he went to America, Muscle Shoals to be precise, and recorded *Atlantic Crossing* with veteran soul producer Tom Dowd. At least in the British market, it did the trick. A Gavin Sutherland song gave Stewart his third British number one: 'Sailing'.

Before 'Sailing' was released, Stewart acknowledged that 'this one's for the terraces'. He knew well it would be used as a chant at football stadia across the country. What he honestly did not realise was how commercial it was. Number one in 1975, it came back a year later when used in a television series about the ship *Ark Royal* and this time got to number three. But it still wasn't a world beater. In America the record company cut off the last majestic moment of the single, fearing radio stations wouldn't play a four-and-a-half-minute record. One thing was certain: they wouldn't play the remainder, and 'Sailing' failed in the United States. There could be no turning to the Faces: they were now officially pronounced defunct.

Once again, Stewart rose to the occasion, with his second-best album *Night On The Town*. There were a few good tracks on this record, but two knockouts. The first was one of the finest seduction songs ever written. 'Tonight's the Night' managed to make lust seem a comforting little feeling between friends, and made the seducer seem a nice guy. It was number one in America for nearly two months, Rod's biggest US hit. But in Britain, it was not the most successful single off the album. That distinction went to 'The Killing of Georgie', yet another example of Stewart's ability to assume the viewpoint of very different but very real people and write about them with understanding and compassion.

It seemed Rod Stewart was back at the top of his form and that the great songs might this time keep flowing. They didn't. Indeed, Rod's most moving single since then, the 1977 'I Don't Want To Talk About It', was taken from his 1975 album *Atlantic Crossing*, because fans had sung it word perfect in the 1976 concerts that were perfect examples of the rock show as communal experience. The last few wonderful hits actually contained the clues. They were all ballads. Rod Stewart, who had a reputation as a rocker, had actually lost the ability to write a good rock song. And the ballads, whose subject matter had once covered a wide range of human experience, became more and more confined to love songs.

Britt Ekland had sounded great as the female voice on 'Tonight's The Night'. But she was fatal to Rod Stewart's image. Their highly publicised affair was embarrassingly portrayed in a BBC television documentary, and Britt's love for the high life took Rod away from the roots that had kept him in touch with his audience. When the punk movement criticised him for his life style, he replied, 'What am I supposed to do with the money I earn? Give it back?'

Rod Stewart's breathtaking response to the kids who accused him of flaunting his fame in their faces was to prove them right. He kept doing it because he and/or his management thought it made good publicity. The tabloids loved it. Now they could print pictures of pretty girls and Rod Stewart at the same time. As Simon Frith observed, it was as if Rod had been willing to become a great artist as a means to the end of becoming a rich man with a lot of women. Once the end was achieved, he didn't need the art. So it seemed on disc.

Blondes Have More Fun was a historic miscalculation. One reason it was such an unusual mistake is that at the time it seemed like a triumph. The first single from the LP, 'Do Ya Think I'm Sexy', was an international number one. Yet even this track left one with a bad feeling. Stewart originally took full composer credit. Then the South American songwriter Jorge Ben pointed out that the hook in the melody line was his. Rod had heard Ben's 'Taj Mahal' on holiday and had used it, perhaps subconsciously without giving credit. In the meantime, he had given the song to UNICEF, performing in the 'Song For UNICEF' concert at the United Nations. But it had not been all his to give, and Stewart finally acknowledged Jorge Ben's contribution.

'Do Ya Think I'm Sexy' was the natural culmination of the building of Rod Stewart's image. He was the male sex symbol of rock . . . and that was all he was. In working hard to cultivate the image, he had weeded out other aspects of his talent. He had typecast himself. Most of the follow-up singles were all as cavalier as 'Do Ya Think I'm Sexy': 'Ain't Love A

Bitch', 'Blondes Have More Fun', and 'Passion'. None was a top ten hit. After fifteen top ten hits in sixteen attempts, Stewart had five in a row that fell short. Only with 'Young Turks' did Rod hint at his former brilliant form.

But those of us who revere his best work like to think that this is not the real Rod Stewart. It's like in the TV series *Soap* – aliens have replaced the Rod we know with a space creature who looks just like him but acts differently, and someday the real Rod, who is now floating out in the cosmos, will figure out a way to reverse the switch. Then we'll get more like 'Mandolin Wind', 'The Killing Of Georgie' and 'Maggie May'. If not . . . we can always listen to the oldies.

JONI
MITCHELL

If angels sang, they would probably have voices like Joni Mitchell, soaring over all they survey and gliding effortlessly from note to note. But if angels did sing, they probably wouldn't sing the songs Joni Mitchell wrote, because God's soldiers are supposed to be always happy, and Joni Mitchell is all too human. Her lyrics are honest, intimate, almost confessional, as if somehow telling the world about failed love affairs and problems of self-identity would make them all better or at least get them out of the way. But it is precisely because Joni Mitchell has told all in a poetic and frank way, singing with the voice of an angel, that she has been a unique artist.

Joni Mitchell was born Roberta Joan Anderson in Alberta, Canada, in 1943. She enrolled in the Alberta College of Art, thinking she might become a commercial artist. One evening in the early sixties she went to a jazz club because her friends liked jazz and she wanted to find out what it was all about. There was no jazz that night, but there was a folk singer, and Joni kept coming back to the club to learn more about folk music. She bought a ukelele and later a guitar, learning to play the latter instrument from a Pete Seeger instructional record.

Joni started performing in Alberta, but gave up art as a possible profession and moved to Toronto. There she found a part-time job and Chuck Mitchell, who became her short-time husband. Chuck and Joni moved to Detroit, where they worked as a duo. It was in the Motor City that they met New Hampshire folksinger Tom Rush, a major figure in the Boston folk scene and a recording artist of national stature. Rush had the uncanny ability to identify major songwriters before they had experienced success. He recorded James Taylor and Jackson Browne songs before they were well-known. In 1966, he took one of Joni Mitchell's songs to Judy Collins, but she didn't want to do it. Tom recorded 'Urge For Going' himself and scored a top ten hit in New England. It was Joni Mitchell's breakthrough as a songwriter.

'Urge For Going' was an unusual hit, not just because it was a top ten regional record that did not spread nationally and was never even released in Britain but because the instrumental accompaniment was so sparse. It was typical of the basic folk style which Joni Mitchell herself employed at the time. The single 'Urge For Going' was the peak of Tom Rush's career to that point, but it never appeared on album. Rush re-recorded it, adding another of Mitchell's verses, and included two more songs by the writer on his next LP. One of them was chosen as the title track, and it was a masterpiece. Joni had a Canadian friend who had been upset at the prospect of turning twenty-one. As she told *Zig-zag*, 'All his life . . . all the things he wanted to do, they said "Wait till you're older". Now he was older, and he didn't want to do those things any more. . . . He was lamenting lost youth at twenty-one!'

Joni Mitchell's friend was Neil Young and the song she wrote about him was 'The Circle Game'. It used the motion of a carousel as a metaphor for aging and brilliantly captured a child's sense of wonder, an adolescent's impatience to grow up and the adult's acceptance that reality is less spectacular than fantasy. I was driving up a hill in New Hampshire one night when I first heard a disc jockey named Dick Summer play 'The Circle Game' by Tom Rush. I pulled over to the side of the road and, in the peace of a New England night, listened to the track in its entirety. Joni Mitchell's words made a powerful impact on me then and there, and they still do now.

The Circle Game by Tom Rush enjoyed a healthy run in the US album chart in 1967. It brought the songwriting talent of Joni Mitchell to all America. Now Judy Collins, who had passed on 'Urge For Going,' carried the torch. She included two of Mitchell's numbers on her LP *Wildflowers*. One was 'Michael From Mountains', a romantic fantasy given an appropriate dream-like arrangement. The other song became one of the great classics of the late sixties. Dave Van Ronk had recorded it as 'Clouds', Judy Collins called it 'Both Sides Now'.

Recorded in 1967, 'Both Sides Now' gave Judy Collins her first American hit single in 1968 and her first British 45 success two years later. 1968 also saw the release of Joni Mitchell's first efforts as a performer. Her eponymous debut album was produced by David Crosby, recently of the Byrds and about to team up with Stephen Stills and Graham Nash. As a matter of fact, Stills played bass on Joni's album. The master tapes were accidentally damaged, and when they were restored the high notes had lost their clarity. Joni later said it sounded 'like we recorded it under a bell jar'. But the voice was still unmistakably hers. From the very first track she sang about her personal life with great emotion and little reserve. 'I Had A King' was about her brief marriage, now past, to Chuck Mitchell. Little had Chuck known when he married Joni that three years later she would tell the world what was wrong about him – that his car was rusty, that he wore Paisley fabrics and drip-dry shirts, that he talked about his ex-wife behind her back. In 'I Had A King', Joni sang of these things, and she had more to say three years later in another track, 'The Last Time I Saw Richard'. 'Marriage Too Soon', she wrote the first time. 'Only a phase, those dark café days', she said the second. It came to be remarked that the worst danger of having a relationship with Joni Mitchell was that you would find yourself on her next album. She was always painfully open about her private life, selling ring-side seats to her heart for the mere price of an LP.

She once said that in the early days Love Lost songs were easier to write than Love Found songs, because Love Found songs 'really take a lot of confidence, not only that you are in love, but that the other person is in love with you. Otherwise you're afraid to say all the things that you want to say. . . . You don't want to look foolish and commit yourself to all these things.'

With the moderate success of her first album, Joni Mitchell gained the confidence to release her own versions of 'Both Sides Now' and 'Tin Angel', which had been debuted by Tom Rush on *The Circle Game*. Joni's performances appeared on her second album *Clouds*, released in 1969. So did 'Chelsea Morning', which showed an up-tempo side of her work not heard before, with richer instrumental backing and, dare we say it, a happy sound.

'Chelsea Morning' cheered *Clouds*, but not everything was sweetness and light. Consider 'Songs To Aging Children Come', used in the film *Alice's Restaurant*, a cinematic expansion of Arlo Guthrie's epic about avoiding the American draft. In the movie a young friend of Guthrie dies, and in the calm that follows the tragedy, we hear 'Songs To Aging Children Come', performed by another artist.

These days it seems absurd that people in their teens and twenties should be obsessed with their own ageing. They are, after all, still very young. But in the late sixties and early seventies, the American generation which opposed the war in Vietnam, resisted racism and constructed a counter-culture was almost by definition narcissistic. Its own beliefs and habits were being constantly affirmed in the face of a hostile establishment.

In a life where to be adult amost certainly meant crossing over to the underworld, where you could 'never trust anyone over thirty', a birthday was a disaster. 'Songs To Aging Children Come' is touching today. A dozen years ago, it was shattering.

'Aging children, I am one', sang Joni Mitchell. Yet at the age of twenty-six she was in her songwriting prime. There is an endless debate as to whether pop lyrics are poems. In Joni Mitchell's case, there is little room for argument. Her best lyrics read as marvellous poems. A case in point is 'Woodstock', the songwriter's reaction to the three-day festival in New York State in 1969. In the words of this piece one can find all the optimism of that courageous if self-indulgent culture, the desire to free one's soul from material encumbrances, and the need to 'get ourselves back to the garden'. It was a lyric that could be performed in almost any style, as two contrasting versions proved. Crosby, Stills, Nash and Young reached number eleven in America with their hard rock version in the spring of 1970. Matthews Southern Comfort went to number one in Britain with soft sounds only half a year later.

Joni's own version appeared on her LP *Ladies Of The Canyon*. This album continued the consistent improvement of her long players in the range of written material, proficiency of musical performance, and extent of commercial success. Each of Joni Mitchell's first six albums reached a higher position in the American charts than their predecessors. A profitable by-product of *Ladies Of The Canyon* was the artist's first British hit single, 'Big Yellow Taxi'.

Other delights include Joni's version of 'The Circle Game', 'Willy', an almost frighteningly frank account of her relationship with Graham Nash, and 'For Free'. 'Willy' was transfixing in its loving yet lucid lyrics, but at least by now Joni's fans were accustomed to her singing about her men. 'For Free' was the first of a new group of Mitchell songs which attempted to deal with her new-found material success. As she explained to her fellow folksinger from the early days, the Israeli-born Malka, 'I had no idea that I would be this successful, especially since I came to folk music when it was already dying. I had difficulty at one point accepting my affluence, and my success and even the expression of it seemed to me distasteful at one time . . . I had a lot of soul-searching to do.'

In 'For Free', Joni addressed this dilemma, by contrasting her playing for pay with the no guarantee, no percentage set of a street-corner busker.

It was the first but not the last song Joni Mitchell wrote about fame and fortune. She kept getting progressively more popular, and deservedly so.

Blue, released in 1971, is one of the finest collections of adult love songs ever released . . . and by 'adult' I do not mean the moaning and groaning 'Je T'Aime' variety. Mitchell wrote about the ups and downs of love as it really is. When it's going well, it seems everyone who is not in love is crazy for missing out; when it's going poorly, everyone who is in love must be mad. *Blue* took Joni Mitchell to number three in the British album charts. She was now more than ever a commercial property, to use show business terminology. In the era of singer-songwriters, *Variety* called her a top 'chirper-cleffer'. Other artists flocked to do her songs. Nazareth took a track from *Blue*, 'This Flight Tonight', gave it an astonishing heavy metal reading, and took it to number eleven in 1973. Bob Dylan recorded 'Big Yellow Taxi' in what proved to be an ill-starred moment. But the wackiest fate awaited 'Both Sides Now' which attracted almost all the top easy listening stars. Perhaps because recording a ballad by an artist popular with the rock audience was a financially shrewd move, and perhaps just because it was a great song, 'Both Sides Now' was cut by Andy Williams, Glen Campbell, Frank Sinatra, Bing Crosby, Mantovani, Neil Diamond and Max Bygraves. With top names like these covering her material, Joni Mitchell made even more money, and in *For The Roses* again took stock and looked at where she was.

For someone who was having reservations about success, it seemed strange to cultivate more of it, but that's what Joni did with 'You Turn Me On I'm A Radio'. 'I've never had a hit record in America,' she told Penny Valentine in one of her infrequent interviews. 'So I got together with some friends and we decided we were going to make this hit . . . destined to appeal to DJs. Graham and David came and Neil lent me his band and he came and played some guitar and somehow it just didn't work.'

Well, not if one was hoping for a top ten single. That came with the next album, in 1974, when 'Help Me' finally introduced Joni Mitchell to AM radio. 'Help Me' reached number seven, but the album it came from, *Court and Spark*, reached number two in the LP list. This has been the high point of Joni Mitchell's career, an album of songs with first-class lyrics, tuneful melodies, and marvellous support by Tom Scott, the *LA Express*, and a host of star instrumentalists. Side One is one of the best sides of an album ever released. There's the title track, then 'Help Me' which stands on its own as a single, 'Free Man In Paris', the ultimate in getting-away-from-the-music-business, and then a coupling of two of the most desperate yet controlled statements of position a songwriter has yet made. In 'People's Parties', Mitchell tells of her inability to cope with the social demands of parties, and in 'The Same Situation' speaking of how, as a woman, she faces over and over identifiable aspects of relationships: the self-questioning, the longing for approval, the hope that this one might work, the doubt that it will. Run together on the album, they seem to constitute a definitive statement on one woman's position in social and romantic affairs.

It sounded agonising. Of course, maybe Joni Mitchell suffered no more than the rest of us, it's just that she articulated it better. But maybe she really did feel caught in an endless cycle of career pressures and romantic entanglements, in which case the only way out would be to change. That's what Joni Mitchell did.

The warning came in an interview with folksinger Malka. 'I really don't feel I've scratched the surface of my music,' Joni said. 'I'm not all that confident about my words. Thematically I think that I'm running out of things which I feel are important enough to describe verbally. . . . Most things that I would once dwell on and explore for an hour, I would shrug my shoulders to now.' This quotation pointed the direction for Mitchell's future work: more musically ambitious, less emphasis on melody, less intricacy in lyric. The process began immediately, with the 1975 album *The Hissing Of Summer Lawns*.

'The Jungle Line' on that album featured Joni Mitchell on Moog and acoustic guitar, the warrior drums of Burundi – and nothing else. The musical experimentation has continued ever since, with a jazz feel pervading the artistically successful *Hejira* and dominating the overblown double album *Don Juan's Reckless Daughter*. In sales terms, the artist's career was now going in reverse.

Jazz records almost never sell as well as pop. There are many devotees who feel Joni got the jazz/pop mix best on *Hejira*, particularly on the haunting song to the aviator, Amelia Earhart.

Since *Hejira*, Joni Mitchell's critics have not been enthusiastic, and her fellow artists have ceased covering her material. *Mingus* was virtually uncoverable, with all the material written by, featuring, or paying tribute to the dying and since deceased jazzman Charles Mingus. By its very nature, that project was a one-off, but there is evidence to suggest that Joni is, as she predicted, having problems or losing interest in writing new material. Two live albums in six releases is always a bad sign. But since she has cleared the bases with her recent work, whatever lies ahead is almost certain to be different. After all, her work has always been a direct reflection of her own life and interests, so wherever they go, so goes the music. She did give notice with that very personal Declaration Of Independence from *Court and Spark*, when she told us how wonderful it was to be free from the star-making machinery behind the popular song . . . how liberating it was to be a 'Free Man In Paris'.

LED ZEPPELIN

If I were to say rock and roll, most of you would say Elvis Presley. If I were to say big band, most of you would say Glenn Miller. And if I were to say heavy metal, what would you say? That's right.

Like Elvis Presley or Glenn Miller, or James Brown or the Sex Pistols, Led Zeppelin define a style. The best work in heavy metal music has been done by the four Englishmen, and if you never heard any HM other than theirs, you'd still know all there is to know about it. But because they came to represent one variety of popular music, we tend to forget that they more or less invented it. True, they weren't the first major hard rock group to feature long instrumental solos, Cream did that; and they weren't the first hard group to have a headbanging hit in America, Deep Purple achieved that in 1968 with 'Hush'. But before Led Zeppelin came along, the term 'heavy metal' didn't exist – a rock critic, appropriately named Lester Bangs, invented it to apply to Zeppelin and their offspring. Zep took rock one step beyond the three-minute pop songs it was accustomed to and on which only the Doors had frequently expanded. They incorporated instrumental virtuosity with distorted amplification, extremely loud volume, a relentlessly pounding back beat, and nearly hysterical lead vocals.

If this maniacal mix was anyone's idea, it was Jimmy Page's. As producer and co-writer of Zeppelin LPs, it was he who chose to place the group at what was in the late sixties an extremity of popular music. Then, as the seventies passed, he watched as scores of other groups and millions of devoted fans followed.

Page had established a solid reputation as a top session guitarist before Led Zeppelin, though you might not know it from his solo single, 'She Just Satisfies'. Page featured on classic singles like 'You Really Got Me' by the Kinks, 'With A Little Help From My Friends' by Joe Cocker, 'I Can't Explain' by the Who, and 'It's Not Unusual' by Tom Jones. Oddly enough, nothing of a high standard was recorded while he was in his first major group, the Yardbirds. Page considered it a gamble to leave a guaranteed income as guitarist for hire to play for a group with a history of personnel changes, but it was a gamble he had to take; session work was 'disgusting' him. The Yardbirds might have been great with both Page and Jeff Beck in the group, but a package tour promoted by American disc jockey Dick Clark killed that prospect. 'It was the worst tour I've ever done as far as fatigue is concerned,' Page remembered. 'It was living on a bus, driving hundreds of miles, doing double gigs every day for four weeks. We didn't know where we were or what we were doing.' Jeff Beck withdrew after two shows and was sacked, leaving Page to play lead guitar in a group that was now better live than on disc. The best record of Jimmy's days in the Yardbirds is the 'Stroll On' sequence in the film *Blow Up*, where Jeff Beck gets extremely upset with his guitar and starts an instrument smashing spree.

While Page was taking part in the final flights of the Yardbirds, the teenage Robert Plant and John Bonham were making music with the Band of Joy, a Birmingham-based group. Plant made two singles with the Band. According to *Record Collector* magazine, they're each worth £60 now. But in 1967, very few people paid anything to get 'Our Song' or 'Long Train Coming'. Despite the lack of sales, success was only a short time coming. When Terry Reid declined Jimmy Page's offer to sing in a reformed Yardbirds in 1968, he recommended Robert Plant. Plant recommended his friend Bonham as drummer. Although he had already discussed the possibilities of a group with Page while working on Donovan's *Hurdy Gurdy Man* album, bassist John Paul Jones was the last to officially join the group. 'I answered a classified ad in *Melody Maker*,' he later joked. 'My wife made me.'

If this is true, it was one of the most profitable commands a woman ever gave her husband. All four musicians were overwhelmed by their first jam session. They seemed to have been perfectly matched to create a powerful sound. Page and Plant realised early on the group could go one of two ways, either towards very intense rock or towards a folk-flavoured, acoustic sound. They were capable of either, and, indeed, from the very beginning recorded material in both veins. But it was the shockingly direct and elemental rock that set the quartet apart from other British groups. Keith Moon joked that an act like that would go over like a lead balloon. In so doing he gave the foursome their name: Led Zeppelin.

'Good Times Bad Times', the very first track from the debut album *Led Zeppelin*, was a minor hit single in America. It was going to be released in Britain but was withdrawn. Four times in their career Zeppelin started pressing singles for British release . . . four times the 45s were pulled back. All are now worth dozens of pounds. When Led Zeppelin named themselves after Keith Moon's witticism, they spelled the first word 'Led' so that no one would mispronounce it. 'Lead' could have been pronounced 'Leed'. The immediate success of *Led Zeppelin* showed that the group shouldn't have worried. It was a top ten success in both America and Britain, with plenty of airplay for both 'Good Times Bad Times' and 'Communication Breakdown', and passed the million mark in sales.

Led Zeppelin II, however, dwarfed its predecessor in both sales and lasting impact. It also caused me one of my worst nervous moments in radio. In late 1969, when it was released, I was working on my first radio station, WDCR in Hanover, New Hampshire. It was my responsibility to choose the Pick Hit Of The Week and to introduce it on my Monday afternoon chart programme. I would always play it just before the top two, to heighten the suspense. But one week I didn't think any of the new singles were going to be hits, so I had to choose an album track I thought would be a hit were it to be a single. The lead cut on *Led Zeppelin II* fit the bill, with two reservations. First, it was over five and a half minutes long. Secondly, the lead singer had a very obvious sexual experience in the middle of the record. This was not just a whole lotta love, this was passion, this was . . . doing it! I could see the main street traffic from the studio window, and I feared that all the faint of heart going home in the rush hour would switch off as soon as they heard Plant's panting. I played the Pick Hit Jingle, gritted my teeth, and started 'Whole Lotta Love'.

My fears were unjustified. Soon released as a single in America, in edited form, 'Whole Lotta Love' was a top five hit. *Led Zeppelin II* began an astonishing string: every one of the group's studio albums from there on in reached number one in Britain and either number one or two in the United States.

'Whole Lotta Love' was the definitive heavy track, with Page playing a classic riff, Jones and Bonham providing powerful backing, and Plant wailing away so far over the top there was nowhere left to go. It's a performance like that that sets standards. Perhaps 'Whole Lotta Love' was the best work by John Bonham. He played longer and harder at other times, but here he set a machine-gun drum voice in the context of the most energetic of songs. It was a prime example of physical rock and roll. Led Zeppelin at the heavy best bypassed the brain and went straight to the body. Some fans generalised the phenomenon and developed an indiscriminative craving for metallic noise, like the lunatic who crawled into then fell asleep in a speaker at a rival group's concert. But where there is free will, there will always be those who make stupid choices.

Zeppelin albums occasionally featured showcase numbers for the individual band members. There was 'Dazed and Confused' on the first album, which became a concert feature for Jimmy Page, who would solo on it just about as long as he wished. *Led Zeppelin II* boasted a track for John Bonham to show his stuff, subtly titled 'Moby Dick'. The attention given driving, pounding, thumping tracks like 'Moby Dick' obscured the soft side of Led Zeppelin. When the group's third album came out, this was no longer the case. Critics reacted as if the foursome were changing style. 'Crosby Stills and Nash had just formed,' Jimmy Page recalled in conversation with reporter Cameron Crowe. 'That LP had just come out and because acoustic guitars had come to the forefront, all of a sudden: LED ZEPPELIN GO ACOUSTIC! I thought, where are their heads and ears? There were three acoustic songs on the first album and two on the second.' Alongside 'The Immigrant Song', the acoustic material was some of the best on offer in *Led Zeppelin III*. But it was on the fourth album that the group found a way to best incorporate the two strands of their work. On 'Stairway To Heaven' the track musically builds from a soft pastoral introduction to a dynamic power-packed conclusion, much as the title would suggest. In one song, Plant and Page got to do almost everything they loved to do and everything at which they excelled. If only numbers like that could happen every album! But 'Stairway To Heaven' was no ordinary song. It was a high point of rock music's still young life, a special occasion on which an artist dared to be great and succeeded. The fans responded in kind, making the album a long-term best seller and voting the track number one on many American radio stations' all-time request lists.

One reason everybody bought the album and asked to hear the song on the radio is that it was never a single. Too long, you might say – but that didn't stop 'Hey Jude' or 'MacArthur Park'. The real reason 'Stairway To Heaven' was never a single – except, inexplicably, on an EP in Australia – is that Zeppelin, particularly manager Peter Grant, wouldn't let it come out. Instead they chose as the American single 'Black Dog'.

Because the fourth LP bore no English language title it is referred to as either Runes, Four Symbols, or Zoso, all references to the album artwork, or simply *Led Zeppelin IV*. Whatever one called it, there was little doubting it had the best single side of any Zeppelin album. Sandwiched between 'Black Dog' and 'Stairway To Heaven' were 'Rock and Roll', the second American single, and 'Battle Of Evermore', featuring Sandy Denny in duet with Robert Plant. British fans were endlessly frustrated that the Americans got all the singles, but it was part of Peter Grant's brilliant strategy. Singles were necessary in the States where, without a weekly pop press, radio keeps an artist in the public ear. But in almost all other respects, Grant kept Zeppelin's exposure to a minimum, to create demand when the boys were on supply either on tour or with a new release. So, there were almost no radio or television appearances, very few interviews, no 'photo opportunities' to give easy publicity. When the product was for sale, it was snatched up, resulting in the number one chart placings and the gigantic concert crowds. Even at the height of his phenomenal American success in the mid-70s, Elton John scoffed at the suggestion that he was the biggest British attraction in the States, saying it was far and away Led Zeppelin. He was correct. The group established box office records almost at will. Even in England, when they played Knebworth, they were the first act to play more than one day.

Zeppelin fans were desperately loyal. Their devotion was complete. They would flock to the shows and buy the new records without waiting to judge the quality. They had total knowledge of the repertoire. If you mention 'Rock And Roll' to a Zep freak, he'd think you were talking not about a style of music but about the track from *Zoso*.

The total domination of their audience did not give Led Zeppelin a broader effect on society, not in the way that Elvis Presley's popularity created a commercial youth culture or the way the Beatles changed life-styles. Society as a whole was not moved by Led Zeppelin; for the members of the group to live outside the world of heavy metal they would have to claim their outside interests for themselves. This they did. The film *The Song Remains The Same* showed these preoccupations in graphic fantasy sequences. Perhaps of greatest interest were the representations of Robert Plant's love of the countryside and of Jimmy Page's fascination with the occult. The guitarist's hobby is a source of macabre speculation for some fans and critics, but since they know less about the subject than Page does, the speculation is as fruitless as it is endless. If the heavy metal champions had to work out their own personal interests, they also had to find for themselves new musical directions. They were stereotyped, they had to try new things without much encouragement, especially from the critics, who had a field day lambasting anything unexpected, including the reggae-influenced track from the 1973 album *Houses Of The Holy* 'D'yer Maker'. Pronounced 'Jamaica', it was a top twenty US hit for Led Zeppelin. *Houses Of The Holy* was a number one album in the US and UK. The critics hated both. 'I just don't care,' Page said. 'I don't care what critics and other people think . . . Otherwise I would have been totally destroyed by the reviews . . . wouldn't I?'

Well, yes. Response to extremely cruel criticism is stoic silence, and Led Zeppelin stayed quiet for almost two years. Had their words been less harsh, the reviewers might have made an astute observation: that having invented the form and provided its definitive examples, there wasn't much point in Led Zeppelin continuing as a heavy metal group, except for pleasure and entertainment. It proved to be the case on *Physical Graffiti*, the 1975 double album, that some of the most interesting material was the different stuff, Page's acoustic instrumental 'Bron-yr Aur' and the track with Middle Eastern influences, 'Kashmir'. Veteran headbangers did get their three-minute fix, though, with 'Trampled Underfoot'.

'Bron-yr Aur' was a tribute to the Welsh cottage where Page and Plant wrote much of *Led Zeppelin III*. Robert told *Rolling Stone* the track 'typifies the days when we used to chug around the countryside in jeeps . . . Zeppelin was starting to get very big and we wanted the rest of our journey to take a pretty level course. Hence, the trip into the mountains, and the beginning of the ethereal Page and Plant.' 'Bron-yr Aur' once again focused attention, if only briefly, on the acoustic side of Led Zeppelin that paid homage to rural Britain and its folk music. The most fascinating things to happen to the group in the next three years were also tangential to their heavy metal sound. The cover of *Presence* is one of the best sleeves of all time. Designers Hipgnosis & Hardie featured a twisting black column called The Object in a series of otherwise everyday scenes. It was a complete concept, with the name of the group and the title of the LP only visible on the spine. One thousand objects were manufactured and distributed to friends and professional contacts; they still adorn the sitting rooms of several music business figures.

The Song Remains The Same was a double album soundtrack, filling a three-year gap between studio efforts.

When Zeppelin did re-emerge in 1979, they did so with another number one on both sides of the Atlantic, *In Through The Out Door*. Immediately a ballad called 'All My Love' became a radio favourite. It confirmed yet again that blues and folk fan Plant had an expressive and soulful voice. He could be gentle when he wanted to. 'All My Love' received so much airplay in America that there was no point in releasing it as a single. Better to put out another track and get exposure for that one as well, helping sales of the album into the bargain. 'Fool In The Rain' reached the American top thirty and helped give *In Through The Out Door* one of Zeppelin's longest runs at number one. What no one could have known was that *In Through The Out Door* would be Led Zeppelin's last album. John Bonham died in 1980, and the remaining three members said they would retire the group. It couldn't be Led Zeppelin any more, so it wouldn't be. It was a statement of refreshing integrity. But without meaning to sound heretical, it perhaps was a time for the men of Led Zeppelin to do something else. A form of music can only be started and its boundaries defined once. Zeppelin did that to heavy metal and they can't do it again. But whatever else they try, no one can take those pioneering achievements away from them.

Jimmy Page acknowledged it would be difficult to reach the heights again when he spoke to Cameron Crowe in 1975 about 'Stairway To Heaven'. 'It had everything there and showed the band at its best,' he said, 'as a band, as a unit. It was a milestone for us. Every musician wants to do something of lasting quality, something which will hold up for a long time, and I guess we did it with "Stairway" . . . I don't know whether I have the ability to come up with more. I have to do a lot of hard work before I can get anywhere near those stages of consistent, total brilliance.'

There might be a few people who would argue with the self-congratulations of that last line, but they aren't listening to this programme.

ISAAC HAYES

'Hold On, I'm Comin'' was a number one soul hit in the summer of 1966. It was written by Isaac Hayes and David Porter and performed by Samuel Moore and David Prater, better known as Sam and Dave. Hayes and Porter wrote a string of hits for Sam and Dave, wonderful celebrations of the excesses of love, delirious passion, as in 'Hold On, I'm Comin'', or intense emotion, as in 'When Something Is Wrong With My Baby'. At the time no one seemed to mind that two men were singing to each other about the love of one man for one woman.

At least Hayes and Porter didn't. Both of them were making their first breakthrough in show business from backgrounds they were understandably trying to escape. Porter was an insurance salesman. Isaac Hayes worked in a meat-packing plant, the last in a series of menial jobs he held by day while he made music at night.

An orphan, who grew up on his grandparents' sharecropper farm near Memphis, Hayes played in Valentine and the Swing Cats and Sir Isaac and the Doodads before getting session work in the city. In Memphis in the mid-sixties, that meant working for Stax/Volt Records, and Hayes, who had got his first job as a pianist knowing only two chords, found himself playing sax and keyboards on Otis Redding records. Stax was a small musical family, and, like most of the folks there, Hayes worked with many artists. He and Porter co-wrote for a variety of Stax stars, but most successfully for Sam and Dave and Carla Thomas, whose string of rhythm and blues hits included the pop smash 'B-A-B-Y'.

David Porter recalled that he and Hayes 'had no set pattern and just each came up with melodies, lyrics and hook lines and phrases. You see, I'm no musician . . . and Isaac could never write music, either, so it was very much teamwork.'

Porter's favourite Sam and Dave hit was one he and Isaac wrote in a friend's house in fifteen minutes. They couldn't write in the studio because Otis Redding was running over. Under such emergency conditions came the ballad classic 'When Something Is Wrong With My Baby'.

It was a number two on the rhythm and blues chart in early 1967. Sam and Dave hit the summit again later that same year with another Hayes–Porter tune, 'Soul Man', which even got to number two in the pop field. In 1969 they hit the British top twenty with 'Soul Sister Brown Sugar'.

The Stax/Volt phenomenon was at its peak for only three years, but during that short time the musicians produced hit singles with over a dozen artists.

Two of Booker T.'s M.G.s also helped Isaac Hayes out on a small piece of self-indulgence in 1967. One night after a champagne party, bassist 'Duck' Dunn and drummer Al Jackson joined Isaac for a rather rough reading of some familiar tunes. The result was the LP, *Presenting Isaac Hayes*. It wasn't very good, but it did give a clue as to what the man might do next. As he worked his way through Erroll Garner's standard, 'Misty', he recited the lyrics against a leisurely instrumental backdrop.

Presenting Isaac Hayes was not a great success, but it sold well enough to justify another album. The chance came in 1969. Stax had changed drastically in those two years. Otis Redding, chosen by *Melody Maker* readers as the world's greatest male vocalist, had died in a plane crash along with most of the Bar-Kays. Sam and Dave were breaking up, and the record company itself had left its distributing label, Atlantic, for Paramount Pictures. To present a new face to the world, Stax decided to issue albums by all its artists, over two dozen in all. Isaac Hayes cut his record with members of the re-formed Bar-Kays, and without any fanfare it was placed in the bottom right corner of the large trade advertisements for the Stax LP release. All the reader could see was the top of a giant bald head, the small name Isaac Hayes and the smaller title *Hot Buttered Soul*.

Of such humble origins do legends emerge. *Hot Buttered Soul* was one of the most successful and influential LPs in the history of black music. Hayes presented a style he had toyed with on his first LP and experimented with on one of the last Sam and Dave albums. He took a familiar pop song, prefaced it with a scene-setting monologue, and then proceeded to half-sing, half-speak his way through it, drawing out every musical possibility in the original and adding a few jazz touches of his own. The epitome of this technique is 'By The Time I Get To Phoenix'. It had taken Glen Campbell two minutes and forty-two seconds to work his way through Jim Webb's song. It took Isaac Hayes over six times as long, yet not a minute was padding.

It was a style that in the hands of others and even later in Hayes' own would become insufferably boring, but Isaac's 1969 version of 'Phoenix' is riveting from beginning to end, from his tribute to Jim Webb through his setting up of the plot, from the stirring entry of the strings to the triumphant salute of the brass, from Hayes' stated intention to talk about 'the power of love', to the crumbled lover's admission that 'I'm gonna moan now'. Everything you ever wanted to hear about soul music is in 'By The Time I Get To Phoenix'.

'Phoenix' was one of two tracks from *Hot Buttered Soul* released on a double-sided hit single. Even in edited form, it was six and three-quarter minutes, ludicrously long for radio purposes. Yet both it and the other side, 'Walk On By', were top forty hits in the United States, so strong was the sound and image of the new incarnation of Isaac Hayes. Suddenly gone was the writing partnership with David Porter. Here was the interpreter of other artists' material.

'Hot Buttered Soul' was an album that had two unexpected effects. First, it made the introductory rap and the extended track popular elements in the soul music of the early seventies. Unfortunately, almost no one could make the approach work, including, after another year of it, Isaac Hayes. Barry White was shrewd enough to take the spoken beginning and graft it onto new songs of single length, and sold many millions of records. Hayes either couldn't or wouldn't do it, and his subsequent albums concentrated on drawn-out numbers too long for singles.

It didn't matter, at least in terms of image, because the second consequence of *Hot Buttered Soul* was that Isaac Hayes became a black superstar. It was ironic, considering that one of the reasons 'By The Time I Get To Phoenix' was so long and laid-back was that he was making a lot of it up as he recorded it in a dark studio. But this deliberation and moodiness were considered signs of wisdom and sexiness. Hayes found himself called 'Black Moses', and rather than reject such a compliment, he made the most of it. He shuffled on stage in sandals, bedecked in chains, wearing a Biblical robe, his eyes covered by sunglasses, his head covered in cloth. Dancing girls attended him and an orchestra embellished his every groan. Audiences went ape with adoration. The film *Wattstax* is documentary evidence. A full stadium of Stax fans applaud Rufus Thomas, the Staple Singers, and Jesse Jackson, but when Isaac Hayes arrives they lose control. It was one of those cases where the members of a subset of society made an unspoken agreement with each other to do something nonsensical for the fun and inspiration of it.

Isaac played along. He accounted for over two-thirds of Stax' financial gross in the early seventies.

It was a tribute to Isaac Hayes' popularity that his version of 'Never Can Say Goodbye' charted while the Jacksons were still peaking with the original. But even so it only got to number twenty-two, and if 'Black Moses' was going to make another strong impact it would have to be in some other way.

Why not films? In America almost every major celebrity of any kind gets a chance in at least one movie. Hayes went to a meeting at MGM. As he later said, 'The essence of the meeting was to come up with a black piece of product, a film aimed at the black market . . . You give me a crack at the lead role, I said, and I'll deal with the music.'

Hayes left the meeting thinking he would get to star as John Shaft, a black private eye fighting for his life with both the syndicate and the Harlem mob. If he got the part, he would be going one up on his old friends Booker T. and the M.G.s, who had made the music for Jules Dassin's film *Uptight* but had not acted.

'Weeks later,' Hayes told *Black Music*, 'I got this call. "I'm sorry, but the casting's already been done, in New York, and the production's underway." But I was stuck with my commitment. I had to do the music anyway.' Every composer should have such a tough break. Isaac Hayes' soundtrack to *Shaft* proved even more successful than his rambling raps. It won him an Oscar, four Grammies and a Golden Globe. The double-album was the fastest seller in Stax history, moving over a million units in three months. The single of the theme tune reached number four in Britain and number one in America.

The theme from *Shaft* became a cliché so quickly it is hard to appreciate that it was once new. It took two hours for Isaac Hayes to write and all of the seventies for its influence to work its way through popular music. The style of guitar playing became a familiar part of American funk: along with Sly Stone and Norman Whitfield, Isaac Hayes was a prime influence in encouraging black youngsters to borrow from white rock, reclaiming the electric guitar for black music.

The sound overflowed to society at large. The Metropolitan Police used a 'Shaft'-sounding instrumental in a television recruiting message. A New York radio station used the brass finale of 'Shaft' as its news jingle. Black exploitation films followed in great numbers, and most popular black songwriters got the idea that they, too, had to write a soundtrack, though only Curtis Mayfield and Marvin Gaye did so successfully.

As a matter of fact, Isaac Hayes once again imitated himself, this time to so little effect most people aren't even aware of it. He got his wish to appear in films with *Three Tough Guys* and *Truck Turner*, but neither the movies nor his music were memorable, though Hayes insisted that a lot of his friends liked 'Pursuit Of The Pimpmobile'. It he couldn't start another trend just yet, he might as well follow one, and follow he did. In the mid-seventies Disco was the new big thing, and Isaac produced, arranged and played keyboards for the Isaac Hayes' Movement's album *Disco Connection*. The title track became a British top ten single in 1976. But the hits did not keep on coming. Album sales shrank and income dropped.

Hayes had always enjoyed conspicuously consuming the wealth he had missed as a child. He always set aside what he called 'mad money', that part of his earnings that would go for material possessions. In 1971 a journalist wrote of his office, 'He's surrounded by good hi-fi, a small colour TV, wild printed walls, fringed carpets, and sci-fi lighting, plus a womb-like chair with speakers in the headrest. It's so freaky that, on my way out, I actually had to enquire which particular panel was the door.' By the mid-seventies Hayes had several luxurious cars. Almost anyone would have been happy to live in his limousine.

This is not to say he wasn't a generous man. He was, engaging in philanthropy on a wide scale and setting up The Isaac Hayes Foundation, a charity designed to help poor and needy old people. But he did not have good financial advice. In 1978, he was three million pounds in debt, the result of what he called 'bad management, legal battles with record companies and the upkeep of a forty-man entourage'.

It seemed a sad send-off to a top talent. Then something miraculous happened to 'Black Moses'. He became successful again, and in 1979 he had three hits. The first was a re-make of 'B-A-B-Y', which had inexplicably never charted in Britain despite being a great American success for Carla Thomas. Rachel Sweet remade the record, and scored a top forty hit in the UK. Sweet was not the only female artist to score with an Isaac Hayes song in 1979. Dionne Warwick had toured with him two years earlier. Now she charted with a song he composed, 'Déjà Vu'. It won her a Grammy, but around the same time Isaac Hayes earned an award that must have meant at least as much: his first gold disc in four years. After years of drought as an artist, he returned to the American top twenty with a remake of Roy Hamilton's 1958 hit, 'Don't Let Go'. The album of the same name sold over a half million copies in the US – and that's what was needed for a gold record.

Hayes was back in the charts as an artist, just as he had come back months before as a writer. In 1981, he achieved his goal of a dramatic part in an important film, appearing as The King of New York in John Carpenter's *Escape From New York*. Where he goes now even he doesn't know for sure. He has goals, all right: he says he wants to be 'internationally accepted as an actor', that he wants to 'cover plays, musicals, things I haven't even begun to touch'. And he says he's toying with the idea of making contemporary music in the style of the seventeenth- and eighteenth-century masters.

It all sounds a bit grandiose, but no betting shop should put anything beyond a man who's already had three successful careers: songwriter, vocalist, and film composer. One just hopes that whatever his next triumph, it'll have the same honesty and feeling that went into his early songs. Before he was an actor Isaac Hayes was, fundamentally and most importantly, a 'Soul Man'.

DUSTY SPRINGFIELD

I can just see the reaction the moment the first notes of music are played. There will be those who leap to their feet, wave their arms in the air, and shout nonsense syllables to work off their excitement. That's the way that some of her fans responded to her. Then there are the others, the ones who merely bought the records – twenty-five hit titles in Britain and America in only six years. Those were the years in the mid- to late sixties when the whole world worshipped Dusty.

Mary O'Brien was born in Hampstead, London, in 1939. Her friends nicknamed her 'Dusty' because she was a tomboy who liked playing football with the boys – although, as she later pointed out, she retired from the sport at the age of fifteen. 'I was a convent girl,' she remembered, 'and I knew from the age of eight or nine that I did have this strange voice. Eventually I got the chance to act out a dream.'

In show business, dreams take a long time to come true, and there's always a period of apprenticeship the public doesn't know about. Dusty got her first experience with the Lana Sisters. She made her stage debut with them at the Savoy Cinema in Lincoln when she was seventeen. It was painful for her – not the show, she fell down a flight of stone steps. The Lana Sisters also appeared on television and on record. Dusty's first performance on disc was on their 1958 single 'Chimes Of Arcady'. The group never charted, but Dusty's next association was more successful.

Her brother Tom was due to play a folk music date with a partner. But the partner fell ill, and Tom drafted a friend named Tim Field to take his place. The show went so well they decided to stick together. They thought they'd add a female voice to give the group a fuller sound. Who better than Tom's sister, who already had professional experience? Tom's trio was called the Springfields and their debut single was 'Breakaway', a top forty hit in the summer of 1961. Their next single, 'Bambino', reached the top twenty. It was based on an Italian Christmas song introduced to them by a friend on holiday in the Riviera. The Springfields were more

popular than their two minor hits would suggest, winning the *New Musical Express* Top Group Poll in 1961 and 1962. But it wasn't until '62 that they had their first million seller. Ironically, the one that sold a million wasn't even a hit in Britain.

'Silver Threads and Golden Needles' was a country and western song that had been written in 1956. The Springfields' version became a top twenty pop hit in the United States. It was an exciting and evocative single and it gave the group the chance to go to Nashville to record an album. But no matter what the success, Dusty was always extremely modest about the Springfields. She joked that in recording sessions she would have to stand on telephone directories to get up to the height of the men. She claimed that much of the time they sang flat, and she said the only reason they sang folk was because it was the only type of music they all liked. The three individual tastes were actually very different.

It seems difficult to imagine keeping calm about the Springfields' achievements in late '62 and early '63, the poll victory as Best Group, the American gold record and then the first big British single. A top five placing and a full half year chart run were earned by 'Island Of Dreams'. Dusty claimed she recorded it suffering from laryngitis.

'Island of Dreams' was followed by another smash, 'Say I Won't Be There', though this one didn't stay in the charts quite as long. It seemed the Springfields were near the top of their profession, so they did what they thought was the only logical thing. They split.

It wasn't that they had anything against success. It wasn't that they didn't like each other. It's just that, as Tom explained, they had done everything they wanted to do. He was also observant, and he must have seen that while 'Say I Won't Be There' was top five, the Beatles were having their first number one. The group scene was changing radically.

Tom had noticed something else too. Dusty had proved a winner in two solo appearances on television, including *Juke Box Jury*, and she'd inspired a fashion following of a sort for her large bows and stacked up hair. Tom thought Dusty could be successful on her own. He was right, but he couldn't have known how quickly she would make it. Dusty's first release entered the charts in November, 1963, and by December it was in the top ten.

'I Only Want To Be With You', an all-British production written by Ivor Raymonde, reached number four in Britain and number twelve in America. It was a sensational start to a solo career. Dusty, as usual, played it down. 'It's marvellous to be popular,' she said, 'but foolish to think it will last. It never does in England.' In her case, it did. She followed her debut with a similar sounding single, 'Stay Awhile'. It was a moderate hit. Then in the summer of 1964, she topped the success of 'I Only Want To Be With You' on both sides of the Atlantic with different records, both written by Burt Bacharach and Hal David. The American release, 'Wishin' and Hopin'', charted first. It was never a single in Britain because it became a hit for the Merseybeats while Dusty's version was in the American top ten. The other half of Dusty Springfield's Bacharach–David top ten double in the summer of 1964 was 'I Just Don't Know What To Do With Myself'. While in the Springfields, Dusty had kept her love of Latin American music and rhythm and blues to herself. As a soloist, she could incorporate these forms into her work. 'I Only Want To Be With You' had been influenced by Tamla Motown, which was entering its Golden Era in the States.

Most Britons knew of Bacharach and David's work with Dionne Warwick. They didn't know about their songs recorded by other artists on Dionne's label, Scepter/Wand. Chuck Jackson had cut a Bacharach classic 'Any Day Now', and Tommy Hunt had scorched his way through the Bacharach–David number 'I Just Don't Know What To Do With Myself'.

'When I first heard the song in New York I was absolutely knocked out by it,' Dusty remembered. She made her own version. But then, as she continued, 'I played it so much I went off it. I begged my recording manager Johnny Franz not to release it.' Against her advice, Philips issued 'I Just Don't Know What To Do With Myself' and found themselves with a top three record.

It was Dusty's biggest hit to date. The follow-up, 'Losing You', didn't do quite as well, but did manage to reach the top ten.

1964 had been a year in which Dusty made an indelible impression on British pop. The music papers carried numerous articles about her. Fans knew her favourite colour was pink, her favourite food and drink syrup pudding and Coca-Cola. Her top group was the Shirelles, and the papers were full of comments about her own soulful delivery. A journalist played Mary Wells some Dusty tracks just before the 'My Guy' star left Motown. She couldn't believe it when he told her Dusty was white. Cliff Richard called Miss Springfield 'the white negress', and Dusty herself explained that 'I have a real bond with the music of coloured artists in the States. I feel more at ease with them than I do with many white people. We talk the same language.'

It therefore should have come as no surprise when, at the end of the year, Dusty refused to perform before segregated audiences in South Africa. Her signed contract insisted she'd sing to multi-racial crowds. After completing five shows, she and her management were ordered by South African officials to sign documents saying she would not play to integrated houses. Dusty and her backing group the Echoes stood by their principles and were given twenty-four hours to leave the country.

The expulsion became a cause célèbre in Britain, and South Africa was bitterly attacked in the press. The artist shrugged her shoulders and said it wasn't a political stand she was taking, it was just that music is for everyone, and everyone should have the right to hear it.

She recruited two of her best black friends to sing back-up on what became her next big hit. Madeline Bell and Doris Troy visited the recording session and were recruited in the studio to sing 'In The Middle Of Nowhere'. But the support on the next 45 was not by them, as critics assumed, but by Lesley Duncan. Dusty herself considers it her favourite of all singles she's done. By the late 70s, it was the only one she still played often at home. She loved the Gerry Goffin–Carole King song 'Some Of Your Lovin''.

'Some Of Your Lovin'' was a top ten single in late 1965, the first of three consecutive years in which Dusty Springfield was voted the World's Best Female Singer in the British pop paper polls. She appeared at the historic New Music Express poll winners concert at Wembley in early 1966, probably the greatest collection of artists Britain has ever seen. It also starred the Beatles, the Rolling Stones, Cliff Richard, Roy Orbison, the Shadows, the Small Faces, the Walker Brothers, the Who, the Yardbirds, the Alan Price Set, the Spencer Davis Group, and others, including Tom's new protégés the Seekers.

But Dusty hadn't been completely happy with 1965. She'd disappeared from the American charts, and publicly criticised her record company there for its choice of singles. She still had hits in Britain, but not as spectacularly as with 'I Only Want To Be With You' or 'I Just Don't Know What To Do With Myself'. Dusty needed a blockbuster.

It came from Italy. She had attended the San Remo Song Festival, where she heard 'Io Che Non Vivo (Senza Te)', the Italian entry.

'I've been crazy about it since I first heard it,' Dusty enthused. 'It's good old schmaltz.' The programme editor of *Ready Steady Go!*, Vicki Wickham, and the manager of the Yardbirds, Simon Napier-Bell, wrote an English lyric for the tune, and 'You Don't Have To Say You Love

Me' became Dusty Springfield's first number one. It also became an international pop standard. Dusty was hot again, and her next release was another top ten winner. It had been considered for a single before 'You Don't Have To Say You Love Me'. Now, it was the follow-up. 'People ask me if I'm trying to give up sounding coloured,' Dusty said when asked about it. 'I'm not trying to give up anything. I think this is the most adult song I have sung.' From her beloved team of Goffin and King came 'Going Back'.

'All I See Is You' became her third consecutive top ten single. Dusty was developing as one of the world's leading ballad singers. Her breathiness and her huskiness added to the emotion of songs she delivered in a voice that seemed to be dripping with feeling. She sounded completely vulnerable, yet determined to improve her position. In 1967 she gave the best qualities of her art to one of the best love songs of the decade. 'The Look of Love' came from the film *Casino Royale*. The song has outlasted the film. It stayed in the American charts for nearly four months. Though later hit versions were enjoyed by Sergio Mendes and Gladys Knight, Dusty's original remains definitive. It helped her career expand, winning her assignments to sing occasional film themes. The only thing it didn't do was give her a British hit.

Clive Westlake had already co-written two of Dusty's hits. Now he wrote one on his own. He gave Dusty his own piano-and-voice demonstration tape of a song she called 'beautiful'. She took 'I Close My Eyes And Count To Ten' to number four in the UK. Still played as an oldie on British radio, the 1968 smash was almost never broadcast in America. Dusty was by now so cross with her American company that she changed labels. She signed to Atlantic Records in the United States, retaining Philips in the rest of the world. Each label was to release titles recorded by the other. So it was that Philips in Britain issued an album recorded by Atlantic in Tennessee.

Atlantic had a reputation for the world's finest soul singers – Ray Charles, Aretha Franklin and Wilson Pickett, to name just three. When asked by a journalist if she thought the company saw her as a soul singer, Dusty naïvely replied, 'I don't think they see me that way at all. Jerry Wexler, the boss at Atlantic, sees me the way I am . . . whatever that may be.'

'Whatever' it was, was a sensitive and soulful artist who could handle almost any kind of material. Jerry Wexler took Dusty to the American Group Productions studio in Memphis. There, she recorded one of the great female vocal albums of all-time, using local musicians rather than the British players to whom she was accustomed. At first she was intimidated. These Southerners listened to a demo and then just worked on the song for a couple of hours without written parts. Dusty felt exposed and on her own. But after about a week, she got into the groove. That groove is heard throughout the LP *Dusty In Memphis* and most certainly in the international top ten hit, 'Son Of A Preacher Man'. Although the title *Dusty In Memphis* might suggest an up-tempo party album, much of the material was in keeping with Dusty's previous ballad hits. 'Don't Forget About Me' was a Goffin–King song originally done by Barbara Lewis, while 'Just One Smile' was the tear-jerking Randy Newman composition made famous in Britain by Gene Pitney. There was another track that became a top forty hit in America. Noel Harrison's version had already been a hit in Britain, so it was American audiences who got to hear Dusty's tasteful reading of 'Windmills Of Your Mind'.

The whole project had proved so successful Atlantic took Dusty to another soul centre. Philadelphia was the base of the emerging songwriting and production giants Kenny Gamble, Leon Huff and Thom Bell and it was there that the woman from Hampstead recorded yet another US hit, co-written by Gamble, Bell and Jerry Butler and produced by Bell, 'A Brand New Me'. You can only go traipsing around the soul capitals of the world for so long. Dusty found that while she was distinguishing herself in one-off projects her home base was eroding. The British pop scene had moved on and, two years later, Dusty Springfield didn't seem to fit in comfortably.

'Nothing could please me more,' she told an English reporter in 1970, 'than to find something different to do, but I can't find it. I am as I am. Where would I go to be different?'

After a couple of years of relative inactivity, she went to a place she'd once said she didn't like, California. Several plans for a comeback were formulated; none came to fruition. Some of the disappointments were due to legal problems. Some halted because, as the unpredictable artist admitted herself, 'I possess this fearsome reputation.' Some auspicious-sounding projects just didn't work out. Her 1973 album, *Cameo*, was produced by red-hot American producers Steve Barri and Lambert and Potter. Her 1978 comeback effort, *It Begins Again*, got the support of one of the most expensive promotional campaigns in Phonogram history. In 1979 she made 'Baby Love' a single written by the Buggles and Bruce Wooley, the team who penned 'Video Killed The Radio Star'.

For the dozen years since her last great success, the world has wished Dusty Springfield well. Anne Murray, the multi-million record seller of the late seventies, says that Dusty is her idol. Springfield has been publicly admired by both Elvises, Presley and Costello. Elton John often spoke of his desire to work with Dusty under the right circumstances and yet for all the support from her fellow artists, and for all the love from her undying fans clearly visible at Drury Lane comeback concerts, Dusty is unable to get to work to get results in today's idiom. Maybe the song was literally true and she just doesn't know what to do with herself. It isn't a question of having something to prove, it's having something to do.

She's living in Toronto now. There are no plans at present. But at least the greatest female pop singer of the sixties must know that whenever she needs them, as she sang in 'You Don't Have To Say You Love Me', her many supporters really are, 'close at hand'.

CHUCK BERRY

Long, long away, in a galaxy far from earth, a spaceship hurtles towards the outer reaches of the universe. It is carrying samples of human civilisation so that any intelligent race can see what kind of life is populating the planet Earth. There are drawings of men and women, and photographs of the kinds of accommodation in which they live. There are samples of their culture: a Bible, a Beethoven symphony, and 'Johnny B. Goode' by Chuck Berry.

Charles Edward Berry was born. Ordinarily one would say with authority when and where, but the reference books cannot agree. He was born in either San Jose or St Louis in either 1926 or 1931. If he was born in 1931, it was either on the 15 of January or 18 October. What is clear is that he was brought up in St Louis, a city where you could hear both country and western and what was in those days named 'race' music, later called rhythm and blues. While in high school Berry bought a six-string used Spanish guitar and eight instruction books. His teenage years were not all fun and music: he spent three years in reform school for attempted robbery.

Back in the outside world, he earned a degree in hairdressing and cosmetology and worked for General Motors. It was his primary ambition to be a hairdresser. He had to work because he had a wife and children to support.

In 1952 he started the Chuck Berry Combo and played a variety of St Louis clubs, including one called The Crank Club. Three years later, he made a rough recording of two of his songs and took it to Chicago, where he made a pilgrimage to see Muddy Waters perform. Berry persuaded Waters to let him sit in on a session. The blues giant was sufficiently impressed with the Missourian's guitar playing that he recommended he see Leonard Chess, head of Chess Records, a white man who was building a family business selling records by local blues artists to the Negro community.

Berry played Chess the two songs he'd written. The one he felt best about was a blues called 'Wee Wee Hours'. 'It was "Wee Wee Hours" we was proud of,' Berry's piano player Johnnie Johnson recalled. 'That was *our* music.' True enough, but so was the B-side, and Leonard Chess liked that one better. It started off 'Ida Red, why can't you be true, oh, Ida Red, why can't you be true?' It was not a typical blues song, but rather a curious mixture of rhythm and blues and country. There were some changes made. The title was altered from 'Ida Red' to 'Maybellene', the name of a cow in a children's book. And a few musical suggestions were made by disc jockeys, Alan Freed and Russ Fratto. So, at least, we are told. Freed, who introduced black music to white radio audiences, occasionally visited the Chess studios and made helpful comments that would increase a number's commercial potential. What we know for sure is that Alan Freed gave 'Maybellene' heavy exposure on his show and that he and Fratto received partial songwriting credit for their efforts, whatever they were. Today such behaviour would cause a scandal. In 1955, it was the way the game was played. There is no doubting the great help Alan Freed gave 'Maybellene'.

'Maybellene' was more than just a successful first release. It was number one on the American rhythm and blues chart for nine weeks in the summer and autumn of 1955. It topped the r & b airplay chart and the r & b jukebox chart. In those days, jukebox play was a very important source of revenue. It was also a top ten hit in the pop chart. To appreciate what a breakthrough this was, one need only look at the first Billboard top 100. The week the music business Bible increased its chart from thirty to a hundred titles, middle of the road music still dominated the pop chart. The only other big names of the new music in the first Top 100 were Billy Haley and Fats Domino. Chuck Berry, at number forty-two in that first chart, was definitely breaking new ground.

Presumably the success of 'Maybellene' compensated for whatever regrets Berry and his pianist Johnson had about 'Wee Wee Hours' not being the A-side. From then on Berry concentrated on his new music, and only occasionally went back to the blues. Still, it was difficult to tell from only one hit what it was that he had done right, and for the next year and a half Berry struggled to repeat his debut success.

His next two releases, 'Thirty Days' and 'No Money Down', did quite well in the r & b field, but failed to cross over to pop. Just when it appeared Berry might be a one-hit artist, he at least got a minor hit. In the summer of 1956, he scraped the bottom of the top thirty with 'Roll

Over Beethoven'.

Elements of style were beginning to emerge. For a successful lyric, include references to which teenagers can relate: cars in 'Maybellene', blue suede shoes and the emerging new music in 'Roll Over Beethoven'. For a successful instrumental track, keep the rhythm flowing, repetitively when possible, with a guitar line that goes back and forth between alternating chords.

Because radio stations today feature oldies almost exclusively from the rock era, an entire generation of music fans is growing up with virtually no knowledge of what happened in popular music before 1955. It's as if God created Adam and Eve and then, in 1955, gave us Elvis Presley and Chuck Berry. But as original as Berry was, he must himself have been inspired by someone. Chuck never denied it. He told reporters his hero had been Louis Jordan.

Jordan's humorous comments on the fashions and habits of his day, performed in boogie and swing styles, made him the favourite of fun-seeking Negroes and hip white youngsters. He was one of the few coloured artists to score pop hits in the forties, and he dominated the jukebox and race lists. In 1949 he spent twelve weeks at number one on the newly-named rhythm and blues chart with a song the young Chuck Berry must have heard dozens of times, 'Saturday Night Fish Fry'. Jordan used scenes from contemporary life in popular song. Chuck Berry did this in the mid-50s. But the new artist had to get still one more element right before he could begin a string of hits. He had to speak in the young record buyer's idiom. Several of his first singles were about everyday life, all right, but they were about problems and, in many cases, adult problems.

Such was the case with the two-sided single that entered the r & b chart in October, 1956. 'Too Much Monkey Business' was too negative sounding, dealing with difficulties at work, in school and in the army. 'Brown-Eyed Handsome Man' was about troubled adults, starting off with a timeless reference to getting in trouble for not having a job. Neither title was fully appreciated for several years – in the case of 'Brown-Eyed Handsome Man', not until Buddy Holly posthumously took the song to number three in Britain in 1963. When neither side was a pop hit, Chuck had the inspiration of directly addressing the adolescent audience that was suddenly buying records in great quantities. 'Up in the morning and out to school,' he wrote. 'The teacher is teaching the golden rule.' So began 'School Day', the recitation of a day in the life of a school child. But it isn't all gloomy, because school gets out at 3 o'clock, everyone heads for the juke joint and dances and romances to their favourite hot sounds. 'School Day' came out in March, 1957, and became Chuck Berry's second top ten single and second rhythm and blues number one. Most incredibly, it stayed in the Top 100 for twenty-six weeks, a full half year. The man had found his groove. In 1958 he had three major hits, 'Rock and Roll Music', 'Sweet little Sixteen' and 'Johnny B. Goode'.

'Sweet Little Sixteen' even made the top twenty in Britain, which was very slow to give Berry recognition.

Both 'Rock and Roll Music' and 'Sweet Little Sixteen' are good examples of the incessant rambling piano playing in Chuck's singles. It was a curious and attention-grabbing feature. You never knew where the pianist was going to go next, but you knew he would be busy. You also thought that since he was usually kept in the background you were on to a secret part of Chuck Berry's success. This added to the sense of participation in the record that came from Berry's lyrics. He talked the teenage language at a time when many adults were still hostile or, almost as bad, condescending. But instead of addressing the audience like an elder, Chuck coolly described the lifestyle and related the action. A young listener could feel he was going through the record parallel to Berry. Teenage America couldn't help but feel a record was about them and for them when their cult programme, *American Bandstand*, was referred to, and when many of their home towns were mentioned by name, as they were in 'Sweet Little Sixteen'.

This massive success burned an impression in almost every teenage brain in America. It obviously influenced Brian Wilson, because when he wrote 'Surfin' USA' for the Beach Boys, he merely wrote new words to the 'Sweet Little Sixteen' tune, ultimately giving Chuck Berry composer credit. 'Surfin' USA' is about as white a record as you can get, performed by a bunch of California boys and talking about something only a privileged few whites ever got to try. That it should be based on a Chuck Berry song testifies to how Berry got through to white kids far more than to black youngsters. Despite his three early r & b number ones, Berry was predominantly a rock and roll star. He appeared in four films, three of which were rock and roll movies (the fourth was a documentary about the Newport Jazz Festival).

Chuck was also a headliner on several of the great rock and roll package tours of the late 50s. He made sensational concert viewing because of his personal trademark, the duck walk. There are two good descriptions of the duck walk. One is just to say that he walked across the stage like a duck. The second came from Nik Cohn, who saw him 'bounding across the stage on his heels, knees bent, body jack-knifed and guitar clamped firmly to his gut. Then he would peep coyly over his shoulders and look like sweet little sixteen herself, all big eyes and fluttering lids.' It was the perfect way to deliver a song like 'Carol', just one of many titles now recognised as rock standards. Berry was the unofficial poet laureate of America's teenagers.

There is a law about teenagers in the United States. It's called the Mann Act, and it says that you can't transport a minor across state lines for sexual purposes. In 1959 Chuck Berry was charged with violating the Mann Act. He'd brought a Spanish-speaking Apache prostitute from Texas to work in his St Louis night club. When she told the police Chuck had violated her, Berry denied the charge. The police believed the prostitute. Berry's first trial was ruled invalid because it had racist overtones. He was less lucky the second time around. Chuck Berry was sent to jail for two years.

He always maintained he was innocent, that the whole point of the exercise had been to punish a black man for becoming rich and famous. If that was the goal, it was achieved. Berry's wife separated from him, a terrible trauma. Unable to record or perform, he disappeared from the charts and the stage. He instantly became a historical figure. He sat in jail while the whole world of popular music left him behind.

Berry's good name was rehabilitated not by the legal process but by the white youngsters he had meant so much to in the fifties. Now they were old enough to perform, and they chose to perform his songs. In 1963, a twenty-one-year-old Indiana guitarist recorded a 1959 song and took it to the American top ten. Lonnie Mack's 'Memphis' remains the best instrumental version of a Chuck Berry composition. While it was in the American top ten, another Berry composition was entering the British hit parade. The Rolling Stones, a white rhythm and blues combo starting to make it on the London scene, climbed to position twenty-one with their debut single, Chuck Berry's 'Come On'. This was the first of many Chuck Berry songs recorded by the Rolling Stones. They turned to him more than any other writer. The Stones knew something that other rock groups would quickly learn: that Chuck Berry's songs were both easy to play and, because of their steady level of excitement, guaranteed crowd pleasers. From the early days of the Rolling Stones, Chuck Berry became the writer out of residence for any new group.

The Beatles were fans of many of the same stars the Stones loved. On *With The Beatles* they paid their tribute to Chuck Berry by turning George Harrison loose on 'Roll Over Beethoven'.

What a wonderful coming-out-of-prison present for Chuck Berry. The new idols of the Western world idolised him! Britain gave him a 'welcome home' gift of its own. Mick Jagger had talked so favourably about Chuck Berry that a release of 'Memphis' prompted by Lonnie Mack's American success went into the British top ten at the very end of 1963.

Being freed was enough stimulus to get back into the studio. To have a top ten hit and prestigious cover versions was further encouragement. In January, 1964, Berry cut two sides that would become hit singles, 'Nadine' and 'You Never Can Tell'. But 'You Never Can Tell' was not issued immediately after 'Nadine'. That distinction went to a song recorded a month after the January session. It became a major hit, taking Berry to number three in Britain and giving him yet another US winner. Chuck was never one to alter a successful formula, so you'd be forgiven for noticing elements of previous hits in 'No Particular Place To Go'.

'No Particular Place To Go' gave Chuck Berry his greatest commercial success to date in Britain. The follow-up may have taken him to a new artistic peak. The lyric evoked the small touches that go into a young romance. Once again, naming actual goods and activities made the song relevant to the people who would be hearing and buying the record. 'The coolerator was crammed with TV dinners and ginger ale', 'They bought a souped-up Jidney, was a cherry-red '53'. 'You Never Can Tell' was a rich record, so full of clever and affectionate touches it seemed the writer must have a wealth of material in the pipeline. He didn't. For the rest of the sixties, Chuck Berry produced almost nothing noteworthy. He dried up.

The transition between 1964 and the rest of the decade was so abrupt there are those who believe that the 1964 hits were songs written before the imprisonment and merely recorded at the first opportunity. Whatever the case, the stars of the sixties made it certain that his reputation was safe for all time. It was nice but unnecessary when Berry released a good album, the 1970 issue *Back Home*. The first track 'Tulane' was in his best blistering story song style. It was followed by yet another excellent track, the blues 'Have Mercy Judge', a continuation of the troubled tale of Tulane and Johnny. Just when he was beginning to come up with good new material, everybody wanted to hear the old stuff again. Rock and roll revival shows became a rage, particularly in the United

States, and Chuck Berry was a natural headliner.

He also continued to appear in Britain, where his ultra-precise business style shocked promoters. It was said that he checked the daily exchange rate to make sure he wasn't losing out on his fee, and others swore that when he counted his pay, he took out bank notes he thought old and crumpled and asked for new notes. When he appeared, he almost always used back-up musicians who couldn't do justice to the material. He played the contracted length of time and no more. The musical legend became a bizarre show business legend.

It was while in Britain in 1971 that Chuck recorded a concert at the Lanchester Arts Festival. A notorious song from that performance gave Berry his long overdue first number one single in both the UK and US. It had nothing to do with his rock and roll and there is some confusion as to how much of it really did have to do with Berry. It had been in his set for almost twenty years under the name of 'My Tambourine', but in 1952 it had been recorded by Dave Bartholomew as 'My Ding-a-Ling'. Both Bartholomew and Berry have taken writer credit on 'My Ding-a-Ling'. If it was 'Johnny B. Goode' we'd argue about it.

In 1975, Elvis Presley had a British top ten hit with 'Promised Land'. For Elvis to record Chuck Berry's saga of how a poor boy earned fame was wonderfully ironic. Each of them had gone from unlikely origins to achieve world renown. One can complain that the personal adulation was distributed unevenly: that because he was black, or because he wasn't particularly good-looking, or because he wasn't young enough, Chuck Berry wasn't the pin-up or the scream dream that Elvis was. But even without that kind of success, and even with, sad to say, a second jail term, this one for tax evasion, Chuck Berry doesn't have too much to regret. His position as the inventor of much that is important in rock and roll is safe. No subsequent change in fashion can deprive a pioneer his status of having been a pioneer. He was the one who talked the teenage language, who worked at it until he got it right, and who turned out its definitive examples. That's good enough. As long as rock and roll survives, the father of rock and roll music will be Chuck Berry.

THE ROLLING STONES

The Rolling Stones were five Englishmen who took their name from a Muddy Waters blues song and who popularised American rhythm and blues in Britain and gave it back to white teenagers in the States . . . who went on to make the most powerful and demonic music of the sixties . . . and who became, after the break-up of the Beatles, the world's most famous rock group.

The Rolling Stones didn't begin so much as coagulate. They'd all been floating around the London blues scene in which Alexis Korner was prime mover. Mick Jagger and Keith Richards had known each other in Maypole County Primary School and had renewed their acquaintance in 1960 when Jagger was at the London School of Economics and Richards was attending Sidcup Art School. Richards joined Jagger's part-time group, Little Boy Blue and The Blue Boys. Brian Jones, a refugee from Cheltenham, was performing blues with Paul Jones under the ethnic-sounding pseudonyms Elmo Lewis and P.P. Pond. Charlie Watts drummed for Alexis Korner's Blues Incorporated, while pianist Ian Stewart had contacts with numerous players.

The cultural isolation in which these musicians worked, and the squalor in which some of them lived, are best evoked by Roy Carr in his book *The Rolling Stones: An Illustrated Record*. It is obvious these blues buffs weren't in it for the money: there was none.

The places they played were not big halls. Most people didn't even know where they were. Take, for example, the Ealing Blues Club. In small press advertisements for Blues Incorporated the public had to be told how to get there: 'Ealing Broadway Station. Turn left, cross at zebra, and go down steps between ABC Teashop and jewellers.'

This obscurity is typical of the cults which have sprung up in British pop music in the past twenty years. There is a very small scene of devotees who attract friends and their friends and then suddenly there's a cult, whether it's punks, New Romantics, or Northern Soul freaks. The

big difference is that the London bluesmen were doing it in the early sixties with no interest from a pop press and no pop music radio station to give support.

But Alexis Korner's Blues Incorporated did get to appear on the Light Programme of the BBC in 'Jazz Club'. The budget only allowed for six musicians, so Mick Jagger, by now one of the group's vocalists, had to be left out. That was not so terrible because it meant that he could get some associates together to deputise for Korner at the Marquee while he was playing on 'Jazz Club'. On 12 July 1962, the Rolling Stones made their debut.

The membership wasn't settled until 1963. Bill Wyman was asked to join because Jagger, Jones, Richards and Ian Stewart needed a bass player and because he had better amplifiers than they did. Charlie Watts agreed to play drums only after agonising over whether he could afford to lose his day job at an ad agency.

A residency at the Crawdaddy in the Station Hotel, Richmond, created word-of-mouth about the Stones that led to their first press mention and a visit from Andrew Loog Oldham, who became their manager and negotiated a contract with Decca. The band's first records were of the rhythm and blues and straight blues that they loved: Chuck Berry's 'Come On' was their first single and songs by Willie Dixon, Jimmy Reed and Rufus Thomas were on the first album. But that initial LP also included the first song Jagger and Richards wrote together, a marvellous harbinger of things to come and, coincidentally, their first American top forty single, 'Tell Me'.

Mick Jagger doesn't quite hit all the notes and the band's timing gets imprecise at the end . . . but none of that matters. 'Tell Me' was an excellent blues song, performed with conviction and intensity. It was credited to Jagger and Richard, the 's' on Keith's name disappearing until the late 70's. Ian Stewart played piano on 'Tell Me' but wasn't pictured on the album sleeve. He remains to this day an unofficial sixth Stone. He looked too normal, and the manager didn't want him ruining the effect. Andrew Loog Oldham wanted to cast the Rolling Stones as the bad boy counterpart to those family favourites, the Beatles. For the LP sleeve he had the Stones photographed against a black background. None of them are smiling. They are all staring at the camera as if auditioning for the movie *Psycho*. No words appeared on the jacket, except the Decca logo.

Oldham's scheme and the group's music both succeeded. In the last

Opposite: The Rolling Stones with Ian Stewart (holding maracas)

THE ROLLING STONES

week of April 1964, *The Rolling Stones* went to number one in the album chart, and stayed there for twelve weeks. Things moved quickly now. The group's fourth single, 'It's All Over Now', entered the British charts the second week of the summer of 1964, the same week 'Tell Me' went into the US list. 'It's All Over Now' was the Stones' first number one, a cover version of the Valentinos' original rhythm and blues smash of two years previous. That one had come out on Sam Cooke's Sar label, and it was to Sam's repertoire that the Stones next turned, embellishing the Cooke treatment of Willie Dixon's 'Little Red Rooster' to achieve another number one.

There is a terrible risk in having a string of hits with other people's material. It's like not having a steady date. You never know where the next one is coming from. The Rolling Stones would be much more secure if they could generate their own songs.

'Tell Me' had been a fine first effort. 'Heart Of Stone', an American single in early 1965, was such a convincing blues composition it was hard to believe it was an original. Both these numbers were rooted in r & b. The Stones had to develop their own style if they were going to be more than just popularisers of their heroes' music. Starting with a repeated guitar figure Keith Richards may have borrowed from James Brown and using a title Mick Jagger may have taken from the Staple Singers, the two writers came up with their first world class composition. 'The Last Time' created a driving hypnotic effect that to this day remains its own.

'The Last Time' began a new phase in the Rolling Stones' career. They moved away from imitations of the blues which, however inspired and altered, nonetheless alienated both r & b purists and pop fans with no interest in r & b. The quintet seized a space in the centre of the action. The press helped. Always looking for an angle, they emphasised the alleged degeneracy of the group. 'Would you let your daughter marry a Rolling Stone?' was asked as often as 'Would you buy a used car from Richard Nixon?' It was a stupid question. Charlie Watts and Bill Wyman were about as straight as celebrities can be, and on the other side of the coin, Brian Jones wasn't interested in marrying anyone's daughter. He wound up having several children by various unwed mothers.

From 1965 on every Rolling Stones A-side was a Jagger–Richard composition. In one year they took the quantum leap from being novice songwriters to penning one of the anthems of rock and roll, one of the three greatest singles of all-time, a song so perfect in its construction, articulate in its lyric, and unrestrained in its feeling, that one cannot imagine how it could be improved.

Bob Dylan had written great songs of protest, but they were usually about specific targets. Mick Jagger protested about the general frustrations of everyday teenage life: the inane commercials on television, the emptiness of the consumer society, the times when your spirit is willing but her flesh is weak. Keith Richard had progressed from being Britain's best Chuck Berry-style guitar player into a musician who could conceive great riffs of his own, as in the fuzz-toned intro to '(I Can't Get No) Satisfaction'.

'Satisfaction' was a work of inspiration. It was a number one single in both America and Britain – but it was more than a number one single. It was simultaneously a state-of-the-art performance and a state-of-society statement. Once someone has gotten into a groove as deeply as the Stones did with 'Satisfaction', there's no point in deserting it until it has been fully mined. This the Stones did with their next two singles. 'Get Off My Cloud', their fifth consecutive number one, voiced irritation at minor invasions of personal territory, while '19th Nervous Breakdown' savagely put down society girls who have nothing going for them but their pedigree and who crack up. Here the Stones entered into a dark and depressing part of real life.

With the next single they went one step farther . . . to despair. Somehow the light of the singer's life has been extinguished. We assume a lover has died. We catch the mourner not at a point of prayer, not at the moment of rationalisation, but in the time of deepest grief. There are no words to describe the pain, nor the blind fury at this undeserved loss. It is a totally subjective look at death.

I'm personally involved, because at school we lost two popular and beautiful friends while this record was a hit. Maybe that gave us a real insight into what Jagger is talking about – how, when you suffer a meaningless and idiotic loss, you want to blot the sun out of the sky. You want to 'Paint It Black'.

'Paint It Black' was an American number one in the early summer of 1966. The Rolling Stones had completed an extraordinary sequence of singles, records written with an insight into the soul and performed with the controlled intensity that communicates emotion far better than an equally furious but undisciplined thrash.

During 1966 the Stones also cut several songs which seemed to cast Mick Jagger as a male supremacist. On the *Aftermath* album there was the title 'Stupid Girl', another track on which Jagger revelled because he now had a difficult woman 'Under My Thumb', and a third on which a self-styled 'clever girl' is told she's 'Out Of Time'. The title of the first 1967 single, 'Let's Spend The Night Together', immediately suggested further female exploitation.

The reaction to the song would lead one to think something about it *was* insidious. Most American radio stations played the other side, 'Ruby Tuesday', while executives of the Ed Sullivan Show made the Stones change the lyrics to 'Let's Spend Some Time Together'. In fact, all that 'Let's Spend the Night Together' was was a celebration of the joy of sex. The partner was treated equally: 'I'll satisfy your every need, and now I know you will satisfy me.' Blatant references to sexuality had been a long-standing fixture of black music, but for a top pop group to even acknowledge the existence of 'doing it' was taboo. In this sense, 'Let's Spend The Night Together' was as revolutionary a record as any the Stones ever made.

'Let's Spend the Night Together' was included on American copies of *Between the Buttons*, the first of two Stones' albums released in 1967. Charlie Watts supplied verse and illustrations for the back cover that were very touching in their simplicity and directness. For example, under a cartoon of one man saying to another 'Say, is that a boy or a girl?' are the lines '"Between the Buttons," behind the dirt, You know at times you're often hurt.' Beneath the hardened exterior and the bad boy image did lie, after all, human beings.

Jagger and Richard managed to cope when charged with drug offences. Jagger even received establishment support in the historic leading article 'Who Breaks A Butterfly On A Wheel?' The editor of *The Times*, William Rees-Mogg, concluded Mick was being victimised for his notoriety.

The effect of drugs charges on Brian Jones was less happy. He visibly began to fall apart. He was twice taken to hospital suffering from nervous strain. Jones was arrested and convicted a second time in 1968. His playing deteriorated and, shortly after leaving the Stones in 1969, he was found dead in his swimming pool.

It could not have helped his ego that the Stones had clearly become the Mick and Keith show. Brian had shared top billing with Mick on some of the earliest gigs, but was later obscured by the dynamic duo. The Stones' first great piece of 1968 had been another Jagger–Richard composition. 'Jumpin' Jack Flash' was the Stones' first number one in two years. It also gave Mick an unintended nickname. Perhaps because the lyric was read in the first person, perhaps because it was a great rock and roll record and the name had to be hung on somebody, the lead singer of the Rolling Stones came to be 'Jumpin' Jack Flash'. During the seventies the live shows would be comparatively restrained until this song was performed near the end of the set. Almost overnight, 'Jumpin' Jack Flash' replaced 'Satisfaction' as the song most identified with the Rolling Stones. The next step was logical. Having acquired overtones of evil, Jagger would become evil incarnate. He did so in 'Sympathy For The Devil', the lead track on the 1968 album release *Beggars Banquet*.

We haven't mentioned many of the Stones' LPs before now. The most outstanding numbers were usually singles. But if one was to get one Stones album outside of an anthology, this would be the one. Many critics have observed that one necessary ability the Beatles and Stones had to get them through the frantic sixties was they could write about what was happening around them. Inspiration was directly at hand.

1968 was a dog of a year. The war in Vietnam was dividing the generations in the Western World, Martin Luther King and Robert Kennedy were assassinated, street riots plagued European cities, particularly Paris, and the Chicago police violently attacked anti-war demonstrators at the Democratic Party Convention. Evil was at large. Jagger acknowledged it. He said, 'Call Me Lucifer'.

'Sympathy For The Devil' was one of the most powerfully phrased and delivered tracks in rock and roll history. It still sounds good. Then it sounded world-shaking. It took on a quality that seemed so genuinely demonic that when a concert-goer was stabbed to death during its performance, at Altamont, in late '69, the Stones retired the song for several years. There were more outstanding tracks on *Beggars Banquet*. Inspired by the student riots in Paris 'Street Fighting Man' seemed to speak for frustrated youth everywhere. 'What can a poor boy do 'cept sing in a rock and roll band?'

The Rolling Stones were in their second great period. After *Beggars Banquet*, they issued the *Let It Bleed* album (with the unforgettable 'Gimme Shelter') and one of the finest two-sided singles ever put to plastic. 'You Can't Always Get What You Want' was a marvellous extended piece. The hit side 'Honky Tonk Women' was a rock classic and the best-sounding single the Stones have made.

After 1967, they dispensed with Andrew Loog Oldham and for several years employed Jimmy Miller as producer. He must have had something to do with honing down of the Stones' singles. Every instrumental voice was heard clearly. What was unnecessary was omitted. You can hear the change in 'Jumpin' Jack Flash' and in 'Honky Tonk Women'.

'Honky Tonk Women' was the last great Rolling Stones record of the sixties. By bizarre coincidence, 1970 was a turning point for almost every major musical act. The Beatles split, Simon and Garfunkel parted, Diana Ross left the Supremes. The Stones went through changes, too, leaving Decca and starting their own label.

Again, they were inviting comparison with the Beatles. Because the two groups were the major British artists of the sixties, it seems natural to try to figure out who was best. The truth of the matter is that they were different. Even in the early days, the Beatles sang American black music in a pleasant pop style, while the Stones were blues merchants. But timing always made the Stones seem the Beatles' inferiors. They became popular after the Beatles, even recording a Lennon–McCartney song for their second single. Their second-rate psychedelic album, *Their Satanic Majesties Request*, followed the Beatles' masterpiece *Sergeant Pepper*. And the Rolling Stones record company began three years after the Beatles started Apple. Add to these considerations the fact that the Liverpudlians were the biggest show business success of the decade in any field and any group looks a distant second. But contributions should be judged on their own merit, not in comparison with someone else's achievements. In this light the Stones still appear wonderfully accomplished. For example, though others have equalled it, no one has produced a better rock dance record than the one they chose to inaugurate the Rolling Stones label: 'Brown Sugar'.

'Brown Sugar' suggested that the seventies might be another great decade for the Stones. It wasn't. There were some fine records, particularly the albums *Sticky Fingers, Exile On Main Street* and *Some Girls*, but the abrasive edge was gone. Rock music was unable to maintain a vital connection with politics. The Stones were no exception. Rock stars lapsed back to being entertainers, like pop stars were before Presley. There's nothing wrong with being a good entertainer, but one is unlikely to mean quite as much to the personal lives of millions as when one was inseparable from an era itself. Of all the seventies bands, only the Sex Pistols were vital in the way the Beatles, Stones and Dylan were in the sixties, and the Pistols were only so for a shorter period of time to a smaller audience in fewer countries.

The Stones, ironically, increased their success in terms of concert grosses and record sales. Their old fans could now afford to pay considerable sums to see them, and both the original Stones supporters and younger fans bought their new releases. The Rolling Stones are a classic case of a show business legend – just manage to survive, keep doing decent material, and your audience will grow and grow long after your initial impact has worn off.

The Stones are still making good records, almost as good as the Pretenders, and their seventies concerts were good, almost as good as the Who's. It isn't downgrading the group to observe that Mick Taylor didn't quite work out as Brian Jones' replacement, that Jagger seems to radiate a detached ennui that comes from living a life of leisure he has earned, that Keith Richard seems dangerously and ludicrously intent on living up to his image. They are just seeing themselves through. What else can grown men do but play in a rock and roll band?

The best moments come when they show they're still in touch: when Bill Wyman releases his witty single '(Sisi) Je Suis Un Rock Star', when Jagger runs through the problems of living in New York on 'Shattered', and when the group musically address a shift in popular taste, as when they blended disco and rock on 'Miss You'.

One is tempted to say one misses the old Stones, and to say that is a criticism of the band. It is actually not a criticism, it is nostalgia. When critics say that, they are simply longing for that part of themselves which is also now gone. The Stones, in case they haven't noticed, are still here.

DIANA ROSS

The most successful female singer in the history of recorded music never had proper vocal training. 'I think that people who aren't professional sing better,' she once said with a straight face. 'They have a newness in their voice.' That quality has given Diana Ross more number one records than can be played in an hour-long programme. It's enough to make everyone who's never had a voice lesson go out and make a record tomorrow.

The success story of Diana Ross began almost literally in her own backyard. It began down the street. Diane Earle was one of five Detroit girls who sang in a quintet supporting the all-male group the Primes. One of the Primes, the ensemble which later evolved into the Temptations, thought it was only natural that their female counterpart should be called the Primettes. The girls, who were still in school, made two unsuccessful singles, 'Tears of Sorrow' and 'Pretty Baby', for Lu-Pine Records, enough of a discouragement for Betty Anderson to leave. Diane Earle wasn't so easily put off. Smokey Robinson lived a few houses down the street, and she saw the Miracles rehearsing on the steps. One day Diane asked Smokey if her group could get an audition at Motown Records.

Robinson arranged it, the Primettes visited Motown, and, by a stroke of luck, Motown founder Berry Gordy happened to walk by as the quartet sang. If this were a Hollywood script, Gordy would be bowled over, sign the Primettes to a long-term contract and immediately hand them to his best producers and writers, but this is real life. The company president thought the girls were, to use his word, 'immature', and suggested they finish high school.

It's harder to get someone determined out than it is for them to get in. The Primettes hung around as much as they could, helping out in small ways in the office and in the studio. Diane got a summer job as an office girl. A co-worker remembered her as 'a secretary who thought she could sing'.

And then there were three. Barbara Martin left the Primettes to get married. Diane, who had been the last to join a quintet, was now one of a trio, sharing lead singer chores with the group's head Florence Ballard. It was Flo whom Berry Gordy told to choose a new name for the group. She solicited over a dozen suggestions from Motown staff members before deciding on the Supremes. Diane Earle changed her name to Diana Ross.

Gordy himself took the Supremes into the studio, producing and co-writing their first single, 'I Want A Guy'. It was released in March, 1961, to almost no response. Even Berry was unconvinced of the long-term potential of the Supremes. He offered employee Robert Bateman a percentage for life if he would manage Diana Ross. Bateman turned him down because, as he told writer Peter Benjaminson, 'No one wanted to get involved with a kid who sings through her nose.'

With their third single, 'Your Heart Belongs To Me', the Supremes were shifted from the Tamla to the Motown label. At least this time they reached higher than they had before, number ninety-five on the Hot 100. This was no overnight success story. Berry Gordy tried writing and producing them. Smokey Robinson tried. Nothing worked. Fellow artists on the Motortown Revue teased the girls, calling them 'The No-Hit Supremes'.

Then someone else got a shot. The songwriting and production team of Brian Holland, Lamont Dozier and Eddie Holland had scored success with Martha and the Vandellas. It was thought they might do the same with a second female trio. Their first collaboration with the Supremes 'When The Lovelight Starts Shining Through His Eyes' became a top forty hit in early 1964. You could tell the producers were bigger stars than the singers: the record started without the group in sight. It wasn't an all-time classic, but it was a breakthrough. By now Berry Gordy had decided that Diana Ross should be the regular lead singer of the Supremes. Florence Ballard and Mary Wilson were supporting vocalists. This rise in estimation still didn't make Diana a star. The next Holland–Dozier–Holland production did poorly, and Motown had to sweet talk Dick Clark into taking the Supremes along on his 1964 Cavalcade of Stars. He offered them a mere five hundred dollars a week, but Motown accepted. The girls had to be seen by the public.

Holland–Dozier–Holland had noticed something about Diana that they decided to showcase. Martha Reeves, had a strong, commanding voice. In the early days of Motown, Marvin Gaye was occasionally drowned out by this backing singer, so he called her group 'the vandals of music', the

Vandellas. Diana Ross had a lighter and more feminine quality to her voice. Even when she growled in 'When The Lovelight Starts Shining Through His Eyes', it wasn't so much the growl of a lioness as the purr of a pussy. Holland–Dozier–Holland put this delicate and sexy quality upfront on 'Where Did Our Love Go'.

It was as if the last place team had suddenly won the championship. After two years of almost complete failure, the Supremes were number one in America. They even got to number three in Britain, the best UK placing yet by a Motown artist. Dick Clark voluntarily gave them a rise. Holland–Dozier–Holland could be forgiven for being pleasantly shocked. They were going to give 'Where Did Our Love Go' to Mary Wells, but when she left Motown they had been left with the song. What the Supremes had done with it was a revelation. The 'Baby, Baby' introduction had hit home in hearts across the world. They made the most of a good thing and called the next record 'Baby Love'.

This became a number one record in both America and Britain. Holland–Dozier–Holland weren't going to drop the 'baby' motif. In the next single, they had Diana Ross sing 'Come see about me, see about your baby'. The first verse of the single after that began 'Baby, baby, I'm aware of where you're going' and in the near future they would have Diana croon 'Baby, whenever you're near, I hear a symphony', and 'My world is empty without you, babe'. It was enough to drive Diana Ross to having kids. But maternity was not what Diana was singing about. She was addressing herself at all times to her anonymous man, and millions of men fantasised they might be the one. It was a completely safe romantic experience. Diana Ross was sexy without being erotic. Indeed, the very application of the word seems defamation of a religious shrine. Diana always sang for effect, but never with so much emotion that the listener felt threatened by the prospect of an experience he couldn't handle. Diana's cooing voice said 'Come hither', but to the candy store, not to the bedroom. She was soulful enough to make the Supremes' records special, but bland enough to make them safe. The result was that the Supremes were the best-selling American act of the sixties, almost always doing better in the pop charts than the rhythm and blues lists. Solomon Burke and Little Milton, r & b singers of extraordinary feeling, reached number one in their field in the spring of 1965, while the Supremes were kept at number two with a record that had no trouble reaching number one in the Hot 100, 'Stop! In The Name Of Love'.

This 45 was cited by John Lennon as an example of production techniques from which the Beatles could learn. The introductory organ swell which built into the first dramatic 'Stop!' was just one of several simple sounds Holland–Dozier and Holland used to get listeners hooked into their singles from the very start. The handclaps on 'Where Did Our Love Go' and the drum that faded in at the beginning of 'Come See About Me' were further examples.

In 1957–8, Elvis Presley had accumulated four consecutive number one singles. No artist had ever achieved five. To the string of 'Where Did Our Love Go', 'Baby Love', 'Come See About Me' and 'Stop! In The Name Of Love', the Supremes now added a fifth, 'Back In My Arms Again'. No home-grown artist has ever duplicated the feat, though both the Beatles and the Bee Gees have surpassed it.

The Supremes were more than the local girls made good. They were a worldwide phenomenon. Gordy tried to make sure they became a show business institution. He had them record albums of material divorced from their hit singles but close to the mainstream – an LP of Sam Cooke compositions, a collection of British invasion hits, and, later on, a Rodgers and Hart anthology and an entire album of material from *Funny Girl*. Motown's famous Quality Control worked diligently on the Supremes, giving them the characteristic choreography where every movement by every member is in unison. The gowns were glamorous and identical. One of the funniest moments of the sixties was in the stage production of *Hair*, when a black female trio in sequined garb huddled around a microphone to sing Supremes style. They backed off during the instrumental break to reveal that they were in fact all crammed into one gigantic dress. Call it training, call it discipline, Diana Ross was happy to submit to it. She was being groomed as a show business superstar, though she might not have known it from her weekly allowance. In 1966, the year of 'You Can't Hurry Love', and 'You Keep Me Hanging On', Berry Gordy said of the Supremes, 'We had some trouble with them at first. You must be very strict with young artists. That instils discipline. But once they get a number one record, they tend to get more independent. They start spending their money extravagantly. . . . After a year, they saw their mistakes and came to appreciate our handling of their affairs.'

Florence Ballard certainly didn't appreciate what she was told to do in 1967. Gordy told her to leave the Supremes. Originally, he had downgraded her to play up Diana Ross. That had resulted in a success so great the demands on the Supremes surpassed Flo's energy. The original leader of the Supremes died in 1976 at the age of thirty-two.

Cindy Birdsong joined Mary Wilson in what was now obviously a back-up role to Diana Ross. Accordingly, Motown billed the act Diana Ross and the Supremes. The first release under this name remains one of the group's distinctive singles. Holland–Dozier–Holland returned John Lennon's compliment and borrowed psychedelic elements from the Beatles for 'Reflections'. It was a great departure for the writer/producers. A few months later they staged another great departure. They left Motown. The men who had built the careers of the Supremes and Four Tops subsequently started their own company, Invictus, which had hits like 'Band Of Gold' and 'Give Me Just A Little More Time'.

This did not help Diana Ross and the Supremes, who floundered through three progressively less successful releases. Berry Gordy couldn't accept anything but the best for his top star, to whom he had grown personally attached. At one point, Diana referred to Berry as 'father, mother, brother, sister, lover', which is more than 'just good friends'. Gordy had several top writers including R. Dean Taylor retire to a hotel room until they emerged with a hit song suitable for Diana. The changing social conditions in America in the late sixties meant that sugary sweet confections wouldn't be enough anymore. The group of writers, referred to on record labels as The Corporation, came out of the hotel and into the studio with a song that was not only up with the times but ahead of them. The lead character was a young woman who had been born illegitimately. She didn't want to fool around before marriage for fear that she might bring into the world another baby with the same stigma. Diana Ross took the role of 'Love Child'.

'Love Child' was the Supremes' eleventh number one record. It was a comeback to be sure, for in the top ten at the same time was the group's duet with the Temptations, 'I'm Gonna Make You Love Me'.

History repeated itself, and Berry Gordy and Smokey Robinson tried their hand at writing and producing the Supremes, just as they had in the early days. Even though the president and vice-president of her label, these legendary talents could not grasp the essence of Diana Ross' appeal. If they could, they couldn't write for it. It was up to Johnny Bristol as producer and co-writer to provide the last hit. Everyone knew it was going to be the last because it was announced in advance that Diana and the Supremes were going to part. The corporate thinking was that Motown would then have two superstar acts instead of one. The risk of which everyone was aware was that neither might be able to make it without the other. At the end of 1969, the chips were on the table: it was double or nothing.

'Someday We'll Be Together' was a love fantasy, but the title was so appropriate for the circumstances the artists were facing in real life that it gripped America and went to number one in the soul chart as well as the Hot 100. The uncredited male voice on the track is that of Johnny Bristol, who sang interjections from the control booth via the intercom. The original intention was to inspire the three women; the male intruder would be erased from the tape later. But the result was so emotionally effective it was retained, and so Johnny Bristol became Diana Ross' first, though uncredited, solo male partner.

Diana Ross began her solo recording career in the spring of 1970. Her first release, 'Reach Out and Touch (Somebody's Hand)', was meant to encourage parents to be tolerant of and helpful to children who had become drug addicts. It was a strange choice for a first solo single. The message the artist wanted to convey was buried between the lines of what sounded like an all-purpose peace and love lyric. It was too bland to become a major hit, though Ross persisted in using it as her signature tune throughout the seventies, walking into her concert audiences and making it an audience participation number. If the spectators consisted of Marvin Gaye and Michael Jackson, the results were exciting. If the fans were almost anybody else, the concert died somewhere between the fifth and sixth rows. Diana nonetheless stayed with the writing and production team of Nicholas Ashford and Valerie Simpson. They had previously made a memorable series of singles with Marvin Gaye and Tammi Terrell. One of those sixties tunes was chosen as Diana's next single.

The full-length version, which many radio stations played even if it was six minutes long, had an extraordinary spoken introduction. We must remember that Isaac Hayes had triumphed less than a year before with his extension of 'By The Time I Get To Phoenix'. Ashford and Simpson tried Diana out on 'Ain't No Mountain High Enough'. It did the trick. 'Ain't No Mountain High Enough' established Diana Ross as a major solo artist, reaching number one in the US and the top ten in the UK. The Supremes had only had one number one in Britain, 'Baby Love', so it seemed that Diana's discs were always doing better in the States.

Not so in 1971. Radio One disc jockey, Tony Blackburn, took a fancy to a track from Diana's second solo album, *Everything Is Everything*, and promised he'd give it heavy airplay if Tamla Motown would release it as a single. They did, he did, and 'I'm Still Waiting' went to number one.

In America it didn't even make the top forty, so Diana got accustomed to thinking it was a flop. When she came to Britain for her next concert tour, she agreed to include the number in her programme, and was shocked when it was greeted by sensational standing ovations.

For her next project Diana was turned in a direction away from all her previous sources. Berry Gordy wanted to get Motown into movies. He wanted to film the life story of Billie Holliday, and he wanted Diana to be the star. Ross herself was dubious at first. She hadn't yet had that many solo hits to be sure she could survive adopting someone else's persona. What if the public liked Ross as Holliday and would never again accept Diana as herself?

It sounded like a blueprint for corporate and career disaster. A company that never made a movie makes an important feature film, and a young woman who has never acted, stars as one of the greatest blues singers of the century. The naysayers overlooked one point of history. Before the Supremes had hits, almost everyone had thought Diana couldn't sing. She sang. Now they said she couldn't act. She acted.

She acted her guts out. Even with slight historical distortion and a bit of showbusiness gloss, *Lady Sings The Blues* was an emotionally moving and musically entertaining film, and the main credit went to Diana Ross. She became her character. When, destroyed by drugs, she had a fit in a padded cell, everyone in the cinema squirmed. You couldn't even think of the Supremes, the portrayal was so convincing. Diana won an Academy Award nomination for Best Actress that year, the first black to ever be nominated in that category. She lost the Oscar to Liza Minnelli, who had been brilliant in her musical, *Cabaret*. Some Ross supporters thought that, given that both performances had been first class, Minnelli had won because she was white. It was more likely, given this was Hollywood, that Diana had lost because she wasn't Judy Garland's daughter.

The single from the film, 'Good Morning Heartache' was symptomatic of Diana's approach to the music in *Lady Sings The Blues*: don't try to copy the incomparable, sing as Diana Ross influenced by Billy Holliday. On screen and in soundtrack album sales, it worked.

It was still unusual for the artist to be absent from the singles charts, so concentration was redirected on making hit records. 'Touch Me In The Morning', an American number one in 1973, was one result. But one could not let the critical and commercial success of *Lady Sings The Blues* pass by. Gordy entered into a deal to make another film, the rags-to-riches tale of a black model nicknamed *Mahogany*.

Confronted with *Mahogany* the critics yelled 'Timber!' Whereas in *Lady* Diana had acted a fully delineated character, here the movie was built around Diana and making her and her personally conceived fashions look good. The other actors and the plot were sacrificed. *Mahogany* was a star vehicle gone off the rails – or, to be specific, off the road, when the effeminate white fashion designer who can't have his virtuous black model figuratively and literally tries to resolve the conflict by driving the car they're in at high speed into a mound of rubble.

Motown didn't learn from its mistake. An actress contributes to a film, the film doesn't revolve around the actress. But in the late seventies the company did it again. They insisted that Diana Ross play the Judy Garland part in the black version of *The Wizard Of Oz*: *The Wiz*. In one sense, this seemed a natural. Diana Ross was even more than Barbra Streisand the successor to Judy Garland's dedicated and emotional following. But Judy Garland had been sixteen when she played Dorothy. Diana Ross was thirty-three. It wasn't that there wasn't a suitable black actress for the part; Stephanie Mills had been a smash on Broadway in the stage version. But who was Stephanie Mills compared with Diana Ross? Twenty-three million dollars was spent on *The Wiz*, a lot of money to ease down any road.

In two easy steps, Diana had gone from being an Academy Award contender to a cinematic embarrassment. The talent must still be there, but it has to be used and not amused.

Diana couldn't even win an Oscar for music. On the 1977 Academy Awards telecast she sang a stunning version of 'Theme From *Mahogany*' via satellite from the streets and canals of Amsterdam. The Best Song award went to 'I'm Easy', performed by Keith Carradine who accompanied himself on guitar sitting on the stage steps.

At least 'Mahogany' had been the bigger record, one of two number ones from the same album. The other, 'Love Hangover', had been released while 'Mahogany' was still climbing the charts because the Fifth Dimension had released a cover version of this obvious hit song. Diana found herself with a back-to-back pair of winners.

Ross has registered in the American charts every year since 1962 and in Britain since '64. This doesn't mean that every release hits the top ten. In the disco–dominated years of the late seventies, Diana found it difficult to adapt. She scored a success in the disco field with her Richard Perry-produced project *The Boss*, but it did not provide big hit singles. For that she had to turn to the most prolific hitmakers of the field, Nile Rodgers and Bernard Edwards of Chic. Diana was reportedly unhappy with the mixes on the album they recorded together and had the tracks remixed so they were more to her liking. But there could be no quarrelling with the results: a multi-million selling album, *Diana*, and her biggest solo single, 'Upside Down'. The collaboration with Rodgers and Edwards was immensely profitable, but it was a one-off. Diana now needed a new direction. She decided she would find it outside Motown. The news shocked the normally unshockable music business. Diana Ross and the Motown sound were inseparable. How could they be parted? Money. Diana wanted money, and other companies were able to pay more for her new contract than Motown could. It was ironic, seeing that Berry Gordy's company had started with a hit called 'Money (That's What I Want)'. As she had in other ways before, Diana was living up to Berry's words.

And, equally as ironically, her last release on Motown before joining RCA in America and Capitol in Britain was her longest running number one. 'Endless Love' recorded with Lionel Richie was also her first extremely successful duet with a male partner (her album with Marvin Gaye had spawned several singles, but no blockbuster sellers).

Diana Ross left Motown as America's top female recording star. She has been willing to be the mouthpiece of the most talented writers and producers of her era. Diana might have been a Pygmalion if she had been the front woman for only one source, but by using them all she stands as the important figure whom others merely supply. If she continues to use this approach, her string of hits very well might turn out to be endless.

BILLY JOEL

Into the Elton John gap he came, riding his Steinway like Billy The Kid, plugging the holes in the airwaves left vacant by Elton's short retirement. There was room for only one piano player in this town, and Billy Joel was now it. Or at least so it seemed when songs from the album *The Stranger* dominated radio in late 1977 and early '78. Reality was much less glamorous. Billy Joel had been making records for almost ten years.

Billy Joel was born in 1949 in the New York suburb of Hicksville, Long Island. His father, a survivor of Dachau concentration camp, went back to Europe when Billy was seven years old, and while he sent a cheque every month, mother had to work at odd jobs to make ends meet. 'Sometimes it was scary not eating,' Joel remembered. 'Do you know what it's like to be the poor people on the poor people's block?' In his leisure hours Billy's dad had been a classical pianist. Noticing that at the age of four Billy had been engrossed by a Mozart piece, his mother signed him up for piano lessons, thinking he might emulate his father. But when Billy was seven rock and roll took over the charts, and Fats Domino, Jerry Lee Lewis and Little Richard were natural models for a piano-playing youngster. This is why Joel concentrated on keyboard rather than go at the guitar. The piano was a rock and roll instrument in 1957; Billy learned it and stayed with it.

In 1964, the Beatles conquered America, and the teenage Joel joined his first group, the Echoes, who became the Lost Souls. A few years later Billy and the bassist advanced to a popular local group, the Hassles, who recorded two albums.

The Hassles fell apart in 1970, but Billy Joel and Hassle drummer Jon Small stayed together to record a duo album as Attila. The album sleeve had them dressed as Huns standing in a meat refrigerator with carcasses hanging over their heads. The music was played as heavily as possible and boasted titles like 'Brain Invasion' and 'Amplifier Fire'. Joel later called it 'the loudest thing you ever heard'.

Attila were under the direct influence of the psychedelic era and guitar heroes like Jimi Hendrix and Jeff Beck. But Billy Joel had other musical interests as well. He loved the melodies of Paul McCartney and longed to be a songwriter himself. In 1971 a demonstration tape won him a contract with Family Productions, and, a year later, his first solo album was released. It was called *Cold Spring Harbor*, after a village on the Long Island shore. The songs are in the style that came to be associated with the artist, but he sounds like he's trying to imitate Roger Chapman. There was a reason. 'The strangest thing happened,' producer Artie Ripp related. 'The 16-track machine ran slow, and when we mixed the final master, Billy sounded like a chipmunk.'

Cold Spring Harbor was received with mild interest, and Billy Joel toured on the strength of it. But he had made several disadvantageous deals. He had reached a point where he had agreed to give to various people nearly 150% of his earnings.

Finding himself in a desperate dilemma, he took the understandable option. He fled. He went to California with his girlfriend Elizabeth, the former wife of the Hassles' drummer. While his finances were sorted out as best they could be, Billy Joel played in a cocktail bar under the name Bill Martin. 'I got free drinks and union scale,' he told journalist Timothy White. 'I took on this totally make-believe identity. I was like Buddy Greco, collar turned up and shirt unbuttoned halfway down. They thought "Wow, this guy is really hip!"' Joel catered to the cocktail crowd playing other people's songs and assuming an artificially smooth patter pattern.

Well-meaning drinkers would slide to Joel's side, saying they had contacts in the music business and that he should get a deal. That was just what he had run away from. But he had also left a song circulating on FM stations in the East. He'd done a live broadcast for a Philadelphia outlet, and the number 'Captain Jack' had been taped and replayed. On the strength of this song particularly, CBS records traced Joel to California and got him to record in North Hollywood in the spring of 1973.

It was understandable that Billy would want to record a song about the life of a late-night bar pianist. What he couldn't have foreseen was that this clearly autobiographical number would become a top twenty single. Paying his dues had supplied Billy Joel with his first hit: 'Piano Man'.

It wasn't particularly well-phrased. 'Making love to his tonic and gin' and 'Shuffles in' has got to be the most forced rhyme in top 40 history. People order 'Gin and tonic', not 'Tonic and gin'. The problem is that words rhyming with 'tonic' include 'platonic' and 'bubonic', not the kind of thing one hears in a typical chart record. Then there's that line about an old man who knew the words of a song when he 'wore a younger man's clothes' which sounds like he's been going through somebody's wardrobe.

Despite these shortcomings, 'Piano Man' succeeded in creating an environment and an attitude. So did 'Captain Jack'. The two-year-old underground favourite finally found a place on plastic on the *Piano Man* LP. It was a major piece about the debilitating effects of drugs.

When he had first left home, Joel had lived in a small flat across the street from a black housing development. 'The slang they used for heroin was "Captain Jack". I didn't mean my song to be specifically about heroin,' the writer told *Melody Maker*, 'just whatever your fix is, to escape from reality, don't abuse it.' More recently, Billy added that he'd seen 'so many friends shovelled under the Long Island dirt. The miracle of modern chemistry killed them if Vietnam didn't.'

Listeners interpreted it from their own vantage points of user or non-user, and it was a controversial track. But 'Captain Jack' was the kind of controversy a young artist finds helpful: it got Joel talked about and it got him played on the radio.

Piano Man went gold quickly and platinum eventually. Yet even after its millionth sale, Billy Joel had profited less than eight thousand dollars. The handling of his financial affairs was still messy. One night he turned to Elizabeth, now his wife, and said, 'Why don't you do it? You're smart.' For a period of several years, Mrs Joel served as Mr Joel's manager until Billy's contractual arrangements were sorted out. In 1981 he was still paying Artie Ripp's Family Productions 28% for having discovered him, but, as he told *Rolling Stone*, 'I signed the papers. Until the situation changes, it's not really healthy to dwell on it.'

One might have thought that coming off a hit, someone with Billy's ability might have been able to consolidate his success. This was not so. The next album, *Streetlife Serenade*, did less well, and *its* show business oriented single, 'The Entertainer', had to struggle to reach the top 40. Billy decided to leave California and come home. His 1976 release *Turnstiles* was suffused with his love for New York: the sleeve showed him in city subway turnstiles, 'New York State Of Mind' was a love song to the town, and 'Summer Highland Falls' alluded to the locale of his new home on the Hudson River. Just as there were all these greetings to the East, there was a farewell to the West. He wrote this song with the Ronettes in mind, and was therefore thrilled when Ronnie Spector recorded it with The E Street Band one year later. It remains his favourite cover version of one of his compositions: 'Say Goodbye To Hollywood'.

'That made me truly happy,' Joel said. Something else happened in 1977 to make him happy. Radio stations all across America jumped on the first single from his new album *The Stranger* and within months Joel had an international smash.

It seemed as if all the ballads he'd ever written were mere warm-ups for 'Just The Way You Are'.

A popular music standard, it's been covered by artists ranging from Engelbert Humperdinck to Isaac Hayes. Ironically, Barry White's version wound up being a bigger hit single in Britain than Billy's original. But because his song fitted all artists, there was a danger that Joel the performer would be overlooked. 'People who've only heard "Just The Way You Are" assume that I'm purely a middle-of-the-road, Barry Manilow kind of performer,' he told writer Steve Clark. 'I hate that. I don't want to exclude rock and roll audiences who might not come to my gigs because of one middle-of-the-road song.'

Fortunately, there were several types of material on *The Stranger*, and more hits, beginning with 'Movin' Out (Anthony's Song)'.

No matter what his talents, Billy Joel at this point was not the kind of artist whose new release was greeted by flocks of fans at the browser bins. He had almost no image. Most British disc jockeys didn't even know his name, and when 'Just The Way You Are' came out many insisted on calling him 'Billy Jo-EL', as if he came from the planet Krypton, home of Kal-EL and Jor-EL, better known as Superman and his father.

Joel had no visual image, either. His previous album jackets had gone out of their way to make him look hideous: he was a black-and-white hippie on his first sleeve, a black-and-white Medusa on his second, and a barefoot boy in chequered shirt and jeans on the back cover of his third – he didn't even appear on the front. He looked like an accountant on the sleeve of *Turnstiles*, but for *The Stranger* he suddenly got class. He was barefoot again, but that's because he was on a bed. What was different was he was wearing a shirt and tie, looking at a mask on the pillow next to him. Hanging on the wall was a pair of boxing gloves.

The mask and the title symbolised that part of persons kept private from others, even those close to them. The boxing gloves represented part of Joel his audience didn't know about – he'd once been a welterweight boxer who had won twenty out of twenty-two fights. The twenty-second had been the last. It was 'against this guy with a head shaped like a bullet', he told *The Daily Mirror*. 'Could he hit! . . . I just lay there in the ring and didn't bother getting up again. I was no fool!'

As an artist he was still hitting, reaching out at targets he felt he should have a go at even if there might be some objections. 'Captain Jack' had been one example of this special kind of courage. From *The Stranger* came another, 'Only The Good Die Young', which was a top twenty hit in the States but never released as a single in Britain. It dealt with what Joel considered the unnecessarily strict and hypocritical morality of the Catholic Church. Equally clearly, he had nothing against Catholics themselves, and he wrote lovingly about the Italians who populated his world. 'Movin' Out (Anthony's Song)' contained references to Mama Leone and Mister Cacciatore, and in the epic, 'Scenes From An Italian Restaurant', the stages of a love affair are related against the backdrop of bottles of vino in the local Italian.

Listening to this work, one is struck at how tight the track is, how atune with each other the players are. That's because this was the first Billy Joel album produced by Phil Ramone, and he had the inspiration to record Billy with his touring band, rather than with session musicians. The men who played together regularly knew the material best, and were able to interact as a unit more closely than session men.

The Stranger sold over five million copies and became Columbia Records' biggest seller in the United States, surpassing even *Bridge Over Troubled Water*. Joel's album went platinum in New York City alone, a reminder that, despite his new-found fame around the globe, Billy was still especially welcome at home. But as he has politely pointed out, it is not really fair to claim that either he or Bruce Springsteen are the pride of New York, since Joel came from Long Island and Springsteen New Jersey. Therefore, Billy and Bruce cannot be competitors, but rather two individuals, both with insightful but different perceptions of everyday life in metropolitan New York and its surrounds.

Whereas Springsteen is considered the Boss of contemporary rock music despite his haunting slow songs, Joel is often referred to as a balladeer despite his up-tempo material. It has always annoyed him, and partly to escape from this tag he gave his next album, *52nd Street*, what he called 'a harder edge' than *The Stranger* had. *52nd Street* was named after the road that once was the swing centre of New York City. Consequently some buyers thought they were purchasing a jazz-flavoured LP, but this was not the case. Still, there were three fine tracks right in a row, 'Big Shot', the ballad 'Honesty' and 'My Life', a statement of quiet but determined defiance that was once said to be John McEnroe's favourite song. The package also included Joel's second stab at a Phil Spector tribute 'Until The Night'.

'Big Shot' proved to be an unexpected zenith of Billy's 1979 appearance at The Royal Albert Hall. Because one associated keyboard antics with Jerry Lee Lewis and Elton John, one didn't expect to see Joel running about the stage, strutting across the boards, and jumping on and off the piano. It was an athletic acting performance that perfectly complemented the music, a rare moment when all aspects of a pop concert fit together for greater effect.

The hero of Hicksville tried to play down his new-found fame and fortune, saying things like 'What does all this money mean? It could all be gone tomorrow!' But he worked in a medium which created stars for its own purposes, and Joel found himself in constant demand for both printed and broadcast interviews. He was pressured to be a middle-of-the-road star while wanting to be the rocker he thought he was. To complicate matters, rock critics were far less kind to him than the easy-listening reviewers. He took his own stand, and on the front cover of his 1980 long player *Glass Houses* was seen about to throw a stone through the glass wall of a country house. It was his own house. 'I know I'm going to get rocks thrown at me,' he reasoned, 'so I'm gonna throw a rock through my window at myself – meaning the whole narrow image people have of me!'

Every track on the first side of the album became a single in the US, UK or both. 'It's Still Rock and Roll To Me' was the most successful in both nations, incidentally giving Billy his first American number one. It had been the last song written for the album, coming as a reply to the spreading popularity of New Wave. He thought the new music was 'good and necessary' and said it should 'give the whole damned industry an enema'. But he counselled that it wasn't *that* new, that the brevity and roughness of New Wave should not be mistaken for originality. 'It's just a reaction to a rediscovered past,' he said. 'It's still rock and roll to me.' Some rock fans considered the remark condescending, others inaccurate. *Rolling Stone* named it the Worst Rock and Roll single of 1980.

These are the reactions of persons who don't understand either Joel's vantage point or his appeal. Billy Joel is an angry young man, but he is an angry young normal man. Despite the hungry nights he suffered as a child, he grew up as a member of the American mainstream. Like other members of his generation, he worshipped the Beatles, loved Motown and Stax, and went to Woodstock. He grew his hair long, then he cut it. He used drugs a little bit, then stopped. He's too typical to make an avant garde statement, and those who wait for him to do so will find that hell freezes over first.

This is also the origin of his appeal. Billy Joel is just that much more talented and just that much more articulate than his peers. They can still relate perfectly to what he says, it's just that they don't have the ability and perhaps the guts to say it themselves. In an era of American music when the safe does better than the innovatory, Billy Joel does best of all by threatening gently.

He remains mildly but pleasingly idiosyncratic, releasing a live album not of old hits but of early songs he felt were never recorded properly. He calls them not *The Best Of* or *Golden Greats* but an actual title: *Songs In The Attic*. It's an act of rebellion not so much against society as against the commercial expectations of the record business. As long as he keeps this kind of attitude and thumbs his nose at the crassest of demands made upon him – he's okay. He's still rock and roll to me.

OTIS REDDING

They called it 'soul', the ability to communicate to others an intangible quality of deep feeling. In popular music, 'soul' had its heyday in the early and mid-sixties, led by men and women who could sing a ballad with such emotion the listener shared the experience, and who stomped through up-tempo material with such gusto it seemed the phonograph needle might go right through the record. The undisputed King of Soul was Otis Redding.

If you just saw a photo of him you wouldn't think he was King of anything. His nose was extremely large, and his cheekbones protruded so far they looked like they were trying to escape from his head. His moustache was always so thin you couldn't tell if he kept it that way out of choice or because he couldn't grow a full one. And he was usually slightly overweight, as if he should be going for a week on a health farm instead of an hour on stage.

None of it mattered. When he started to sing, he took his audience to a world within, where emotions fought to be recognised, expressed, and purged. The voice of Otis Redding got under one's skin and fought to get out. When it did, it provided an exhausting but exhilarating catharsis.

Redding was born in Dawson, Georgia, in 1941. His father was a minister, and soon moved the family of six children to the larger city of Macon. This had been the home town of Little Richard, so it was he who was the original model for the teenage Otis. In 1960, Redding cut 'Shout Bamalama', clearly influenced by Little Richard. It was released by Confederate records, a local company that had the questionable taste of putting a confederate flag on the label; not, one would have thought, the ideal artwork for a rhythm and blues song. In his book *Making Tracks*, Charlie Gillett relates the reaction of a New York record man who turned down an offer to pick up 'Shout Bamalama' for national promotion: 'This was when Little Richard was in his gospel phase and that sound was as dead as could be, so I didn't follow it up at all.' Bethlehem Records did take the single, and made its money back years later repackaging the track on compilation albums with genuine hits from the King catalogue.

Two more unsuccessful singles were recorded. No one wanted to know Otis Redding except his manager, Phil Walden. Though a white man, Walden felt like a brother to Redding.

Atlantic Records wanted to cut a single with another of Walden's clients, Johnny Jenkins and the Pinetoppers, a group for whom Redding had sung while a teenager. Jenkins had registered a minor regional hit called 'Love Twist' without Otis, and Atlantic wanted a follow-up. Phil Walden made sure that his friend drove the group to the session at the Stax studios in Memphis. When, after two and a half hours of the three-hour session, it became clear that nothing good was going to come of the Jenkins material, Atlantic promotion man Joe Galkin suggested that the young singer get a chance. He'd brought along a song of his own. In storybook style, Otis Redding stepped to the microphone and recorded a hit: 'These Arms of Mine'. This showed an aspect of Otis Redding's talent not displayed before. It wasn't recognised at first by Stax head Jim Stewart, who had agreed to produce the record in exchange for a percentage of the publishing rights. Stewart gave his part of the two songs on Otis' first single to a Nashville DJ, but kept the right to release the sides on his new Volt label. The DJ was only too willing to play 'These Arms of Mine', and through his exposure the record started to break. Otis Redding made his debut on the rhythm and blues chart in March, 1963. The record spread slowly across America, and by May it had entered the Hot 100.

Stax were still unaware of the great artist they had on their roster. Eight months elapsed before Otis Redding cut his second Volt single, a version of Allen Toussaint's 'Ruler of My Heart' called 'Pain In My Heart'. It was slightly more successful than 'These Arms of Mine', sufficiently so to justify Redding's first LP.

Steve Cropper had made very distinctive contributions to Otis Redding's first two hits. On 'Pain In My Heart', he played the catchy guitar licks. On 'These Arms of Mine', he had been on piano, laying down an infectious repetition of chords. Booker T. Jones had been on the first single as well, playing organ, and Booker T. and the MG's formed the nucleus of the backing of all of Otis Redding's hits. The Memphis Horns, as they were called, made memorable contributions on several occasions, as evidenced by Otis' output in 1965.

This was his greatest year in terms of artistic achievement, though the peak of his commercial success did not come for two years. In 1965, Redding released no fewer than six sides now considered soul classics. The first two were both on the same single. Otis Redding went not for the ears but the heart with the A-side, one of the deepest soul hits of all time, 'That's How Strong My Love Is'. It was almost immediately covered by the Rolling Stones for their album *Out Of Their Heads*. Being Otis' first good up-tempo track, the B-side, 'Mr Pitiful', brought him his greatest pop success, taking him to the verge of the top forty. Atlantic Records, which distributed Stax, recognised they had a major talent on their hands, and in the early spring of the year dispatched star engineer and later producer Tom Dowd to Memphis to supervise Otis' studio work. Dowd reported that 'Those guys knew what they were doing and worked very well together', and played down his own importance.

Whatever Dowd's influence, the fact is that *Otis Blue*, the album that came out of those sessions, was a masterpiece. If a new record buyer wants one sixties soul album for his collection, this should be the one. The range of material goes from the most moving and tortured of ballads to the most energetic and exciting stompers, and the first single taken from the album is one of the greatest 45s ever pressed.

'I've Been Loving You Too Long' was co-written by Otis and Jerry Butler. The recorded performance is a case study in controlled delivery as Otis starts by stating the title, gradually building the case for his emotional helplessness while the instrumentalists build behind him, and then breaking loose in a peak of frenzy. In his moment of greatest hopelessness he does what might be expected of a minister's son: he calls out the name of the Almighty. In one sense, it was nice that Tina Turner brought the song to a wider audience when she made it the climax of her live show; but she made it a sexual farce, licking and stroking the microphone to make the word 'suggestive' an inappropriate understatement. The song itself is not about sex: it is about love in the fullest sense, a love so complete it refuses to die even when unnourished. 'I've Been Loving You Too Long' was Otis' first top forty hit. 'Respect', from the same album, was his second. In Britain, *Otis Blue* gave him his first chart success: 'My Girl'.

'My Girl' entered the British charts in the autumn of 1965 and remained for nearly four months. It was a cover version of the Temptations' American number one, but for almost all Britons it is the definitive performance of the Smokey Robinson song.

Otis Blue contained several covers, including three remakes of Sam

Cooke numbers. After Little Richard, Sam had been Otis' hero, and the late star was represented by new workings of 'Wonderful World', 'Shake', and 'A Change Is Gonna Come'. It wasn't the only time Otis paid a tribute to Cooke: on other occasions he did 'You Send Me' and 'Chain Gang'.

The most unusual cover on *Otis Blue* was of a recent smash not by a soul star but a rock group. The Rolling Stones had cut 'That's How Strong My Love Is'; now Redding cut their number one hit 'Satisfaction'. Steve Cropper suggested he try it, thinking it might help Otis make a further impression on the rock audience. Otis later admitted he hadn't liked the idea but had done it anyway. Though the artist was unhappy with applying his own style to a song from another form of music, a process which inevitably resulted in a dilution of Redding's artistic purity, a co-writer was not upset. Keith Richard had anticipated while composing the music for 'Satisfaction' that the introductory riff might be played by a horn section instead of, or as well as, his guitar. That's what happened on Otis Redding's version.

'Satisfaction' eventually gave Otis Redding another moderate hit, but it paled next to his last 1965 release, a no-holds-barred belter titled 'I Can't Turn You Loose'. I've used the word 'stomper' to describe some of Redding's up-tempo pieces because that's what he would call them. He felt the old shuffle beat was out and the stomp was in. You can hear it on 'Respect' with its thumping beat, and it's a prominent part of 'I Can't Turn You Loose'. It's as if there were series of peaks on a seismograph, rather than a straight line from the beginning to the end of the track. It was on 'I Can't Turn You Loose' that Redding gave his finest televised performance. He seemed like a man possessed by St Vitus' Dance as he strutted and stomped across the stage, half-singing, half-spitting out his own lyrics. It was almost frightening to be in the presence of such energy.

Critic Clive Anderson called the repeated 'gotta gotta' phrase in 'I Can't Turn You Loose' 'a demented turkey gobble'. Well, no wonder: the record entered the r & b charts Christmas week, 1965. But it was far too manic to be played on pop stations, and sensing that the best chance for mass acceptance lay in ballads and cover versions of rock songs, Otis paid attention to these forms in 1966. 'Satisfaction' was finally released as a single and the Beatles' 'Day Tripper' was given a ferocious reading on the LP *The Otis Redding Dictionary of Soul*. This album wasn't a sell-out. The slow songs were performed with as much earnestness as before. Otis and Stax sensed that these were his forte and that he was the best singer in the field, so he posed on the cover in a teacher's cap leaning against a book that was called *Complete and Unbelievable, The Otis Redding Dictionary of Soul*. It was a way of saying: this man is the master of this music.

He proved it especially well on two singles from the album. First came 'Fa Fa Fa Fa Fa', subtitled 'Sad Song'. It sounds like a title even Abba with their love of nonsense syllables might have thrown away. In fact, it came about by fortuitous mistake. Otis was singing what he wanted to be a horn line. He wanted the brass to go fa-fa-fa-fa-fa at these points of the song. Record executive Jerry Wexler told him to retain the line as a vocal, and it became the title of an international hit. It showed yet again both Otis Redding's natural ability to sing a slow song with feeling and the comfort with which he played with his Memphis mates. Perhaps the best example of this rapport is heard on Otis' version of 'Try a Little Tenderness', a standard from the thirties. The gradual build-up on 'I've Been Loving You Too Long' had been a great success, and on this song it was taken to its utter extreme. No record could begin more gently and end more wildly than 'Try a Little Tenderness'. Melancholy tenor saxes establish the mood, then Otis calmly recites a young girl's predicament. Pianist Isaac Hayes, who played on so many of Redding's hits, trades short but distinct solo phrases with organist Booker T. Jones and guitarist Steve Cropper. Al Jackson, Jr strikes up a faster tempo, the horns grow dramatically tense, the keyboard players get more excited, and Otis breaks the chains that bind him like an emotional Hercules.

'Try A Little Tenderness' was an object lesson in how to construct and perform a hit record. To this day many rock musicians who might find Redding's straighter soul ballads too intense cite it as one of their favourite singles.

'Tenderness' became a hit in early 1967. This was the year when radio rewarded Redding as it had been reluctant to do with his most soulful performances. First it supported 'Try A Little Tenderness'. Then it hopped on an international smash written by Otis and his protégé Arthur Conley and recorded by Conley, 'Sweet Soul Music'. Perhaps we should say 'the younger' Arthur Conley: for all his accomplishments, Otis was still only twenty-five-years-old. Yet in the four years since his first success, he had made historic achievements in music and shrewd investments with his earnings. He had started a record company, a publishing company, a real estate business, and a ranch, the three-hundred-acre Big O Ranch.

Both Roy Orbison and Otis were called 'The Big O', but there is no record of Orbison going home to the ranch by mistake.

Exulting in a nickname like 'The Big O' does take a bit of cheek, but it makes sense in the interests of publicity. Otis wanted fame. In 'Respect' he had written 'All I want is a little respect when I come home'. In 'My Girl' he had rewritten Smokey Robinson's line 'I don't need no money, fortune or fame' to 'I don't need no money, all I need is my fame'. He had written himself into the line-up of soul greats in 'Sweet Soul Music', and now he agreed to be cast as The King of Soul in a duet album with Carla Thomas, *King and Queen*. Rufus' daughter Carla never justified the title Queen of Soul despite several fine singles, but she did make a good album with Otis. They had a hit duet with a remake of Lowell Fulsom's 1966 top ten r & b soul, 'Tramp'.

Otis Redding was now recognised as Stax' most important star. When the firm had its artists record special messages for a 'Don't Be A Drop Out' campaign, Otis led off to the promotional disc supplied to radio stations. This limited edition LP, perhaps the greatest Redding rarity, boasted an open letter to young people from then-Vice President of the United States Hubert Humphrey, who wrote 'Those who learn more . . . earn more. My young friends, that's where the action is!' Otis phrased his message musically, singing 'If you didn't go back to school this year, then you're not groovy.' The rarely heard message to would-be school-leavers contained clever references to his successful 'Tramp' duet with Carla Thomas. A second track from *King and Queen*, Eddie Floyd's 'Knock on Wood', gave the pair another well-received outing. But the work of another female vocalist gave Otis even greater reward than Carla's efforts. Aretha Franklin took 'Respect', delivered it in a nearly non-stop line compared with Redding's stomp style, and added the r-e-s-p-e-c-t spell-out and the riveting contradiction of having the secular catch phrase 'sock it to me' chanted gospel style. 'Respect' was the first and only number one hit by the real Queen of Soul.

It was a wonderful year for Otis Redding: hits for himself, hits in a duet, hits as a songwriter; smash live engagements in Europe and at the Monterey Pop Festival. *Melody Maker* readers chose Otis the world's leading male vocalist. It seemed as if 1967 was the beginning of a long and luminous career. It was, instead, the end. On the afternoon of 10 December, Otis Redding's private plane crashed in Lake Monona, Wisconsin, killing its owner and several members of the Bar-Kays.

It seemed impossible that so vibrant and vital a man could die at the age of twenty-six. For soul music it was a loss as profound as it was shocking. The pallbearers at Redding's funeral included Joe Tex, Percy Sledge, Solomon Burke, Johnny Taylor, Don Covay, Joe Simon, and Sam Moore of Sam and Dave. All were great artists, but none had the Big O's charisma or his wide range of talents. Just when soul music was taking off in the pop charts as well as the r & b lists, its foremost practitioner had to die. The white audience's interest in soul didn't die immediately, but by the early seventies top forty stations would once again be, as the show business phrase goes, 'vanilla'. Otis Redding had nine posthumous chart titles in the two years after his death, including his first number one, 'Dock of the Bay', a mournful, reflective piece that now seemed ironic and prophetic. In Britain, he also reached the top twenty with a pop-oriented tune called 'Hard to Handle'. Other releases included the American hit 'The Happy Song' and the touching piece written by Otis' wife Zelma, 'I've Got Dreams to Remember'.

We've got records to remember, and the unhappy realisation that Otis Redding was cut down in the middle of a great career. He was becoming recognised as a great recording artist and live entertainer, and the Memphis Sound of which he was the biggest star was earning wide popular acceptance.

It really hasn't been the same since he died. Stax made some appalling business decisions, and almost all the label's artists vanished along with the label. Soul music itself began to fade in popularity just as its triumph over r & b was confirmed by the changing of the title to 'soul' charts. With the notable exception of Al Green, the major black artists of the seventies devoted their energies to disco and funk rather than soul. A style which once seemed it would be with us forever faded just like any other pop style.

The difference is that soul was a style that retained its beauty even after it fell out of fashion. Anyone who ever feels lonely or downtrodden can put on one of Otis Redding's from-the-heart records and realise that someone else has felt the same way. Just knowing that makes it feel better. Otis transmitted emotion to vinyl better than any man has ever done. That is soul.

THE
BEACH
BOYS

California got lucky. It could have been known as a place with a desert, where the temperature frequently rose over 100 degrees Fahrenheit and human beings stayed inside during daylight. It could have been called The Earthquake State, where killer quakes can occur at any moment. It could have been famous for all the no-hopers and crackpots who, having failed to make a living in the rest of the United States, had gone as far west as they could go.

But no, California got lucky. It had three unofficial publicists who gave it an image of a fantasy world free of care. First, there was Hollywood, second Walt Disney and third, the Beach Boys. With those three on your side, even a garden shed would seem like the place to be. The Beach Boys sang of the sun and the sand all right – but not the desert, the beach.

The Beach Boys are America's favourite homegrown rock group. The Four Seasons have had approximately the same success on record, but they never claimed to represent a way of life. When one thinks of the Four Seasons, one thinks of Frankie Valli's falsetto voice. When one thinks of the Beach Boys, one thinks of sunshine, surf, and beautiful bronzed bodies. It's no insult to Frankie Valli to say which has more appeal.

The very name of the group evokes a way of life: 'The Beach Boys'. It's certainly more gripping than the Wilson Family or the Hawthornes, which could have been used as alternatives. Brothers Brian, Carl and Dennis Wilson are the nucleus of the group, along with cousin Mike Love and Hawthorne, California neighbour Al Jardine. They were billed in their earliest appearances at school dances as Carl and the Passions or Kenny and the Cadets.

In 1961, Dennis Wilson, who was literally only sixteen, suggested it was time someone wrote a song about his hobby, surfing. Teenage surfers wanted suitable music both to celebrate the sun and sea lifestyle and to play at the parties that were an inevitable part of youth culture. Dick Dale and the Del-Tones were the originators of the instrumental surf sound, but like the Ventures their party music didn't have lyrics. Brian Wilson took his brother's suggestion to heart and, with Mike Love, wrote a song about surfing. What else to call it but 'Surfin''?

It was released on the unimportant Candix label, yet it still made the Hot 100 in early 1962. The quintet had stumbled upon a subject obviously worth further examination. They had also stumbled upon a name. They had chosen Beach Boys simply because it was appropriate to the single 'Surfin''. Now it was theirs for the rest of their career, a stroke as lucky as it was brilliant.

Real-life Beach Boys did live for the beach, hanging out on the sand and in the sea whenever possible. To most of landlocked America, they were mysterious mythic figures. Even many Californians only dreamed about surfing itself. It has always been a minority sport, open only to the daring or the foolhardy willing to paddle into the ocean and then ride the waves back to shore standing alone on a board. It sounds easier to walk on the moon. But surfing seems so heroic, the subject is fascinating even to those who have never been to the beach. Record-buyers were typical teenagers, and they responded in great numbers to Wilson and Love's second surfing single, 'Surfin' Safari'. This was a top twenty success in the second half of 1962. The Beach Boys had been signed to Capitol Records by producer Nick Venet, and now enjoyed first-class national distribution. The only drawback, if there was one, was that regardless of their other interests, they were America's foremost surfing group, and as long as the fad was going strong, they should capitalise on it, even if Dennis was the only one who actually surfed a great deal. Brian put new words to Chuck Berry's 1958 winner 'Sweet Little Sixteen' and came up with a top three smash, 'Surfin' USA'.

Shortly after that fell off the charts in the summer of 1963, the biggest surf hit of all went to number one. Ironically, it wasn't by the Beach Boys. It *was* composed by Jan Berry with Brian Wilson, and acknowledged the influence Jan had had on the Beach Boys' sound. He had applied the falsetto lead vocal and close harmony sound of the Negro doo-wop groups to his own singles in the late fifties, first with Arnie Ginsburg and then with Dean Torrence. Brian Wilson developed this approach with the Beach Boys, so it was only fitting he help Jan Berry with the Jan and Dean number one, 'Surf City'.

1963 was the peak of popularity for surf music. Besides 'Surf City', the Chantays and the Surfaris had top ten instrumentals with 'Pipeline' and

'Wipeout', and the Trashmen scored with the unforgettable and unbelievable 'Surfin' Bird'. When a trend explodes in pop music, it's like a nova, a star that shines brightly briefly and then burns out. Brian Wilson, already the group's musical leader, must have known this, and showed evidence that he could move beyond the novelty. While everyone else was doing up-tempo surf material, he wrote a ballad that transcended the trend. It was called 'Surfer Girl', but from the sound of the record and the concern in the vocal, it could have been about any kind of loved one. Not only was it beautiful, it was commercial, the group's second top ten hit.

On 'Surfer Girl' one hears quite clearly the influence The Four Freshmen had on Brian Wilson. The Freshmen were a close harmony group who had success in the mid-50s. Their big number was 'Graduation Day', which for a long time was aired every year when degree ceremonies were held. The impact they had on the adolescent Brian Wilson is obvious not only by the harmony technique he used with the Beach Boys but from the fact that his group also recorded 'Graduation Day'.

Water sports are not the only teenage recreations in California. It is a gigantic state with almost no public transport, so the individual motor car is an object of obsession. An outgrowth of this motoring mania in the early 60s was drag racing, and the B-sides of early Beach Boys' singles were about dragging. '409', 'Shut Down', 'Little Deuce Coupe' – while they were popularising the surfer's way of life, the group were also documenting the dragster's. 'Little Deuce Coupe' was a top twenty hit in its own right, even though it was the flip side of 'Surfer Girl'. It also provided the melody the Beach Boys used for their Christmas single, 'Little Saint Nick'.

They had sung about surfing and cars. If they were going to complete a chronicle of teenage Californian life, they were going to have to get around to high school. They did in late 1963 with the almost unbelievably innocent 'Be True To Your School'. This record was completely lost in the UK. The lifestyle of the Beach Boys was so alien to Britons they might as well have been from Mars. 'Be True To Your School' was typical. It contained, without cynicism, that crass American invention, the cheerleader, the short-skirted girl with pom-poms who led the chants at school football games. America loved it. Britain turned its head.

Unquestioning loyalty and pride for one's school – it must have been a different America. While 'Be True To Your School' was in the charts,

President John Kennedy was shot in Dallas. This event was the Great Divide of our times. Everything before it suddenly seemed part of another era. Coincidentally or not, the Beach Boys never again issued a single specifically about surfing, high school or the joys of drag racing. Brian Wilson was showing evidence of musical growth anyway. On the B-side of 'Be True To Your School' he put 'In My Room', a song he co-wrote with Gary Usher about retiring to one's private sanctuary when problems loom too large. It was the first sign that the Beach Boys knew life wasn't always a lark. It was also the first evidence of Brian Wilson's troubled psyche, which first drove his group to historic musical peaks and later lost control.

The Beach Boys and Four Seasons were America's most popular artists, but that didn't mean too much in early 1964, when the Beatles finally broke in the States and did so in unequalled style. All their previous British hits went into the top ten in a space of three months, and in early April they had the top five to themselves. 'Fun Fun Fun' was a top ten hit that winter, but seemed insignificant in the midst of Beatlemania. Here was a challenge the Beach Boys met. In May they released their best two-sided single yet, and both songs became hits. As usual Mike Love sang the up-tempo side and Brian Wilson the ballad.

Getting to number one was accomplishment enough: no male American vocal group had done so in nine months. But this single was also a great artistic achievement. 'I Get Around' was a far more complicated single than the Beach Boys' previous hits, with unusual chord changes and harmonies. 'Don't Worry Baby' was a brilliant ballad, taking the formerly carefree setting of drag racing and using it as the background for a tale of insecurity and nervousness. Its subtlety became appreciated with the passage of time, and in the 1970s it was recorded in Britain by Bryan Ferry and Keith Moon and in the States by B.J. Thomas, who took it to the top twenty.

Through clever exploitation of a novelty, the Beach Boys had earned the resources to develop fully their abilities, just at the time they were most suited to do so. Brian Wilson felt inspired by Phil Spector and challenged by the Beatles, and he spurred himself on to a series of remarkable records. The follow-up to 'I Get Around', 'When I Grow Up (To Be A Man)', showed a maturity unusual for the 1964 charts and almost unbelievable for a group which had been singing about high school football a year before. 'Will I dig the same things that turn me on as a kid?' the Beach Boys sang anxiously.

The responsibilities of leading the band as well as the brothers were too much, and Brian suffered a nervous breakdown in early 1965. He decided to stay off the road and concentrate on recording work. Glen Campbell joined the touring group for a short time, followed by Bruce Johnston, who became the off-and-on honorary Beach Boy for years to come. They weren't the first temporary members: David Marks had been a Beach Boy for half a year early in their career while Al Jardine had gone to dental school. Jardine was not only back but up front on the group's first big hit of 1965. It originally appeared as a track on the album *Beach Boys Today*, one of seven consecutive US top ten LPs, and was re-arranged for release as a single. 'Help Me, Rhonda' was the Beach Boys' second number one, peaking in the late spring of 1965. It was a perfect set-up for a good summer song, and the Beach Boys had one in hand. It was the last contribution to their Californian cultural canon: surf, cars, school, sunshine and – 'California Girls' which was the Beach Boys' ninth American top ten hit. Incredibly enough, only 'I Get Around' had reached the ten in Britain. The subject matter of the songs was still too rooted in foreign culture. But that changed in 1966.

First came 'Barbara Ann', the singalong from *The Beach Boys' Party* album that had originally been a hit for the Regents in 1961. This simple song could apply to any English-speaking country, and out of the blue it became the first of four consecutive UK top three hits. The second was an adaptation of an old folk song, anthologised by Carl Sandburg, popularised by The Weavers under the title 'Wreck Of The John B.', and taken into the British charts in 1960 by Lonnie Donegan as 'I Wanna Go Home'. According to writer Joseph Murrells, there actually is a boat called the *John B.* lying in Governor's Harbour, Nassau, that was the direct inspiration for the song the Beach Boys called 'Sloop John B.'.

Observant Beach Boys' fans would have noticed that the last two singles had not been written by Brian Wilson. Surely he must have been concentrating on some major project. He was. He had teamed up with lyricist Tony Asher to work on the LP *Pet Sounds*. In retrospect, Mike Love said that Brian invented the concept album with this record. At the time, it was rumoured that some of the Boys were upset with their main man, wondering what he was doing masterminding an album of mostly slow, reflective material, including a track of dogs barking at a passing train. Critics consider the album a classic, and voted it the twelfth best long player of all-time in a 1977 poll. But though it was the most successful of the group's LPs to date in Britain, it was the least successful of the last half dozen in America.

Pet Sounds is a fine album, giving wide evidence of the possibilities of acoustic sounds in popular music. The best numbers on the album are almost bone-chilling in their troubled lyrics, measured delivery and precise backing. 'Caroline No', Brian's solo set closer, is an example. But this type of music has never been particularly commercial, and the album's American hit, aside from the incongruous 'Sloop John B.' stuck on the end of the first side, was the track most in keeping with Beach Boys tradition.

'Wouldn't It Be Nice' was a wonderful fantasy about what it would be like to have a lifelong partner. The other side of the single, which turned out to be a lasting classic, was about the other side of the relationship: what would it be like to *lose* someone you want to stay with for life? 'God Only Knows'. Together they made the Beach Boys' second truly great two-sided single. It *was* nice that 'Wouldn't It Be Nice' and 'God Only Knows' were hits. But the relative failure at home of *Pet Sounds* hurt Brian Wilson.

For six months he worked on a new single, trying and trying again to get the right sounds. This is very difficult when you're working with a Moog-theremin, sleigh bells and tambourine, but Brian kept going, also using a harpsichord amongst his panoply of instruments. He arranged the backing singers behind Carl as a layer of voices, pre-dating by nearly a decade the complex arrangements of Queen and 10 c.c. The result was 'Good Vibrations', a masterpiece that can be appreciated on several levels: as a hit record, as an example of symphonic pop, or as an outstanding piece of experimental music.

It was ironic that the peak of the Beach Boys' career artistically and commercially, a number one in both the US and UK, should have been so atypical of their work. Perhaps it might have had a broader context had Brian Wilson been able to realise his greatest plans. It is a sad fact of rock history that he was not. Wilson was working on an album called *Smile* with Van Dyke Parks, a lyricist who was publicised as one of the great talents of the late sixties before he actually did anything. His own LP, though well-received by some, flopped miserably, and *Smile* never saw the light of day. Legend has it that Brian Wilson heard the Beatles' *Sgt. Pepper*, realised he couldn't equal it, and declared 'no contest'. Of the fifteen songs intended for *Smile*, only nine ever appeared, and only a few of those on the next album, *Smiley Smile*. The single from the set, 'Heroes And Villains', seemed incomplete – no wonder, it was part of a much longer unreleased whole. It was a terrible setback to Wilson when he naïvely brought the single to a Los Angeles radio station personally, expecting the disc jockey excitedly to play the exclusive. The DJ needed the permission of his executives before airing anything, and Wilson slinked away, back into a solitude that has become legendary.

Did drugs really damage his mind? Did he really have a sand pit in the middle of his living room? Why, in the late seventies, did the Beach Boys persist in bringing him on stage, when he almost always just sat at the keyboard looking like a former human being? Tom Petty summarised the dilemma perfectly when he said after meeting him in a restaurant, 'I thought Brian was a perfect gentleman, apart from buttering his head and trying to put it between two slices of bread.'

We will never know what further heights Brian Wilson could have reached because the old Brian Wilson succumbed to paranoia and drugs. The only touches of brilliance heard since 'Good Vibrations' came in 1971 on the album *Surf's Up*, which included not only Bruce Johnston's fine 'Disney Girls' but what had been intended to be the centrepiece of *Smile*, the title track 'Surf's Up'. Heard now, it seems an almost unbearably sad elegy for a brilliant composer and a great group.

Surf's Up triggered a return to respectability for the Beach Boys in 1971, and there have been sporadic successes since '66: 'Do It Again', a nostalgic look backward that went all the way to number one in Britain in '68, *Holland*, a good new album, *20 Golden Greats* and *Endless Summer*, good compilation albums that went to number one in Britain and America respectively in the first half of the seventies, and one-off returns to the top ten in the two countries, 'Lady Lynda' and 'Rock And Roll Music'. Despite this erratic performance, their live audiences have been larger than ever in the last half-dozen years. They stole the show from Elton John and the Eagles at Wembley Stadium in 1975, and in the States over half their current fans are too young to have been born when 'Surfin' Safari' was a hit.

It all demonstrates the durability of a dream. No matter how aging or hitless the Beach Boys may be, they are forever a fundamental part of a fantasy everyone wants to keep alive. Put on one of the old hits and you can 'Do It Again', go back to the innocent world of sun, surf and sand. It only took three hits about surfing and three further years of singing about California to persuade people the world over that even in troubled times it is possible to find a place that is nothing but 'Fun Fun Fun'.

STEVIE
WONDER

Stevie Wonder had his first number one record in 1963. So did Paul and
Paula, the Singing Nun, and Kyu Sakamoto. The difference is that nearly
two decades later, Stevie Wonder is still having hits. To be precise, he's
had more American top ten hits in the rock era than any artist except
Elvis Presley and the Beatles. And he's catching up.

Stevie was born on 13 May 1950. That we can say with certainty, it's
the surname that gets people confused. His father's name was Judkins,
but on his birth certificate he was called Stevland Morris. When he was in
school he took the name Judkins, and signed his first songwriting contract
that way.

The blind boy began singing, as he put it, 'as soon as I could holler',
and began performing professionally when he was nine. A friend of his
was a cousin of Ronnie White of the Miracles, and through White,
Stevland won an audition with Motown Records President, Berry Gordy.
The founder of the Detroit Sound liked the youngster, who could already
play harmonica and drums, but he wasn't crazy about the name Stevland
Morris. Since Gordy thought his talent was a marvel, a wonder, they
considered calling the boy Wonder Steve . . . Little Wonder . . . and
finally Little Stevie Wonder.

He *was* little, so Gordy put him under Motown's wing. Martha Reeves
had to baby-sit for him as one of her secretarial duties. Stevie was given
an allowance of two and a half dollars a week. Henry Cosby and Clarence
Paul were told to write songs for him. And Marvin Gaye played drums on
the Cosby–Paul song that was Stevie's first release: 'I Call It Pretty Music
(But the Old People Call It the Blues)'.

It was issued in August, 1962. The very first song he recorded wasn't
put out for two years – 'Thank You (For Loving Me All The Way)',
which sounds risqué for a twelve-year-old but was actually a song about
mother.

The problem was that Stevie's voice still hadn't broken and no one at

Motown could figure out how to use it on record. Listening to the first few bars of 'Sunset', a number the artist co-wrote with Clarence Paul, makes one realise that the powerful young singer was as jarring as he was exuberant. It was a boy banshee who wailed into the 'Sunset', a boy who had a lot of talent but hadn't yet been shaped as an artist. Tamla, the Motown family label he was on, tried something obvious by having Little Stevie record an album called *Tribute to Uncle Ray*, a respectful but unimaginative salute to Ray Charles, who, also being black and blind, was the artist to whom Wonder was most likely to be compared.

Tribute to Uncle Ray didn't make it, nor did *The Jazz Soul of Little Stevie*, a reference to the fact that Stevie could play several instruments with a jazz feel. Tamla eventually found the best setting for its child prodigy inadvertently. The excitement of Stevie's still undisciplined voice was conveyed better in live performance than in the studio. A number that had been only mildly interesting on the *Jazz Soul* album became a sensation when played before an audience. 'Fingertips' was never meant to be a single – it was seven minutes long – but the concert recording was so exciting it was put out on two sides of a 45, with the second half getting radio attention. 'Fingertips Part II' is one of the most exciting singles of all-time. Stevie's frenzy clearly affects the audience and the band; a musician frantically cries 'what key? what key?' when the compere demands a reprise.

'Fingertips Part II' was a truly historic hit. Number One for three weeks in August '63, it was the first live record to ever top the American singles chart. Stevie was the youngest artist to lead the list since the twelve-year-old Jimmy Boyd had scored in 1952 with a Christmas number one called 'I Saw Mommy Kissing Santa Claus'. But Boyd didn't have a number one album. Wonder did: *The Twelve-Year-Old Genius*.
It was a lot to live up to, and for over two years Stevie didn't. He was still unable to focus his talent on a three-minute studio recording. Appearing in two of the beach party films so common at the time, *Muscle Beach Party* and *Bikini Beach*, also did nothing to further his reputation as a genius.

The first sign that Wonder might have a lasting career came in November 1965, when a song he had co-written was released. It was the first A-side he had composed, not just the music, but also the central phrase: 'Everything is alright, uptight, out of sight'.

'Uptight' was his return to the top three. It was also his first British chart entry.

Stevie Wonder's voice had broken. He could sing with discipline and control as well as soul. As his billing indicated, he was no longer 'Little'. But, as before, there were difficulties with a follow-up. 'Nothing's Too Good For My Baby' *wasn't* good enough, and for his next try Stevie opted for an off-the-wall choice.

While being driven between towns on a UK tour he had worked out an arrangement of Bob Dylan's 'Blowin' in the Wind' with Clarence Paul. Back in the States, Paul produced Stevie's version, on which he duetted without credit. It wasn't the first time they'd sung together, since Paul had vocalised with Stevie on Wonder's second single, 'Little Water Boy'. This time the result was more successful, and Dylan done Gospel style gave Stevie his third number one r & b hit.

In 1966 it was still the policy of most record companies to follow a hit with a single that sounded quite like it. This had happened to Stevie in the case of 'Uptight' and 'Nothing's Too Good For My Baby'. Now 'Blowin' in the Wind' was followed by another reflective ballad, 'A Place in the Sun'. The change was that 'A Place in the Sun' was another hit. For the first time in his career, Stevie had scored on two consecutive outings.

The big British breakthrough was now only a few months away. In the summer of 1967, 'I Was Made to Love Her' was a top five smash in both the US *and* UK. Stevie was now a genuine international star, and attention was drawn to giving him a coherent and consistent release schedule in 1968. He had a major hit, 'Shoo Be Doo Be Doo Da Day', a minor hit, 'You Met Your Match', and a joyous piece of self-indulgence called *Eivets Rednow*, an album of harmonica solos released under the pseudonym of his own name spelled backwards.

At the very end of the year, a great step was taken in Stevie's growth as an artist. He recorded a cabaret ballad originally brought to the Hot 100 by Tony Bennett, and though the coupling seemed unlikely, it proved a smash on both sides of the Atlantic.

'For Once In My Life' reached number two in America, kept out of number one only by label-mate Marvin Gaye's 'I Heard It Through the Grapevine'. In Britain it began a string of four consecutive top ten hits. Stevie fought for the release of the ballad 'My Cherie Amour', and watched with delight as it took over from the A-side 'I Don't Know Why' to become a worldwide hit. 'Yester-Me, Yester-You, Yester-Day' followed, giving Stevie his second British number two and becoming part of a very strange achievement: Wonder has had four number twos without getting a number one. No artist has equalled this record of frustration.

'Never Had A Dream Come True' started 1970 off in top ten form, but the following single was of greater significance. For the first time, Stevie Wonder produced himself. Furthermore, his co-writers included people close to him personally – the woman he would soon marry as well as produce, Syreeta Wright, and his also blind friend, Lee Garrett. Though Motown never released sales figures, Stevie referred to 'Signed Sealed Delivered I'm Yours' as 'the biggest thing I'd had'.

It was released in July, 1970, the same month as 'It's a Shame' by the Motown Spinners. Both singles were produced by Stevie Wonder, making his debut as a disc director a double success. Slowly but surely, Stevie was becoming a self-sufficient artist, and on his twenty-first birthday in 1971 he became a free artist.

He received one million dollars from the trust fund Berry Gordy had set up with his royalties, and he negotiated a contract which freed him from most of the restrictions Motown placed on its artists. He could work on the projects he wanted, and in a burst of artistic and personal unity co-wrote and produced an album with his wife Syreeta while she co-wrote an album for him, *Where I'm Coming From*.

It sounds as if Gordy gave away a great deal in Stevie's new 120-page contract. But there actually was little reason not to let him have his way with his LPs. The cold fact was that after the *Twelve-Year-Old Genius* album, the teenage Wonder failed to return to the top twenty of the American long play list, and only made a short solitary entry in the British top twenty with the *My Cherie Amour* set. Stevie Wonder's albums had been hodge-podges of two or three hits, a few B-sides, and several tracks that seem to have been thrown together at random. The Supremes, Four Tops and Temptations sold albums in volume. Stevie Wonder did not.

Why not let him have his own way? The old way hadn't worked.

The first fruit of his self-sufficiency was *Music of My Mind*, released in early 1972. With the exception of two instrumental solos, the performances were all Stevie's, and for the first time most of the tracks on an LP were written by him alone. 'Keep On Running' was tense and exciting, 'Superwoman' moody and moving, but because neither was a hit single the album was only a moderate success. The mass audience learned of the new Stevie Wonder when, in the following winter, a classic single leapt out of the radio and grabbed it by the ears.

'Superstition' began the third phase of Stevie Wonder's popular acceptance, as surely as 'Fingertips' had earned him fans as a boy and 'Uptight' had as a teenager. But had Motown not insisted, 'Superstition' would never have been a single, because Stevie had earlier given the song to Jeff Beck, thinking it would be perfect for his group. Wonder wanted 'Big Brother' as his next 45, but he didn't finish it in time and Motown went with 'Superstition'.

The single was perfect. The album that shortly followed was astonishing. On *Talking Book* Stevie Wonder suddenly did everything he had ever done right all at the same time, and found new things to do well, too. Once again he played nearly all the instruments, carrying on the fusion of rock and soul pioneered by Sly Stone and Jimi Hendrix. With the assistance of synthesiser programmers Malcolm Cecil and Robert Margouleff, he made explorations of the Arp and Moog. He sang up-tempo numbers with the power he'd had at his command ever since 'he could holler', and he softly swathed his slow songs in the soft style he'd developed from the ballads he'd insisted on doing in the sixties. 'I Believe (When I Fall In Love It Will Be Forever)' is one of the most inspiring testaments to love ever recorded, and 'You are the Sunshine of My Life' one of the most commercially successful. Incidentally, it wasn't Stevie singing the first two lines of this song, but rather Jim Gilstrap, who later had his own hit 'Swing Your Daddy'. So every disc jockey who talked up to the vocal saying 'Here's Stevie Wonder' was wrong. 'You Are The Sunshine Of My Life' was Stevie Wonder's second consecutive number one single. More importantly, *Talking Book* won over both critics and the rock album buying public. Stevie had recently courted this crowd by supporting the Rolling Stones on tour, a reversal of early form when they had opened for him in 1964. But it had been rock musicians who had done most of the experimenting with popular electronic music, as he loved to do, and Stevie found it only natural to play this crowd.

An even wider audience loved the new Stevie Wonder. Frank Sinatra recorded 'You Are The Sunshine Of My Life'. The National Academy of Recording Arts and Sciences presented Wonder with three Grammy Awards for 'Sunshine' and 'Superstition'. Stevie maintained the momentum by releasing his third album in a year and a half: *Innervisions*.

For some reason, perhaps because he only has himself to discipline himself, on Wonder's LPs there are usually one or two lengthy concessions to current rhythmic trends that won't stand up and one or two tracks where his great and sincere love for God and the universe are trivialised by banal lyrics. Not so on *Innervisions*: the pace was varied but the standards always high. There was one of the most accessible yet devastating stories of black awareness ever put to plastic, 'Living For the City'.

The full-length version, too long for release as a single, contains a powerful playlet in which a young black man arrives in the city, is unjustly framed, and winds up in prison. It enhances rather than clutters the album.

The great irony of the LP was 'Higher Ground', its first single. It contains the lines 'I'm so glad that he let me try it again/Cause my last time on earth I lived a whole world of sin'. On 6 August 1973, three days after the release of *Innervisions*, Stevie Wonder was seriously wounded when the car he was in collided with a logging lorry. For four days the twenty-two-year-old lay in a coma, his survival uncertain. For several days thereafter he drifted in and out of consciousness. Much of that time his friend, Ira Tucker, sat by his side and sang the words to 'Higher Ground'. When Stevie next came to England, choosing to make his comeback concert at the Rainbow, he stated that the aptness of the song was too great to be a coincidence. He did believe he had been given a second chance to reach 'Higher Ground'.

Innervisions won Stevie Wonder a new set of Grammy Awards, and so did his 1974 album, *Fulfillingness First Finale*. When Paul Simon got the nod the following year, he thanked Stevie Wonder for making it possible by not releasing an album.

The three award-winning albums did seem a natural trilogy, one of the most brilliant in pop history. Stevie Wonder became the musicians' musician, the man most cited as a favourite artist or a great influence. In the rush to salute his recordings, one shouldn't have forgotten some of the great songs he'd already co-written for other artists.

By the end of 1974 these included 'Tears Of A Clown', cut by Smokey Robinson and the Miracles in 1967 to become an international number one in 1970, 'Loving You Is Sweeter Than Ever', a 1966 gem by the Four Tops, 'It's a Shame', the 1970 effort for the Detroit Spinners, 'Until You Come Back To Me', recorded but not released by Stevie Wonder in 1967 and given to Aretha Franklin years later, 'Tell Me Something Good', an American number one by Rufus, and 'Your Kiss Is Sweet', part of his second album for Syreeta, no longer the wife but still a friend.

The ultimate acknowledgement of Stevie Wonder's worth to Motown came when he signed his fourth recording contract. The previous papers had been for five years each. This covered seven years and promised

Stevie thirteen million dollars. It was the most expensive recording contract in music business history, though other artists such as Paul McCartney and Elton John have obtained higher royalty rates. Stevie also won the right to determine his own release schedules. This is another way of saying he had the right not to release anything if he didn't think he was ready.

Fans waited two years for the double-album *Songs in the Key of Life*. The demand for another piece of product from the man was so great he wrote a disclaimer on the lyric sheet, saying 'Thank you everyone for being so patient'.

Beginning with this album, Stevie Wonder the artist used his superior musical talent to convey messages of love and tribute other record-makers have been too embarrassed or unable to state. His tribute to Duke Ellington, 'Sir Duke', gave him another American number one.

It was the natural first single from *Songs in the Key of Life*, but the natural second single never appeared. Stevie now had complete control over which tracks were taken from LPs, and he didn't want 'Isn't She Lovely' out as a 45 because it would have to be shortened . . . and he was not going to edit a song about the birth of his daughter.

'Isn't She Lovely' is one of the few pop songs that can be appreciated by almost the entire human population. When these rare moments come along, they are greeted by exultation, and, once more, Stevie Wonder was profusely honoured. But this time he refused to supply the demand for more material as quickly as he had before. It took him three years to prepare his next work, the soundtrack to a film called *The Secret Life of Plants*. It was, at least in comparison to his recent output, a non-event. For one thing, he had chosen a flop film. Showings of the documentary have been rarer than those of *Muscle Beach Party*. A second factor is that whereas 'Isn't She Lovely' was accessible to all, the notion that plants communicate and have something that could be called a 'secret life' seems bizarre to the majority of humans. Thirdly, by concentrating on music suitable to the screen, Stevie failed to provide material that sounded good on the radio or in the sitting room. *Stevie Wonder's Journey Through the Secret Life of Plants*, cherished by a few fans who think they relate to what it's about, sits undisturbed on the shelves of hundreds of thousands more record buyers to whom it never communicated.

Stevie, to whom communication is all, must have realised this, because in his 1980 concert dates he presented a history of his career that almost completely ignored *Plants*. Instead he unveiled his *Hotter than July* album, which included his celebration of freedom, 'Master Blaster'. The reference to Zimbabwe and Bob Marley proved that despite his appeal to the full spectrum of races, he hadn't forgotten he was a black man. His people hadn't forgotten him, either: *Songs in the Key of Life* had topped the US Soul LP chart for twenty weeks, then the longest run at number one ever, and 'Master Blaster' was number one on the soul chart for seven weeks in 1980. Stevie's 'Let's Get Serious', performed by Jermaine Jackson, was the Number 1 soul hit of that year.

The best moment on *Hotter than July* was saved for last as Stevie Wonder paid his tribute to Martin Luther King. Campaigning to make the late civil rights leader's natal day a holiday, Stevie said 'Happy Birthday' in a way that was simultaneously an all-purpose birthday greeting, a dynamite dance number, and a commitment to King's crusade. To make a piece of music work on so many different levels *is* genius. To spread messages of love and tolerance to millions around the world *is* to carry on the work of Dr King in a subtler but no less potent way. Stevie is not only the leading recording artist of the last decade, he is a source of personal inspiration to people around the world. His achievements are tremendous, not for a blind man, not for a black man, but for any man. He once wrote 'I do believe . . . Stevie Wonder is the necessary vehicle on which Stevland Morris must be carried on his mission to spread love mentalism'. The mission continues.

ERIC CLAPTON

His manager called him 'Slowhand' . . . even though he played the fastest instrument in town. His fans called him 'God' . . . even though he said 'I'm only the guitar player'. His greatest song was about unrequited love . . . but he later got the girl. Most of his hits were under some other name . . . but everybody knew he was Eric Clapton.

The first great guitar hero of rock was born on 30 March 1945, in a Surrey town called Ripley. Eric Clapton was brought up by his grandparents – he called it 'semi-adopted'. He was dismissed from Kingston Art College, partly because he spent so much time listening to records rather than doing schoolwork. Clapton was one of many future rock heroes who were not popular with their classmates. As he bluntly recalled, 'I was the one that used to get stones thrown at me because I was so thin and couldn't do physical training very well.'

Clapton found release in American blues records. His first favourite was Chuck Berry, who influenced the young guitarist directly. As a matter of fact, Eric admitted that anyone listening to his initial recordings would have a tough time telling that it wasn't Berry.

One of the early London blues buffs, he went to the Ealing Club, where he occasionally stood in for Mick Jagger as singer of Blues Incorporated. He busked for drinks and sandwiches in Kingston and Richmond.

Clapton played briefly with first the Roosters and then Casey Jones and the Engineers. In October 1963, Eric replaced Tony Topham to become lead guitarist of the Yardbirds, who themselves took over from the Rolling Stones as the resident band at the Crawdaddy Club in Richmond.

The Yardbirds have the distinction of having fostered a series of young guitarists including Clapton, Jeff Beck and Jimmy Page, yet their first recordings were not particularly guitar-oriented. Lead singer Keith Relf played blues harmonica, and his instrumental prowess was spotlighted as much as Clapton's. The group made three singles, an EP and a live LP with the art student-turned-musician. Something strange happened with

the second single: it made the top 50.

'Good Morning Little Schoolgirl' reached the list in November, 1964. The temptation was obvious: make an out-and-out pop record and go for the top ten.

This was exactly what Eric Clapton didn't want. The more he played the more he developed a liking for bluesmen like Big Bill Broonzy, Robert Johnson and Skip James. He loved the work of harmonica player Little Walter Jacobs and claimed it had affected his own, saying that what he did on the mouth organ could be applied to the guitar.

The Yardbirds stepped away from the blues. This is not to say that 'For Your Love' was an artistic sell-out: in its segmented construction and emphasis on the harpsichord it was avant-garde for its day. But it was a pop record, and for Clapton it was the last straw.

Eric quit the Yardbirds shortly after the session. He didn't wait for it to become the top three hit it did.

In an interview with Jann Wenner for *Melody Maker* in 1967, Clapton told how the attractions of fame, money and available young women had drawn him to the group, and that he had indulged. 'But when you find something else that can occupy your mind,' he remembered, 'like when you find that you're actually into playing the guitar, then I don't think you could do both things.'

He worked on a building site with his grandfather for two weeks clearing his head of the Yardbirds experience. Then John Mayall phoned.

Mayall was one of the key figures in the British blues boom. The Manchester man had come to London at the suggestion of Alexis Korner and had played Chicago style blues with five line-ups before asking Eric Clapton to join him for the sixth.

The axeman cameth, and the results were historic. In Mayall's Bluesbreakers Clapton had found an outlet for playing with both emotion and strength. As John Mayall and Bluesbreakers, Eric Clapton, John McVie and Hughie Flint were only together from April to August, 1965, at which point Eric went to Greece for three months, and again from November to the following July, but those months were enough to change Clapton's life. His brilliant solos, both on instrumentals like 'Steppin' Out' and 'Hideaway' and on Mayall's vocal numbers, established him as Britain's finest blues guitarist. The fans who packed out the group's club dates thought even more highly of him. 'Clapton Is God', said the graffiti on the underground wall, and soon the scrawl was all over London. 'Very funny. Very strange,' the subject of the adulation recalled. 'Nothing else was happening in England except me.'

The pressure didn't show on the one album the group left behind. *Blues Breakers* by John Mayall with Eric Clapton remains one of the finest blues LPs any white band ever made. It did something almost no blues LP does: it went to the top ten. The album was one of sincerity of purpose and achievement in performance. As Clapton put it, 'I really got into my music and developed it more than I'd ever done before, 'cause they take it seriously.'

During the two calendar years he was with the Bluesbreakers Eric was so 'into his music' that he found time to cut several tracks with other musicians, including a few with Jimmy Page that were later released on anthologies of English blues and a threesome of tracks for a sampler album called *What's Shakin'*. On the latter set he played alongside Jack Bruce and Stevie Winwood. Clapton took the lead vocal on Robert Johnson's 'Crossroads Blues'. He would play the same number with Jack Bruce singing lead in the not-too-distant future.

The Bluesbreakers had brought Eric national celebrity. Even pedestrians and motorists who never listened to popular music could tell from the graffiti that to somebody, somewhere, Clapton was God. For the man himself, it was time once more to move on. This time it wasn't because he didn't have a chance to play the blues. He'd had it. Now he wanted to play something else: he felt he had to apply his style to rock.

Clapton left Mayall's Bluesbreakers in the summer of 1966. He and drummer Ginger Baker suggested to Jack Bruce, with whom Baker had also worked, that they form a trio. As he later told Steve Turner in a major interview for *Rolling Stone*, 'Cream was originally meant to be a blues trio, like Buddy Guy with a rhythm section.'

The new group stumbled onto their trademark at their first major engagement, the 1966 Windsor Jazz and Blues Festival. They ran out of songs and had to improvise. They made up extended versions of blues songs. These marathons came to feature lengthy solos. Since there were only three men on stage, every one could get a chance to take the spotlight.

It seems odd at first that a group with such long concert numbers should have accumulated seven chart singles. But Cream were a different band in the studio, recording pop songs of mostly their own composition rather than blues standards.

Originally intended to be a band that would play in small clubs rather than large halls, Cream proved too successful for its own purpose. 'We didn't want to be big in any way,' Clapton said, but every release made the charts, and the second album, *Disraeli Gears*, was an international sensation. It included a British hit, 'Strange Brew', a song which was to become an American top ten single when re-promoted a year later, 'Sunshine Of Your Love', an FM radio-favourite, and Eric Clapton co-wrote with artist Martin Sharp, 'Tales of Brave Ulysses'.

Disraeli Gears punned on the derailer gears found on racing bicycles. It was the first Cream album to sell over a million copies, although *Fresh Cream* later topped the figure and subsequent LPs also went over the mark. *Wheels of Fire* sold a million double-albums.

The trio found themselves one of the world's leading live attractions. From an early appearance in one of Murray the K's package shows, an endurance struggle for which both Cream and the Who performed several brief sets a day, the power trio played to thousands at a time, concentrating on venues in the United States. Their amplification suited the size of their audiences, as waves of nearly deafening sound cascaded over the ears of the auditors. A fifteen-minute drum solo from Ginger Baker eventually felt like it was being played inside the listener's head.

The five-month-long American tour wearied Clapton. He tired of the relentless pace and the relentless music. One night he stopped playing in the middle of the number to see if the others would notice. He claimed they didn't, and finished the piece without him.

A negative review in *Rolling Stone*, calling the guitar hero 'the master of the cliché', convinced Clapton the group should stop. Before they did they undertook a series of farewell appearances, including a final date at the Royal Albert Hall filmed by Tony Palmer. They cut one last album, *Goodbye*. The LP boasted a marvellous track co-written by Clapton and his good friend George Harrison, inspired by the mellower music on the *Big Pink* record by The Band: 'Badge'.

It featured a guest appearance by Harrison, on whose Beatles song 'While My Guitar Gently Weeps' Clapton had recently appeared. It was a far gentler number than the manic material Cream were known for, and fans could only wonder which type Clapton's next group would emphasise. Eric had attracted a large following that would accept almost anything he offered them. It was therefore appropriate that the new band was called Blind Faith.

Eric and Ginger Baker joined forces with Stevie Winwood from Traffic and Rick Grech from Family. Blind Faith had great musical possibilities. But it also had great business possibilities, and the operation was doomed from the start. As Winwood related, pressures to hurry up and tour and hurry up and record were so great that the quarter had to present product to the public before it was perfected. Nearly a hundred thousand attended the group's debut concert in Hyde Park. The eponymous LP went to number one in Britain and America without the benefit of a hit single. Blind Faith remain the only act ever to go to number one in the UK and US album charts with their debut disc and never release anything else.

The album itself was not the best work the four men could do, but there were high points, including a moving piece Clapton had written in his new home in Surrey. Away from the London scene and the police who were chalking up drug busts of top pop stars, Eric reflected on his new-found religious faith and wrote the serene song 'Presence of the Lord'.

Clapton realised quickly how unhappy he was in the supergroup. On the second night of the American tour he met Delaney and Bonnie Bramlett, whom he'd requested be the support group. He realised that even though they were getting almost no audience reaction he'd rather be with them than with Blind Faith because, as he put it, 'they were playing soul music'.

He did tour with the Bramletts. An album was recorded under the billing 'Delaney and Bonnie with Eric Clapton' *On Tour*. It was another example of the guitar hero's incredible modesty. At the peak of his profession, he was willing to take second billing to an unknown American duo. When he could have been making money doing solo records, he was always willing to help out on sessions, guesting with over a dozen major stars and making a particularly effective contribution to Aretha Franklin's *Lady Soul* set.

The partnership with Delaney Bramlett continued as the American produced and arranged Clapton's long-awaited first solo album, which used many of the Delaney and Bonnie musicians. Just as 'Badge' had been a reflection of Clapton's appreciation of *Music From Big Pink* by The Band, the *Eric Clapton* package indicated respect for another mellow American artist. Eric had a US hit with his version of J.J. Cale's 'After Midnight'.

'After Midnight' peaked in December 1970 just when Clapton's new album was released. It was an ambitious double called *Layla and Other Assorted Love Songs*, a rather downbeat title. The group's name was Derek and the Dominos, a rather ordinary monicker for a pop ensemble. The name concealed the identities of Eric Clapton and three friends from the Delaney and Bonnie band, and the title hid the sensational news that here was some of the most intense and emotional music the star had ever played. He was in a personal turmoil, having fallen in love with George Harrison's wife Patti after George, his dear friend, had cheated on her. The conflict of feelings, especially when Patti returned to George, was almost unbearable, and the pain spilled over onto the plastic. There are several outstanding tracks on the double disc, but the title number is in a class of its own. 'Layla' is rock's greatest song about love given and not returned. Clapton and guest artist Duane Allman played their guitars as if their lives depended on it, and Jim Gordon played the most beautiful piano coda yet attached to a rock song, a peaceful return to equilibrium after the journey into the emotional maelstrom.

Perhaps because of the subterfuge over the group's name, the album was a relative failure, and, after a tour and live LP, Derek and the Dominos split. Eric Clapton emerged from his home only rarely, appearing at Harrison's Bangla Desh concert and a Leon Russell show at the Rainbow. It was at that theatre that he played a comeback concert two years later in 1973, urged on by Pete Townshend and other famous friends. The blues lover had fallen victim to the dark side of the soul, and had become a heroin addict. He had lost Patti (though, ironically, they eventually married), and both Jimi Hendrix and Duane Allman had died unexpectedly. He admired Hendrix, his fellow guitarist deity, but cursed Jimi for dying without taking him along. Duane had become a friend during the *Layla* sessions, and his death hurt personally.

Clapton was cured of his addiction through a course of acupuncture that was still novel in the West. He hesitated after the Rainbow return, but finally gathered enough material to tell manager Robert Stigwood he wanted to record an album. Seizing the time, Stigwood had him in Florida within a week. Eric stayed at 461 Ocean Boulevard, giving the album a convenient title, and recorded a ten-song programme that included Bob Marley's 'I Shot The Sheriff'.

The lawman may have been killed off, but the career was brought back to life. Eric Clapton had his first American number one single and another British top ten hit. It did more for the composer than any other cover, because Bob Marley was just starting to succeed with Wailers LPs when the number one came along. Johnny Nash's devotion to Marley was more sustained, but had started too soon to have a great impact on the public.

Clapton's version of 'I Shot The Sheriff' was a bit more restrained than the original, and this laid-back approach typified his work in the seventies.

It wasn't that he wasn't capable of playing power guitar, he was. And it wasn't that he'd deserted the blues; an exciting show with Muddy Waters, which featured the men playing separately and together, proved that. But Eric found a new interest in country music, particularly the style of the ultimate relaxed singer-guitarist, Don Williams. This influence was reflected in a series of albums beginning with the late 1977 issue, *Slowhand*. The title was the ironic nickname Yardbirds manager Giorgio Gomelsky had given his lightning-fingered charge while introducing him at the Crawdaddy Club. Now Clapton did indeed play slower, trying to convey emotion with economy. *Slowhand* included a song written by Don Williams, a marvellous and moving Clapton original called 'Wonderful Tonight' that was in the Williams style, and a country ballad penned by Eric and female vocalist Marcy Levy that became a worldwide smash: 'Lay Down Sally'.

One place where it wasn't a big record was the artist's home country, Great Britain. The music scene there had moved on to a sequence of fads created and quickly dispensed with by teenagers who had never known Eric Clapton at his peak and were not very interested in him now.

It was apparent that many who have attended Clapton's recent shows come for the old material, not the good current stuff like 'Wonderful Tonight' or the American hit 'I Can't Stand It'. In particular, they chant for 'Layla' from the start of the show until it is finally played at the end.

It's a shame they aren't very interested in hearing the material that interests Eric Clapton the artist at this time. He's clearly interested in current music, having started his own label. But then one does have to sympathise with the fans who have handed over their hard-earned pay. They know something record-buyers in 1971 didn't: that 'Layla' is one of the twenty or so greatest works in rock. On reissue in 1972, the single was a top ten hit in first the UK and then the US, in edited form in Britain and in its full seven-minute magnificence in America. 'Layla' has gone on to become one of the standards of rock.

There's a lot of irony here, not only that Eric Clapton should have recorded his greatest hit under a pseudonym, but that a man who became famous playing blues style guitar should have his finest moment with a rock song he wrote himself, and that he managed to convey as much sorrow and desperation in that rock song as blues singers have done in their field.

Heaven knows how many guitar players have been inspired by Eric Clapton, how many rock fans were turned on to the blues through him,

and how many people who aren't interested in either the blues or the
guitar have been moved to tears by 'Layla'.

THE DRIFTERS

You couldn't call them the Fab Four or the Dynamic Duo – there were as many members of the group at various times as there are days in February. But something about them attracted the top writing and production talents of the last thirty years. They changed pop music with the help of Wexler & Ertegun, Leiber & Stoller, Goffin & King, Pomus & Shuman, Cook & Greenaway, and even Phil Spector.

You have to identify the lead singer on one of their songs because the Drifters have had a dozen of them. But before you start thinking this is a football team rather than a vocal group, rest assured: only four of them have been of great distinction. The first was almost certainly the greatest. His name was Clyde McPhatter.

The son of a preacher, McPhatter was a boy gospel star who formed his first professional group, The Mount Lebanon Singers, when he was fourteen. Three years later, in 1950, he joined the Dominoes, a group assembled by singing coach Billy Ward. The Dominoes were the first massively popular rhythm and blues vocal group.

The Ink Spots and Mills Brothers had previously enjoyed great success, but they were traditional harmony ensembles. The Dominoes added rhythm to the music and applied the emotion and intensity of gospel singing to secular lyrics. The results were sensational: nine top ten r & b hits in three years, including the number one of 1951, a straightforward rhythm number called 'Sixty Minute Man', and the number two of 1952, 'Have Mercy Baby'. Clyde McPhatter sang lead on 'Have Mercy Baby' and also took the spotlight on a perfect example of the religion & rhythm fusion, the 1953 hit 'The Bells'.

The devotion and hysteria one might expect from a supplicant of the Lord were applied to the subject of a love affair with a woman. The effect was electric, and Clyde McPhatter became a national favourite. Billy Ward had reacted to the group's success by giving himself top billing: Billy Ward & the Dominoes. Clyde was so popular he began to

Opposite: The longest lasting Drifter, Johnny Moore (second from right)

think he could make it on his own. He was either persuaded to leave or was fired – the stories conflict. What we do know is that Ahmet Ertegun, who frequently attended Dominoes' performances, noticed the tenor's absence one night. When told Clyde was no longer in the group, Ertegun got McPhatter's number, had dinner with him the next day, and signed him to Atlantic Records. As the executive recalled in Charlie Gillett's book *Making Tracks*, McPhatter collected some friends to sing with him on his first Atlantic session. Ertegun considered the product sub-standard and rejected it, wanting more of a gospel sound, so Clyde suggested using the Thrasher Wonders, religious-singing friends of his. This combination worked. The new quartet was called Clyde McPhatter And the Drifters, and their very first release, 'Money Honey', topped the r & b list for eleven weeks.

A press release said the act got its name because 'the members had done a lot of drifting from one group to another'. It's just as likely that Drifter was a close relation to the Thrasher Wonders' original name, the Thrasher Wanderers. 'Money Honey' was a pop classic, selling over two million copies. Yet at the time of its release, relatively few white people heard it. This uninhibited sound was too wild for music radio. In 1953, pop stations played what would now be called easy listening. Not until after 'Rock Around The Clock' would the mass audience get a chance to hear the exciting music of black America.

So it was with the second Clyde McPhatter and the Drifters' single. 'Such A Night' was a top ten r & b smash but for the pop field it was covered by Johnny Ray, who took it to number one in Britain. In America, even Ray's version was a bit racy, and the greatest success of the song did not come along until 1964. That was by Elvis Presley.

The Atlantic quartet were recording songs months before release. In November, 1953, when 'Money Honey' was still number one, they had a historic session with producers Ahmet Ertegun and Jerry Wexler. In three hours, they made four tracks, and three of them became major hits.

The first was the group's second number one. Co-written by Jerry Wexler and Clyde McPhatter, 'Honey Love' spent eight weeks at the top of the r & b chart in the summer of 1954. As with several of McPhatter's biggest hits, it could have been a religious song with a simple change of lyric – if it had been 'Holy Love', for example, instead of 'Honey Love'. But putting all this passion into a clearly carnal context made the pretty McPhatter a female favourite. More importantly, Clyde was the inspiration for a generation of soul singers, who entered the charts themselves in the late fifties and early sixties. Jackie Wilson, who replaced him in the Dominoes before going solo himself, was directly influenced. Other top tenors, like Smokey Robinson, studied McPhatter's use of falsetto, the way he flirted with notes before landing on them, the way he drew words out into more syllables than were on the printed page.

In an interview with *Record Mirror*, Clyde recalled that he'd started embellishing melody and lyrics while with the Dominoes. He was nervous in the recording studio, and felt relaxed only when Billy Ward gave him the liberty to take liberties. So started a classic style, heard at its most brilliant on the Drifters' treatment of 'White Christmas'.

Seeing as Bing Crosby had cut what remains the world's number one of all-time with this song, another version might seem automatically redundant. But Clyde and the Drifters' performance was so daring, so different, it breathed new life into the used-up number, which became an r & b standard. Bill Pinkney sang bass.

For four different Yuletides the Drifters' 'White Christmas' graced the charts. It stemmed from that one session which also produced 'Honey Love' and an Ertegun song called 'Whatcha Gonna Do'. As was his custom, the writer spelt his name backwards in the composer credit, which read 'A. Nugetre'. Partner Jerry Wexler told Charlie Gillett he considered 'Whatcha Gonna Do' to be 'Ahmet's greatest tune'. He added, ' "The Twist" was stolen outright from it, and we could have sued, but we never like to draw attention to ourselves as writers.' Hank Ballard, shall we say, 'borrowed' the melody and added a dance lyric for the song that became a gold disc earner for him and a multi-million seller for Chubby Checker.

'Whatcha Gonna Do' completed a great sequence: seven top ten hits in only six outings (one single was a double-sided winner). The only person not around to enjoy this chart success was Clyde McPhatter himself. He'd been drafted in 1954, and only managed a couple of sessions on leave from the Army. His previously recorded Drifters singles ran out in 1955, by which time he'd already cut his first solo tracks. McPhatter left the Drifters to go it alone with a new manager, but ex-mentor George Treadwell had the last laugh: he kept the rights to the name, the Drifters. Treadwell made a fortune with a succession of singers united only by the fact that they were each at one time Drifters.

The years 1955 through '58 were the low point of the Drifters' career. Three lead singers failed to lead the group back to the heights they'd enjoyed with McPhatter. To be fair to Johnny Moore, one of the early substitutes, he might have had more luck building a following had he not been drafted as well. The two most familiar numbers cut during the lean years became best-known in retrospect when Dion took them to the top ten in 1963. That's Dion DiMucci, not Dionne Warwick, though she, too, eventually figures in the Drifters' story, giving the group the bizarre and perhaps useless distinction of being the only act in history to be associated with both of the Dion(ne)s of pop.

Dion's two revitalised Drifters songs were 'Ruby Baby' and 'Drip Drop'. 'Ruby Baby', with Johnny Moore taking lead, and 'Drip Drop', with Bobby Hendricks outfront, were both written by Jerry Leiber and Mike Stoller. During the mid-fifties the songwriting and production team were busiest attending to the Coasters and Elvis Presley, but they got a chance to concentrate on the Drifters in 1959. At least, they were called the Drifters. The group hadn't existed for a year, having been sacked by manager Treadwell in 1958. Then he was reminded he'd signed a contract with Harlem's top venue, The Apollo Theatre, to present the Drifters twice a year for a decade. He took a group who were low on the Apollo bill, The Crowns, and called them the Drifters.

Leiber and Stoller chose a song co-written by the Crowns' lead singer, Ben E. King, under his real name, Benjamin Earl Nelson. In the definitive history *The Drifters*, by Bill Millar, King revealed that he didn't actually write music, he composed it on an old guitar with only three strings left. 'No one else could possibly play it,' he admitted, 'but I pick out tunes and, when I hear something, I'll play it for someone who can write it.'

Leiber and Stoller chose a song co-written by the Crowns' lead singer, recording it. 'The session was falling apart,' Leiber remembered, 'so we started to fool around.' Arranger Stan Applebaum wrote a string accompaniment that sounded like pseudo-classical Russian folk. The tympani was out of tune, so a drummer pounded out rhythm in an unchanging pitch. A Brazilian instrument called the baion was introduced because Leiber and Stoller liked it. The Drifters sang in a key of their own, reciting lines that didn't even rhyme. When the producers took this collage to the Atlantic supervisors, Jerry Wexler told them to go back and try it again. But like Leiber and Stoller, Ahmet Ertegun was fascinated by the jumble, and after it was cleaned up by engineer Tom Dowd, it was released as a 45. To the men who made it, 'There Goes My Baby' always sounded like two different records being played at once. To the public, it was a great pop single.

'There Goes My Baby' was not only a number one r & b hit but number two in the Hot 100, giving the Drifters a breakthrough into the pop market they would hereafter address. The Latin rhythm would be more heavily featured in later Drifters' records and find its way onto other r & b discs. The greatest innovation was the use of strings. The Skyliners and Frankie Lymon were black artists who had previously used strings, but on predominantly pop-oriented platters. After 'There Goes My Baby', strings became an integral part of almost every r & b arrangement, especially those which hoped for a crossover to the white audience. The Motown Sound would have been inconceivable without this dramatic development.

Leiber and Stoller knew they'd stumbled onto a good thing, and put strings on both sides of the next single. 'True Love True Love' gave a one-off lead vocal to Johnny Lee Williams, but the side which emerged as the international hit, giving the Drifters their first British entry, was Ben E. King's 'Dance With Me'.

A hit in late 1959 and early 1960, 'Dance With Me' was credited to boss George Treadwell, Ben E. King under his real name of Nelson and Leiber and Stoller under their pseudonyms Lebish and Glick. The duo preferred writing witty and perceptive songs like they'd done for the Coasters, not teenage love songs. They now assigned the writing chores on the Drifters to New York City's top songwriters, who for some reason always worked in teams. First came Doc Pomus and Mort Shuman, who wrote five important numbers for the group, including two that have been hits for more than one artist. 'This Magic Moment' was years later a top ten record for Jay and the Americans, and in less than two years 'Sweets For My Sweet' provided the Searchers' first UK number one.

In late 1960, Ben E. King went solo. 'Save The Last Dance For Me', which he sang and which Pomus and Shuman wrote, was climbing to number one in the Hot 100 and number two in Britain, but King was making his own sides for 1961 release. He had expert assistance from Leiber and Stoller and their protégé, the twenty-year-old genius Phil Spector. As a matter of fact, Bill Millar speculates that though uncredited, Spector must have worked on 'Save The Last Dance For Me', as it showed his 'Wall Of Sound' in the initial stages of development.

At any rate, Ben E. King was gone, and Rudy Lewis had taken over. He'd also been a gospel singer, but for the purposes of Drifters' records he was kept strictly in the pop mode. In his first full studio session he and the group cut four tunes, all of which became hits. The talent involved would now cost vast sums to assemble. Leiber and Stoller produced, Burt Bacharach arranged, Dionne Warwick, her sister Dee Dee and Doris Troy sang backing vocals, and the songs themselves were provided by the teams of Bacharach and Bob Hilliard, Pomus and Shuman and Carole King and Gerry Goffin. This was a supersession before the phrase was invented.

The song 'Some Kind Of Wonderful' was supplied by King and Goffin, who had offered four songs for the selection. Tony Orlando sang the demos, and, as he reminded Charlie Gillett, the three rejected ditties didn't do too badly either. 'Will You Love Me Tomorrow' became a number one for the Shirelles, 'Bless You' was a US and UK winner for Orlando himself, and 'Halfway To Paradise' did well for Tony in the States and Billy Fury in Britain.

Carole King said that writing songs in the competitive atmosphere of the Brill Building, Broadway, was like being in a 'musical chicken coop'. It certainly produced results. Bacharach got valuable songwriting and arranging experience and, most importantly, discovered Dionne Warwick singing in that high-powered backing trio. They set off together with Hal David to start their own historic string of hits in 1962. In that year King and Goffin, still clucking away in the Brill Building, came up with one of their greatest songs, and Rudy Lewis had the honour of singing the best lyric ever penned about escaping from the cares of the city.

'Up On The Roof' was a top five smash, staying in the charts for twenty weeks as 1962 became '63. It was a bit of fantasy to suppose that one could find a panacea for one's problems by sitting on a boiling hot roof in between the television aerials. But for its time the song was exceedingly socially conscious, and its acknowledgement of real-life urban pressures intrigued Leiber and Stoller. They followed it up by helping Barry Mann and Cynthia Weil write another Drifters' True Life Adventure: this time about the young musician determined to make it in an indifferent business in an uncaring town. 'They are wrong, I know they are,' Rudy Lewis sang, ''cause I can play this here guitar.' (The guitar solo was actually by Phil Spector.)

'On Broadway' was another top tenner. The Drifters had entered another golden era, but it was short-lived. Leiber and Stoller carried the big city saga too far for commercial tastes with 'Rat Race', a fascinating experiment in sound and lyric co-written with the young Van McCoy. It's one of those records that was admired rather than bought. After 'I'll Take You Home', a moderate hit which seemed like the answer to 'Save

Your Last Dance For Me' three years on, Rudy Lewis never again led the Drifters to the Top 40. In May 1964, he died, allegedly of a drug overdose. Ironically, the last song he had cut with the group was 'Vaya Con Dios'.

Even more morbidly, the Drifters had a session scheduled the very day of Lewis' death. Johnny Moore stood in as lead singer, the first time he'd assumed the role in seven years. Knowing the circumstances of its recording explains why 'Under The Boardwalk', a seemingly cheery song about finding seaside contentment, should sound so tragic. Johnny Moore's voice carries a pathos that makes the disc a soulful rather than a novelty record. No other version, including that of the Rolling Stones, has captured the unique quality of the Drifters' 'Under The Boardwalk'.

Written by Artie Resorick and Kenny Young, it was the first great Drifters' success produced by Bert Berns, a legendary music business figure whose many accomplishments did not help him with this act. Berns took the Drifters into a middle-of-the-road, Latin-flavoured path that gradually lost them support.

Their last two gasps of American chart success came with records dedicated to having a good time at weekends. It sounds like one of the most over-used subjects imaginable, but it was one to which listeners were guaranteed to react favourably.

'Saturday Night At The Movies' and 'At The Club' were moderate hits for the Drifters at the end of 1964 and the beginning of '65. The group then lived up to its name and drifted for a couple of years, occasionally registering a minor success. Bert Berns died in 1967, the last year the Drifters made the American charts. They continued to record with Johnny Moore and Bill Fredericks alternating as lead singers, but made no progress.

Then something strange happened. As part of the procession of oldies that marched up the British chart in 1972, a coupling of 'At The Club' and 'Saturday Night At The Movies' reached number three, the Drifters' best showing in a dozen years. As if to prove it wasn't a fluke, another reissue, 'Come On Over To My Place', also made the top ten. The record business can always smell a pound, if only when it's staring it in the face. Fay Treadwell, who took over Drifters' management after the death of her husband, signed a contract with Bell Records, and the British writing and production team of Roger Cook and Roger Greenaway and their songwriting friends continued the string of UK hits as if the intervening years had never existed. They registered half a dozen top ten singles in four years, including an affectionate homage to the past, 'Kissin' In The Back Row Of The Movies'. A British number two in 1974, it was typical of the bland but pleasant fare the Drifters turned out for UK audiences in the mid-seventies. It's easy to knock this material, which was the sort of airplay-conscious creation Clyde McPhatter was fighting against over twenty years before. But pre-punk UK teenagers wanted it, so they got it. At least it gave Johnny Moore steady work, though a variety of new Drifters passed beside him.

For early rock and roll fans, r & b freaks, and the entire American audience, it's the work of the first dozen years that counted, twelve years in which various Drifters and their Svengalis revolutionised rhythm and blues. Without them we might not have the great falsetto singers who emulated Clyde McPhatter, we wouldn't have The Twist, we wouldn't have had Dionne Warwick's hits with Burt Bacharach, the Latin beat might not have come into r & b, Ben E. King would never have met Leiber and Stoller and we never would have had 'Stand By Me', Phil Spector might not have developed production techniques as he did, strings might not have become acceptable in black music and we might have missed the Motown sound. We owe the Drifters a lot. The least we can do is save Ben E. King the last dance.

BOB DYLAN

'I conned a generation,' Bob Dylan allegedly told one of the top singer-songwriters of the seventies. 'I am not a spokesman for any generation,' he said to a reporter in 1978. 'I want to emphatically deny that.'

'I didn't create Bob Dylan,' the singer once told *Rolling Stone* correspondent Jonathan Cott. 'Bob Dylan has always been here . . . always was . . . Maybe I was best equipped to do it.'

One shouldn't put too much stock in what Dylan has said in interviews, because his public remarks have almost always been either contradictory or confusing.

But there may have been some truth in that statement. Certainly in a time of both great social protest and a proliferation of music for young people, there was a place for an artist who could communicate the terms of that protest in the context of the new music. Robert Allen Zimmerman sought and achieved that role. When a British journalist visited Robert Kennedy, the late President's brother said, 'This is what the young people of America are thinking' and handed him a copy of a Bob Dylan album.

He was born in Duluth, Minnesota, on 24 May 1941, and grew up in the mining town of Hibbing. After graduating from Hibbing High he enrolled at the University of Minnesota in Minneapolis, where he spent a good deal of time in the student quarter of the city, unfortunately called Dinkytown.

While singing at Dinkytown clubs, Zimmerman first took the name Bob Dylan, assumedly borrowed from poet Dylan Thomas. He became a devotee of Woody Guthrie, whose folk songs had eloquently championed the downtrodden of America, particularly during the Depression. Dylan tried to telephone Guthrie, who lay dying in a New Jersey hospital from the incurable disease Huntington's chorea. Guthrie was too ill to take the call, or at least so the doctor said, so Dylan, with his parents' approval, set off to New York City to sing in clubs and visit Woody Guthrie in nearby

New Jersey.

His first professional recording came not as a vocalist but as a harmonica player. He'd attracted attention in Greenwich Village and was hired as a session musician for Harry Belafonte's album *Midnight Special*. But after recording the title track, he argued with producer Hugo Montenegro and left the studio. Bob Dylan's disc debut earned him a session fee of fifty dollars.

Dylan's harmonica playing also led to his own recording contract. The last week of September 1961 was a very good one for the twenty-year-old. He began a two-week engagement at Gerde's Folk City and won a favourable review from *New York Times* critic Robert Shelton, who wrote the famous words 'It matters less where he has been than where he is going, and that would seem to be straight up.'

Dylan then played harmonica on a Carolyn Hester session. The producer was John Hammond, the justifiably legendary head of Columbia Records' Talent Acquisition Department. Hammond, who had recorded Bessie Smith and Billie Holliday and recently signed Aretha Franklin, invited the young player to a meeting at Hester's home, where he began discussions that quickly led to a deal with CBS.

The *Bob Dylan* LP was recorded for around four hundred dollars – at the time, less than a hundred pounds. Dylan just went into the studio and sang to his own accompaniment. Only a couple of the numbers were originals, one almost obligatory for the Guthrie fanatic he was: 'Song To Woody'. The *Bob Dylan* album sold only five thousand copies in its first year, and around CBS the artist was nicknamed 'Hammond's Folly'.

There were more problems for the fresh-faced flop. Booked to appear on the *Ed Sullivan Show* on CBS-TV, he won the host's approval to sing the controversial 'Talkin' John Birch Society Blues'. But a CBS executive objected to a line which suggested that members of the ultra-right wing organisation supported 'Hitler's views', even though, as listeners were told in the obvious rhyme, the Führer had killed 'six million Jews'. Dylan declined to appear on the programme rather than be censored. He was later shocked to discover Columbia Records also banned the song. A young corporate lawyer named Clive Davis feared the company could be sued for libel should the track appear on the album. The lawyer, Clive Davis, later became Chief Administrative Officer of Columbia, but was relieved to discover that Bob Dylan, then a major star, did not seem to associate him with his previous role.

Because the John Birch song was out, something new had to be

Opposite: Bob Dylan in Greenwich Village with Suze Rotolo

recorded for Dylan's second album. John Hammond had resisted pressure to drop his protégé, but dropped out of the second album himself when he had rows with Dylan's manager, Albert Grossman. Tom Wilson recorded four more tracks, which replaced four cuts including 'Birch'. The new album was withdrawn, creating a choice collector's item, and the four songs substituted.

All that was the bad news. The good news was that in the year since his debut, Dylan had created strong word-of-mouth awareness of his new material. Clubgoers spread the news that this youngster from Minnesota was writing songs that mattered: songs about the growing civil rights movement and the horrors of nuclear weapons. The rumours were confirmed when *The Freewheelin' Bob Dylan* appeared in 1963. The writing was articulate and impassioned. In the early sixties millions feared imminent death from nuclear catastrophe. Indeed, the Cuban missile crisis of October 1962 had brought the United States and the Soviet Union to the very brink of war, and, as one writer phrased it, friends made appointments to meet the following week not knowing if they'd be able to keep them.

Bob Dylan was one of those who didn't know if he'd be able to finish everything he'd set out to do. He wrote a song of first lines: 'Every line in it is actually the start of a whole song,' he explained. 'But when I wrote it, I thought I wouldn't have enough time alive to write all those songs so I put all I could into this one.' He called the image-laden nightmare about nuclear war 'A Hard Rain's A-Gonna Fall'.

For all the impact of 'Masters Of War' and 'Hard Rain', for all the beauty of 'Girl From The North Country' and 'Don't Think Twice It's All Right', the *pièce de résistance* of *The Freewheelin' Bob Dylan* had to be the opening track 'Blowing In The Wind'. The song asked in the form of several beautifully phrased questions why social and racial injustices had to occur and why there had to always be more wars. 'The answer, my friend, is blowing in the wind', was Dylan's reply, suggesting that change and improvement were just around the corner. The song was the sensation of the 1963 Newport Folk Festival. It became an unofficial anthem of the burgeoning civil rights movement. And Peter, Paul and Mary, a trio formed by Dylan manager Albert Grossman to win success in the pop market, took their pretty version of 'Blowin' In The Wind' into the top ten. When asked in the late sixties which of his albums most fully realised his intentions, Dylan replied 'the second one'.

The Times They Are A Changin', his next LP, was a logical successor to

Freewheelin'. Once again there was anti-war material, such as 'With God On Our Side', and songs about wronged black people, including 'The Lonesome Death Of Hattie Carroll'. And, as before, there was a theme for the young protesters: 'The Times They Are A Changin''. These two LPs remain the all-time classic protest albums. A movement had a hero, and Dylan found himself a top twenty artist in America and, in the case of *Freewheelin'*, a number one chartmaker in Britain.

For the first but not the last time, he risked losing his audience. He issued *Another Side Of Bob Dylan*, a set of less controversial material that included love songs like 'It Ain't Me, Babe' and 'All I Really Want To Do'. It sold less well than the previous two albums on both sides of the Atlantic, and for a few months it appeared Bob Dylan might have peaked. All such thought disappeared in the spring of 1965.

'Subterranean Homesick Blues' was Dylan's second UK top ten single in two months (a late success of 'Times They Are A Changin'' had been the first). But more importantly, it was a historic track. Here was a folk artist singing under the clear influence of Chuck Berry with a rock and roll backing. It had never been done before. It was either an innovation or heresy, depending on one's point of view. *Bringing It All Back Home*, the album led off by 'Subterranean Homesick Blues', remains an astonishing collection of songs. There was the ballad 'She Believes In Me', containing the lines 'She's got everything she needs, she's an artist, she don't look back', which provided the title for the Dylan British tour documentary, *Don't Look Back*. There was 'Maggie's Farm', a hard-rocking number that found renewed relevance in Britain in 1980. And there was 'Mr Tambourine Man', a six-minute rambling acoustic piece about a fantastic pied piper who may or may not be turning his followers onto marijuana. It's no secret that Dylan introduced the Beatles to smoking pot. 'Mr Tambourine Man' and all the numbers on the acoustic side of *Bringing It All Back Home* were rich with descriptive imagery and, surprisingly for a writer so strong with words, good melodies. The Byrds proved that when they issued a two-minute version of 'Mr Tambourine Man' and took it to number one in both America and Britain.

A chart-topping single in the summer of 1965, it was important for several reasons. First, it launched the career of the Byrds, whose greatest successes were often covers of Dylan songs. Secondly, it was the first Dylan composition to go to the very top. Thirdly, 'Mr Tambourine Man' made the folk-rock Dylan had pioneered a commercial cult, and during the same summer Sonny and Cher went to number one with 'I Got You

Babe' and Barry McGuire topped the American charts with 'Eve Of Destruction'.

Dylan, the man who was responsible for all these developments, might well have thought, why shouldn't I have a hit single? Noticing that his fans seemed to also be fans of the Beatles and Rolling Stones, and knowing that he had feelings of mutual admiration with the British stars, it seemed only natural to him to make a rock and roll record. And, only naturally, it was the best one ever made.

'Like A Rolling Stone' caused chaos at the 1965 Newport Folk Festival. The only problem is, to this day, nobody is quite sure why, even people who were there. Some say it was the appalling sound. Others think it was simply because Dylan had got the idea of playing with the Paul Butterfield Blues Band backing him only the night before, and the results were rough. Then there's the popular view, appealing if only for its sense of drama: the folk purists heard Dylan going electric and booed him off the stage. Of course, the bulk of the record-buying public had no idea that this had occurred. They just knew they loved the single, which was a top five hit in the US and UK and became the theme song of protest-minded American youth. Feeling they'd been betrayed by a country which in the course of three years had given them Kennedy's assassination, the murder of civil rights workers and growing military involvement in Vietnam, they could identify with the 'how does it feel?' chorus.

Dylan himself was delighted to finally have a smash single, and was determined to have a follow-up hit. He recorded with Al Kooper and Mike Bloomfield, as he had on 'Rolling Stone', but the content could never have been predicted. Dylan issued the most dismissive, contempt-filled single ever put out. 'Positively Fourth Street' is, quite simply, full of hate. His old friends on the folk scene worried it might be about them; they may have been right. If so, it was a low blow, but a great record.

Dylan liked being a pop star, and wanted to make the ultimate rock record. He didn't realise that with the *Highway 61 Revisited* album, including 'Like A Rolling Stone', he had already done so. He now cut an even tougher-sounding single, but this time the lyrics were alternately obscure and silly. He played the result to fellow folk hero Phil Ochs. According to Dylan biographer Anthony Scaduto, Ochs said, 'That's good.' Dylan, furious that he hadn't said 'Great', played it again. Ochs repeated – it was good, but it wouldn't be a hit. They got into a limousine, but Dylan ordered the driver to stop the car and made Ochs get out. A friendship was terminated because Phil Ochs wasn't overly impressed by 'Can You Please Crawl Out Your Window'.

Ochs was right; the record was only a minor hit. Not only had Bob Dylan alienated his purist folk fans, some of whom shouted 'Judas' at a Royal Albert Hall concert, but he had misjudged his new rock fans. A subsequent single 'One Of Us Must Know' didn't even make the Hot 100.

The setback was only temporary. In the summer of 1966, he released a double album, *Blonde On Blonde*, that broke new ground yet again. An entire side of the set was devoted to 'Sad-Eyed Lady Of The Lowlands', a musical ode to his new wife, the former Sara Lounds. Several other artists later recorded lengthy epics of their own.

The short single from the package, 'Rainy Day Women Numbers 12 and 35' was an international top ten hit even with explicit drug references, but the classic of the album was one of several fine love songs, 'Just Like A Woman'.

Bob Dylan was at the peak of his profession. With the Beatles and Rolling Stones, he was shaping the culture of a generation. To the dismay of the writer who had once said 'Don't follow leaders, watch the parking meters', members of the growing protest movement viewed him as a messianic figure. Typically he then did something no saviour ever had done before. He fell off a motor bike.

It was no minor accident. Some disbelievers think it was no accident at all, that Dylan just wanted to retreat from dealing with the consequences of his fame, but if the reports were to be taken seriously, Dylan had nearly died in the incident. During his year's convalescence in rural New York State he recorded a series of tracks with the Band, a group of Canadian musicians with whom he had toured. The so-called 'Basement Tapes' weren't released until eight years after they were made. Bootlegs flourished in the interim. Indeed, Dylan is probably the single most bootlegged artist in rock history, a dubious distinction since he got no royalties from illegal discs. But buffs who believed his every word and movement meant something, tried to collect everything: concert recordings, taped interviews. One Dylanologist analysed his garbage. Of him Dylan said: 'He oughta take a rest . . . this boy's *off.*'

Knowing that anything he did would be wildly misinterpreted, he deliberately put a strange photo on the cover of his comeback album, the 1968 release *John Wesley Harding*. He was pictured standing in a wood with two singers from India and a local labourer, as if to say 'Make something of this'. Make something of the contents his fans surely did.

John Wesley Harding, named after a nineteenth-century cowboy equivalent of Robin Hood, was another British number one album, and Jimi Hendrix made 'All Along The Watchtower' a worldwide favourite. The style of the LP was, again, radically different from Dylan's preceding work, being a reflective and laid-back album with numerous religious references.

He changed direction again the following year when he recorded a country album in Nashville. In the late sixties country music was associated with the rednecks who most hated the radical youth culture. This move was like going into the lion's den, sticking your head into the lion's mouth, and calmly singing 'Lay Lady Lay'. The success of 'Lay Lady Lay' and *Nashville Skyline* started a synthesis of country and rock that has since proved successful for many artists.

But it was at this point that the career of Bob Dylan started to lose its impact, although the popular reception to the double album *Self Portrait* belies the poor reputation it has now. This collection of originals and covers of favourites by other artists was a number one in Britain and a top ten seller in the States, just as was *New Morning*, the second 1970 release.

With the turn of the decade, many of rock's greatest groups split. Some of its most distinctive personalities died from drug overdoses. New artists appeared in the charts to take the places of the dead and departed. The student protest movement in the United States was effectively terminated. For these reasons alone, Bob Dylan suddenly seemed like a figure from another time. His work, even a protest single like 'George Jackson', seemed to lack urgency. Then, just when it seemed Dylan fans would have to put their expectations away, he returned with a masterpiece. His marriage to Sara had deteriorated, and the only way he could release his feelings was by going into the studio and recording *Blood On The Tracks*. If you considered the title a pun, you wouldn't be far off the mark. The pain oozed from the tracks of the album. Here was a man clearly suffering, articulating his agony to produce bone-chilling art.

'Idiot Wind', intoned with intensity, was just one of the astonishing cuts on *Blood On The Tracks*. There was a heartbreaking ballad, 'If You See Her, Say Hello', and a magnificent narrative tale, the eight-minute 'Lily, Rosemary And The Jack Of Hearts'. The critic Geoffrey Cannon called it 'The best of Dylan, and Dylan's best'.

At the end of the decade came the big change, one that was no greater in substance than some of his previous leaps, but this time one that many fans refused to follow. Bob Dylan, one of America's most famous Jews, found Jesus and was born again, though he resented the label 'Christian' when a well-meaning interviewer attempted to apply the tag. The first album in his religious series was *Slow Train Coming*, co-produced by the famed Jerry Wexler and the talented instrumentalist Barry Beckett and featuring Mark Knopfler of Dire Straits on guitar.

The venom that had oozed through 'Masters Of War' and 'Positively Fourth Street' was now applied to non-believers, but done so at first in an emotionally convincing manner. Then came the artistic downfall. He recorded two more religious-oriented packages without Jerry Wexler and Mark Knopfler. *Shot Of Love* he co-produced himself. Here was the go-in-and-get-out attitude to studio work he'd shown in the early days and had led Phil Spector to remark in 1969, 'He's never been produced'. Other artists had many hits with his material, including to his greatest liking Manfred Mann, because they had bothered to concoct pop productions for play on the radio. Dylan almost never took the effort, and in the late seventies this attitude caught up with him and his sales dropped.

The fans who felt cheated said he was finished, neglecting that some fellow believers were truly touched by what Dylan was doing. When he appeared at Earls Court in 1981, someone yelled out 'Judas!' Was he aware of the irony? Was he aware someone had shouted that out fifteen years before in the Royal Albert Hall?

Bob Dylan has pointed to the example of Muddy Waters, sixty-five and still performing, and said he guesses he will be, too. That's a quarter century of creativity left – more than we've heard so far. And while it is too much to ask for Dylan to mean as much personally to his fans as he once did, it is clearly far too early to write him off. Will he come back? He hasn't even gone away yet.

These are hard times. There is evil in the world, and in the odd absence of any major contemporary artist to raise objection to these wrongs, Dylan still is the most appropriate artist to ask the questions whose answers are still blowin' in the wind.

DAVID BOWIE

'I feel like an actor when I'm on stage, rather than a rock artist,' he said in 1972. 'I very rarely have felt like a rock artist.'

At first it sounds a strange thing for the most influential rock star of the seventies to say. But when it sinks in it makes perfect sense. Like an actor, he played a series of roles, adopting one guise and then discarding it. The difference is he went through musical as well as clothing styles, always a step or two ahead of the next trend, making David Bowie pop music's forerunner of fashion, its champion of change.

Bowie's first important change was his name. He was born David Robert Jones on 8 January 1947. His father Haywood was the head of public relations for Dr Barnardo's homes. David's first group was George And The Dragons, an outfit of Bromley Technical High School students. The other noteworthy school group of the time, The Little Ravens, included the young Peter Frampton, whose father taught David Jones art. The earliest copies of a Jones performance are tapes of him playing saxophone from the time he was taking lessons from Ronnie Ross, but these have never been available commercially.

The first record, the 1964 release 'Liza Jane', came under the billing Davie Jones with The King Bees. Jones played sax in addition to singing lead. The group had originally been called The Hooker Brothers, an apparent tribute to blues singer John Lee Hooker. 'Liza Jane' appeared on the Vocalion Pop label, the first of seven labels on which David Bowie has had records released in Great Britain. He didn't have his first hit until 1969, and he wasn't a major star until 1972. This meant there are eight years of obscure Bowie material, making him one of the most challenging and expensive artists for enthusiasts to collect. A very good copy of 'Liza Jane' is now worth over £85.

That's more than Bowie himself made off the original release. Only three and a half thousand copies were pressed, and only some of them were sold. Furthermore, he didn't get any writer's royalty, because the number was written by King Bees' manager Leslie Conn. The first David Jones composition to be recorded was 'Take My Tip', the B-side of his second single, this time as part of The Manish Boys. They spelled Manish with one 'n' rather than the usual two, distinguishing themselves from the obvious inspiration for their name, Muddy Waters' blues classic 'Mannish Boy'.

Five more unsuccessful singles followed, many of them pop-rock rather than blues numbers. The next release 'The Laughing Gnome' sounded like Anthony Newley backed by The Chipmunks. There were two good reasons for this strange similarity. Bowie's manager was now Kenneth Pitt, who had formerly worked with Newley. Secondly, the Bromley lad genuinely admired the pop star-turned-playwright. 'I was Anthony Newley for a year,' David admitted. 'He was once one of the most talented men that England ever produced.'

'The Laughing Gnome' became a top ten hit in 1973, six years after its release. The gnomes on the record were people who happened to be around the studio whose voices were speeded up technically. One was the engineer of the single, Gus Dudgeon, who produced Bowie's next 45.

If that makes it sound like the tunes were made back-to-back, it's misleading. More than two years separated the singles, during which the artist cut his first album, simply titled *David Bowie*, made his television debut in an ice-cream commercial, and appeared briefly in a TV play and two movies.

He opened a Tyrannosaurus Rex tour miming about the Chinese invasion of Tibet. He had far more popular success with the new single, the release of which was delayed to coincide with the Apollo Moon landing in July 1969. After an unpromising start, David Bowie came up with a classic: 'Space Oddity'. It appeared in the UK Top 50 for one week in September 1969, and then dropped out. At the end of the month the single re-entered the charts and climbed to number five.

The British public now knew the name David Bowie. The artist had taken the pseudonym because he didn't want to be confused with Davy Jones of The Monkees. 'Bowie' was a reference to the hunting knife, and since the bowie knife was popularised by the frontiersman Jim Bowie, who died at the Alamo, the pop star's name should most accurately be pronounced David Bo-hie, or even the down south pronunciation of Jim's name, Boo-ie.

Partly because no one had expected great things of 'Space Oddity', it was recorded rather quickly. In typical fashion, Bowie would give one or two takes and then disappear, leaving the producer to tidy up. In this case Dudgeon called on the unknown Rick Wakeman to compose a synthesiser accompaniment. Wakeman only heard the track once before deciding on his now-famous part, a keyboard performance so fine he was called back for what became Bowie's second great space epic two years later. During that interval David ran the Beckenham Arts Lab, toured with a backing band called Hype, issued singles totally unlike 'Space Oddity' and totally unsuccessful, and released two more albums.

He became known for his bisexuality and for wearing a dress – two different habits altogether, but ones that were easily confused in the mind of the naïve or prejudiced viewer. Bowie was the first pop star to state publicly 'Yes, of course, I am bisexual', and cleared the way for other rock heroes to do so in the seventies.

But the wearing a dress – that, he said, was misunderstood. By posing for the cover of *The Man Who Sold The World*, in drag, reclining on a settee, he was trying to parody the nineteenth-century painter Gabriel Rossetti. The joke went over almost everybody's heads. He seemed to be trying to look like Lauren Bacall and succeeding.

The commercial breakthrough finally came with *Hunky Dory*, the second 1971 album. Bowie was now writing material that was both lyrically imaginative and musically infectious, like 'Changes' and 'Life On Mars'. The latter featured notable contributions from Rick Wakeman on piano and Mick Ronson playing guitar and doing the string arrangements. On the album there is a parenthetical remark next to the song title: 'Inspired by Frankie'. This was a reference to Bowie's unsuccessful attempt in 1968 to get a recorded version of his lyrics to Claude François' French hit 'Comme d'habitude'. Frank Sinatra, who loved the tune, asked Paul Anka to write a lyric, and 'My Way' became Sinatra's signature tune. It was only just that the Englishman based the music of 'Life On Mars' on some of the chords of 'My Way' and had a major hit with it.

The single sales didn't come until after the great breakthrough of 1972, when *The Rise And Fall Of Ziggy Stardust And The Spiders From Mars* made David Bowie a major international star. It was the complete concept: to record an album of songs with a central idea, in this case the creation and the corruption of a glamorous rock idol, and then to live out the character both on stage and in public life. In his shining suit and platform boots, Bowie was the direct inspiration for the glam-rock of the early seventies, and for the first of many times his stage persona was copied by clones who attended his concerts. For the star and the audience, Ziggy Stardust was a way of life.

I was given a lift across town by one of Britain's leading serious composers shortly after *Ziggy Stardust* came out. The first single from the album came onto the car radio, and he nervously turned up the volume and said 'What do *you* think of this? I've always liked rock and roll, but I can't get into this. Listen to his voice, it's so shrill.'

His voice was one of the revolutionary features of David Bowie's approach to music-making. He made no attempt to sing in the traditional American-sounding way. Ever since Elvis, pop stars had tried to sound American whatever their speaking voices were like. Bowie made no such attempt. He was obviously an Englishman, and furthermore one who was more interested in effect than a pleasant vocal noise. In this way, Bowie was the direct predecessor of Johnny Rotten and the New Wave singers who followed the Sex Pistols. David Bowie liberated the English rock star's voice.

'Starman' became a top ten single and *Ziggy Stardust* a top ten album in the summer of 1972. David Bowie experienced a career explosion. He had fifteen top thirty singles in three and a half years. He was the best-selling UK rock album artist in 1973. 'Space Oddity' and *Ziggy* finally broke him in America, and even his outside activities were successful. His co-production with Lou Reed, *Transformer*, was an international chart LP, and 'Walk On The Wild Side' was the most sexually explicit hit single ever.

Bowie had long admired Reed and his pioneer group from New York City, the Velvet Underground. Some of his tracks are direct descendants of Reed material. 'Queen Bitch' from *Hunky Dory* was acknowledged on the sleeve to be inspired by the group. On *Ziggy* the best out-and-out rocker was also in the Lou Reed vein, perhaps the best Bowie track which never became a hit: 'Suffragette City'. 'Suffragette City' gave Bowie concerts an intense excitement, particularly the anticipation leading up to and the release derived from the line 'wham bam thank you mam'.

And then, a year after Ziggy mania started, Bowie finished it. He announced from the stage of the Hammersmith Odeon that it was 'our last show'. The fans were stunned. They milled around the foyer suddenly without a reason for looking the way they did, with no hope that their appearance would ever again make sense. What they and the press, who had a field day with Bowie's 'retirement', failed to realise is that the artist was referring to the last show of Ziggy Stardust And The Spiders From

Mars, not the last concert by David Bowie. He was destroying the character in life just as he had on LP.

Stars had changed image before. They had never changed identity. Johnny Rotten did five years later, and the reaction was just as hysterical. Fans wanted Bowie to be Ziggy, but Bowie was now to be somebody else. He had got what he wanted out of the character. 'I packaged a totally credible plastic rock star,' he later said, 'much better than any sort of Monkees' fabrication.'

The elimination of Ziggy left a void Bowie did not immediately attempt to fill. The songs on the next album, *Aladdin Sane*, had only tenuous links to each other. Indeed, one of them had already been a number two as a single: 'The Jean Genie'.

This cut contained David Bowie's second veiled allusion to Muddy Waters. He had once borrowed the title of the bluesman's 'Mannish Boy'; now he took the guitar riff, as it had descended in rock through the Yardbirds and was to appear again soon in the Sweet's 'Blockbuster'.

'The Jean Genie' was a tribute to another of Bowie's American music heroes, Iggy Pop, whom he would later produce. But his most satisfactory production of another artist came in the same year 'Jean Genie' was released, 1972. Fearing that Mott the Hoople might break up for lack of success, he gave them one of his best songs, 'All The Young Dudes'. 'All The Young Dudes' made the British top three in 1972 and achieved its purpose: Mott the Hoople stayed together to make a series of memorable hits. Bowie had given them their first.

What was most impressive about David Bowie's work, aside from its frequent high quality, was that he usually did get there first. Because he was interested in far more aspects of the arts than the conventional rock star and several different kinds of music, he was aware of new developments in art and music months or years ahead of the herd. His use of the new legitimised it in the pop field, and inspired others to work with the material. Consequently he both anticipated and set trends.

Thus 'Space Oddity' preceded Elton John's 'Rocket Man'; *Diamond Dogs*, his 1974 set based on George Orwell's *1984*, came seven years before Rick Wakeman's album on the same theme; the sleeve of *Diamond Dogs* by fashionable Belgian painter Guy Peellaert preceded a Rolling Stones jacket by the same artist. To be fair, Mick Jagger had requested his drawing first, but Bowie not only got his out first but took the trouble to go to Peellaert's London exhibition. In 1975 Bowie beat the Bee Gees in recording white man's disco.

DAVID BOWIE

His *Diamond Dogs* tour, though an expensive and complex venture that featured David singing 'Space Oddity' suspended over the audience by crane, was an overambitious flop. In late '74 the Philadelphia sound ruled radio stations and dance floors, and Bowie changed his act to a slick soulish set. Recording in Sigma Sound studios in Philadelphia, he cut the majority of *Young Americans*, adding two tracks recorded in New York with John Lennon. One of these became his first US number one. It also gave him a hit in the soul charts and an appearance on black music's television showcase, *Soul Train*, perhaps no surprise since recently added guitarist Carlos Alomar, a former player with James Brown, borrowed the recurring figure from his old boss.

'Fame', co-written by David Bowie and John Lennon, gave the younger man a touch of the American number one fever Lennon had already experienced twenty-one times. He was a bona fide show business celebrity, and made a film, *The Man Who Fell To Earth*, in which he played an alien who found great difficulty fitting into this planet's society. Many critics thought it was an appropriate role. Bowie later admitted that the Los Angeles environment was unhealthy for him . . . not just for his mind, but for his body. He became heavily involved with cocaine, which directly influenced his 1976 work, *Station To Station*. Certainly at his Wembley appearance to promote this album, on the famous 'black and white' tour where all stage lighting was white and clothing was either black or white, David seemed to be influenced by the drug, brilliantly summoning up reserves of energy to present the most precise and perfected rock show I have ever seen in this country. There is even a reference to the white powder in the haunting title track, *Station To Station*.

Bowie managed only one major hit from *Station To Station*, 'Golden Years', yet his career seemed to have more momentum because only a month before 'Space Oddity' had gone to number one on re-issue, the only record ever to achieve that feat. But the artist himself knew he was temporarily burned out, and retreated to Europe, first to France, then to Germany. Reacting early to the novel work by synthesiser-based group Kraftwerk, he teamed up with Brian Eno to produce a trilogy of albums that once again inspired a legion of admiring imitators.

The first two albums, *Low* and *Heroes*, were predominantly instrumental albums, their mood established by doomy and sometimes randomly programmed synthesisers that captured in bone-chilling fashion both the severity of Eastern Europe and the uncertainties of the artist. As he admitted, the main reason there weren't many words on the two LPs is that he had run out of things to say. But the mood of the tracks seemed to speak for an entire way of life, and this found its finest articulation when the albums were used as the soundtrack of a 1981 film, *Christiane F.*, a German movie about teenage drug addiction. Based on a true tale of widespread narcotic misuse and adolescent prostitution, *Christiane F.* was deservedly one of the German box office hits of all time, with Bowie's music terrifyingly illustrating the harrowing scenes of hopelessness.

'Sense Of Doubt' was one of the tracks used in the *Christiane F.* film, as were 'Warszawa', Bowie's impression of Poland that included nonsense syllables rather than conventional lyrics, and 'Heroes', a fantasy narrative based on two real-life lovers who regularly rendezvoused underneath a guard turret on the Berlin Wall near the recording studio. *Low* and *Heroes* were triumphantly successful experiments, certainly artistically, as evidenced by the numerous awards voted in the British press, and in some places commercially, the United States being a painfully obvious exception. Bowie and Eno's collaborations inspired a whole genre of synthesiser-based acts, the most successful being Gary Numan.

In 1980 David once again showed he was in touch with the latest in fashion by borrowing from The New Romantics, who had started copying him. He borrowed Steve Strange personally for the video of his unexpected follow-up to 'Space Oddity', 'Ashes To Ashes', which continued the story of Major Tom in a tone that was, for an astronaut, depressingly down to earth. It was David Bowie's second British number one. Within a year he recorded another chart-topper, a duet with Queen called 'Under Pressure' that was born when the two acts met in a German studio.

For over a dozen years Bowie's audience has been getting his message and translating it into new styles. The way that Bob Dylan hauled American rock music behind him with every move he made in the sixties, Bowie had British pop as his train in the seventies. Every musical move he made gave several new artists a good living and he has inspired the most fervent fan following in recent British pop. They have created a market for Bowie bootlegs and for Bowie books, the most valuable of which are *An Illustrated Record* by Roy Carr and Charles Shaar Murray and *In His Own Words* by Miles.

After his relative success in *The Man Who Fell To Earth* and his great success on Broadway as *The Elephant Man*, it is certain that Bowie will be paying more attention to acting in the 1980s. He says he's growing less interested in music. It would be music's loss if he exercised his artistic prerogative and devoted most of his time to other forms of expression. But even if he never records another note, for what he has already done, for its own worth and for the influence it has had on others, David Bowie is one of rock music's greatest heroes.

ERIC BURDON AND THE ANIMALS

This programme is for the Hollies . . . and the Lovin' Spoonful . . . *and* Creedence Clearwater Revival . . . and all groups who have had plenty of hits but because they lacked a certain charisma or because they didn't revolutionise pop music never have programmes done about them and never have books written about them. These are the acts that are the backbone of rock, comprising the bulk of the chart while the superstars fly high. It's time we gave a salute to one of them – Eric Burdon and the Animals!

'Look out for the Animals,' Ray Coleman wrote in the *Melody Maker* of 8 February 1964, calling them 'unsophisticated, crude, raw and eye-catching'. Rarely has a pop prediction proved so accurate so quickly. Within two months the group had their first hit and within four months their first number one, breaking out in America six months to the day of Coleman's column.

In the late fifties, Eric Burdon, Alan Price and John Steel had been together briefly as the Pagan Jazzmen. Burdon didn't join them for regular work until 1962. At that time they were called the Alan Price Combo, a modern jazz trio featuring income tax officer Price on organ, technical illustrator Steel on drums, and apprentice instrument maker Chas Chandler on bass. Organ, bass and drums was an unusual line-up for any group, so it was not surprising that the Combo soon added designer Burdon on vocals and machinist Hilton Valentine on guitar.

The five men were black music devotees. Burdon had been introduced to rhythm and blues by a merchant seaman who lived in the flat beneath him. Eric decided he wanted to sing like a black man, and shouted in a husky, loud voice in Combo gigs in the quintet's native Newcastle. Local fans called the wild men 'Animals', and the musicians decided they might as well use the nickname professionally.

New Wave fans may think that the independent label was strictly a phenomenon of the late seventies. But the Animals sold five hundred

copies of their own EP as 1963 gave way to '64.

Independent producer Mickie Most, who had returned from being a pop star in South Africa, liked their raw style, and recorded their first nationally distributed single: 'Baby Let Me Take You Home'. The Animals had heard 'Baby Let Me Take You Home' on the debut album by the American newcomer, Bob Dylan, who called it 'Baby, Let Me Follow You Down'. Their version reached number twenty-one in the spring of 1964, a good placing for a first disc. Their next single was the next track on that Dylan album and its success changed their lives. 'House Of The Rising Sun' was a traditional blues song Dylan had learned from Dave Van Ronk. The Animals recorded it twice, changing the house from a bordello to a gambling spot. Both versions were dominated by Alan Price's eerie then frantic organ playing and wailing by Eric Burdon that would have drowned out a foghorn. The composer credit on this classic single reads 'Traditional, arranged Price' and although Chas Chandler claimed years later that Alan hadn't even been present when the group arranged the piece, the prominent role given the organist suggests it was his arrangement.

Chas Chandler recalled that of all the Animals' achievements, he was proudest that 'House Of The Rising Sun' had broken the time barrier for singles. Most hit 45s up to that point had been under three minutes in length, and 'House' was over four, but in the United States the claim couldn't be accurately made since most radio stations played a three-minute edited version.

It didn't matter. The record was a number one on both sides of the Atlantic, and suddenly the Animals were in the thick of the British invasion of America. The United States record company quickly re-promoted the other side of 'Baby Let Me Take You Home', 'Gonna Send You Back To Walker', a version of Timmy Shaw's 'Gonna Send You Back To Georgia' with the name of Eric Burdon's birthplace substituting. But after only a fortnight this chart entry was quashed by the official UK follow-up, 'I'm Crying'.

It was an adequate though not sensational follow-up to a double number one. More exciting was some of the material on the group's first album, simply titled *The Animals*. Original and standard blues songs were featured, demonstrating that Burdon could sing like a black man better than any white man. 'It just doesn't happen,' he said. 'One has to feel it, and I feel it strongly, and it's this feeling that I try to project when I sing.' He kept a book with hundreds of lyrics of black singers, with the

Opposite: Eric Burdon (centre) and the Animals

ERIC BURDON AND THE ANIMALS

word 'Blues' written on the first page in his own blood. He had cut his finger just for the ceremony. Circumstances and conviction had caused Eric Burdon to immerse himself in the blues. How else could he so convincingly sing John Lee Hooker's 'Boom Boom'?

White boys played the blues well without patronising the form. In the era of civil rights reform, this was one of the ultimately fashionable things to do. America's foremost Negro magazine *Ebony* gave the Animals a five-page spread. They appeared by invitation at The Apollo, Harlem's mecca of black talent, the only British rock group to do so. The distinguished critic Nat Hentoff wrote: 'The Animals have more comprehension of Negro blues styles than any other British rhythm and blues group.' For all these tributes, the Newcastle lads didn't seem to have impressed Bo Diddley when he had seen them at the Club A Go Go in 1963 – at least, not by their account. They turned the encounter into an amusing celebration of blues and a quick-fire history of rock and roll.

'The Story Of Bo Diddley' was a minor masterpiece of improvisation and humour of the sort one doesn't find often on single releases. It appeared as the first track on the first Animals LP, though in the States, it was held over for the third album. In America at this time, fewer tracks appeared on long players and some of those were single A- and B-sides which didn't customarily appear on British albums. US Animals LPs thus had very different track listings than the originals. In the bizarre case of *Animal Tracks*, the group's second British set and third American anthology, the liner notes of producer Mickie Most were retained word-for-word, with different song titles inserted. The annotator was saying precisely the same sentiments about different tracks.

One thing was the same in both countries: 'Don't Let Me Be Misunderstood' became an important hit in February 1965. Mickie Most knew, as he would later prove as one of Britain's most successful producers, that what makes a good album track doesn't necessarily make a good single. In April of 1965 the Animals' treatment of Sam Cooke's 'Bring It On Home To Me' was released, and Eric Burdon told *The New Musical Express*: 'I seldom like any of our more commercial numbers. It was Mickie Most's idea, and he knows what sells. I wanted it to be faster and (have) a lot more rave appeal.'

'Rave appeal' or not, Most did know what sold. 'Bring It On Home To Me' became the Animals' fourth consecutive top ten record.

While it was in the charts, Alan Price left the group. It wasn't just the usual musical differences, although the repertoire was steering in the commercial direction. The main problem was that Price loathed flying with a passion and found it terrifying to make the air trips necessary for an act as globally in demand as the Animals.

Alan's last album with the group was *Animal Tracks*. On the cover, the Animals are sitting on a railroad line, all wearing military costumes and pointing their weapons straight at the record buyer. The photo was inspired by Eric Burdon's grisly hobby, collecting antique weapons. His London flat was lined with old knives and guns, World War II souvenirs and a hunting rifle with a telescopic sight.

Price escaped without injury. Appropriately, the next Animals single was called 'We Gotta Get Out Of This Place'.

'We Gotta Get Out Of This Place' was the Animals' second biggest British hit, reaching number two in the summer of 1965. But it was a greater departure from 'House Of The Rising Sun' than the one chart place might suggest. The new success, far from being a traditional blues song, was a song designed for the pop market by ace New York songwriters Barry Mann and Cynthia Weil. Indeed, chart success was such a consideration that two different versions of the single were released in the UK and US, the latter effort deemed more likely to succeed on American radio.

The Animals returned to their roots for a one-off concert at the 1965 Richmond Jazz Festival. They were joined by several leading British jazzmen to form the Animals Big Band, but after the event they reverted to the five-man format. 1965 was a year the group did several unusual things, including touring the Southern United States under the sponsorship of an orphans' home. The Magnolia Boys Town of Laurel, Mississippi, promoted the shows, and Eric Burdon promised: 'If for nothing else than those kids, we'll be singing and playing our hearts out.'

The year ended with another clearly commercial cut, 'It's My Life', but 1966 began with something that was avant garde in comparison. 'Inside Looking Out' was a song about being in prison that sounded different from anything else in the charts at the time and would later be recorded with greater volume and less effect by Grand Funk Railroad. For the Animals it was a daring departure that didn't quite work, as Burdon acknowledged when he said that those who heard it seemed to like it but didn't want to buy it. The record peaked at number twelve, breaking the Animals' string of top ten hits. In America, it was the least successful release in over a year. The next single had to be good, and it was.

The first thing I ever did on my own in the music business was to promote the Animals in concert at my high school. It turned out to be tremendous value for money as the group played all their hits and their forthcoming album and the auditorium sold out.

The high point of the concert came when Eric Burdon introduced 'Don't Bring Me Down', an exciting pop number by Goffin and King that had recently been premiered on the radio. The intro of the song built to a dramatic fuzz tone guitar riff by Hilton Valentine, and as the seconds ticked by the guitarist frantically fiddled with his fuzz pedal, the audience wondered whether he would get set in time for his big chord. He made it – though to this day I don't know whether he was actually panicked or just milking the moment for dramatic effect. 'Don't Bring Me Down', recorded in Nassau while supposedly on holiday, restored the Animals to the thick of the hit parade. But while it was in the charts, in the summer of 1966, the ultimate bring-down occurred: the group broke up.

John Steel had prefaced the split with his own departure in the spring, saying he wanted to spend more time with his family. With Price gone the preceding year, the spotlight had focused almost entirely on Burdon anyway, and now he made a brief attempt at a solo career.

The American record company was having nothing of it, at least not until they'd made the most of the group's current album, *Animalization*. They lifted another single from the album, a rocking version of the r & b standard 'See See Rider'. It turned out to be the Animals' most successful US single since 'House Of The Rising Sun'. In the autumn of 1966, a group that no longer existed was in the top ten. No wonder MGM Records in America looked unfavourably upon Eric Burdon's desire to go solo. They would lose a chart act. A compromise was reached. Burdon, who was contracted as part of the Animals, agreed to the new billing, Eric Burdon And the Animals, and the company consented to the album title, *Eric Is Here*. Burdon had the taste to record for this LP two songs by the then little-known writer Randy Newman. At first he wanted 'Mama Told Me Not To Come' to be the single, but he thought British audiences wouldn't understand the drug references. He settled instead for 'Help Me Girl', a straightforward pop song by other writers.

'Help Me Girl' was a top twenty record in Britain, but in America it didn't do as well. Its release was delayed by the success of 'See See Rider', and by the time it came out a group called the Outsiders had got a one-month jump on Burdon And the Animals. The versions wound up splitting mediocre chart honours. If Eric Burdon was going to make something of his new career, he would have to offer a more individual vision.

This he did with his 1967 releases. Burdon had long been a champion of civil rights. Spending much of his time in the United States, he now found himself espousing the causes of the American young people who bought his records. In 1967 this boiled down to the double-barrelled cliché 'Peace and Love'. Burdon adjusted his perspective publicly. His first major hit in America, 'When I Was Young', was heavily sitar-flavoured, reflecting the brief boomlet in raga rock. In the UK he scored with 'Good Times', an apology for past indiscretions he admitted was autobiographical. The music-hall flavour made it too British for American consumption.

'When I Was Young' and 'Good Times', a double dose of public penance, pointed Eric Burdon And the Animals in a new direction. With their next release they took several giant steps that way. Burdon had been completely converted to the Californian alternative life style. He called the new album *Winds Of Change* – perhaps the only influence Harold MacMillan ever had on rock and roll – and wanted MGM to put on the jacket a photo of a Los Angeles policeman beating a man to death. The record company, which happened to be based in L.A., refused, so Burdon wrote liner notes for the front, illustrated only by a tattered book, and wrote more liner notes for the back. 'I love you all,' the artist wrote, 'and want you to gain something from these new sounds as I gain from listening to my saints in past years.'

It was the message of a man blissed out on a new life style, and here was the great irony: the white man who had a pop producer help him make blues records now had a black producer, Tom Wilson, helping him make pop records. At least one of them typifies its time: 'San Franciscan Nights' which was an international top ten hit. It now sounds charmingly, colossally naïve, but for Eric Burdon it had seemed a logical step to go from love of the underprivileged black people to love of everybody. There were other reasons he liked being in California. 'Because of the movies,' he explained. Not content with watching old films on late night L.A. TV, Burdon hoped to get into pictures himself. In 1968 he planned a film called *The Death Of Harry Farmer*, a desert movie in which he hoped to get Karl Malden to play his father and Rudolf Nureyev to dance a ballet. These plans never came to fruition nor did other cinematic schemes.

He did put all his interests together at least once. His strong feelings against war, his almost contradictory fascination with weaponry, and his love of the visual all came to play in 'Sky Pilot', a seven-minute twenty-seven-second epic in which a conventional pop song about a minister in the military was followed by a few minutes of air battle and bagpipe sound effects and a soothing, message-filled musical coda. Projections were shown on the backdrop during live performance, and Burdon was genuinely excited by the acceptance of this song, which was a hit in the States and, he claimed, a number one with the troops in Vietnam. Radio stations played either the first part or the whole shooting match – an expression which in this case was literally valid.

'Sky Pilot' was a top twenty American hit for Eric Burdon And the Animals in 1968. 'Monterey', instant nostalgia about the Californian pop festival of the same name, enjoyed the same success. 'I'm still accepted in America because I've been going through the same changes that the American kids are,' Burdon explained. But the new emphasis was a flop in Britain, and the group broke up for good that December.

Eric had one more brief grab at glory when, in 1970, 'Spill The Wine', a single he recorded with the soul act War, reached the American top three. One critic observed that Burdon had finally achieved what he had always seemed to want to do: sing for a black group. But despite a serious effort to work together, the two entities went their separate ways.

The seventies were very successful times for War. They were also good for Alan Price, who followed his sixties success with The Alan Price Set, and became a long-term mass appeal soloist. Indeed, the seventies were profitable for Chas Chandler, who had guided Jimi Hendrix in the late sixties and gone on to manage Slade. The new decade wasn't so hot for Eric Burdon. He tried several times with different musicians, but never got the right combination of material, performance and support. The one-off reunion album The Animals did record in 1975, issued in '77, was not of great consequence.

At one point Burdon looked back in frustration if not anger and said 'I didn't try to be seriously involved with the Animals because I was drunk all the time and that was a case of singing for my supper'.

But many artists cannot recognise what they do well. Eric Burdon was the finest white blues singer English rock ever produced. He may have briefly prolonged success on the singles chart by following the flower-power fad, but he deserted his strength. When the fashion went out of style, Eric Burdon had no one left to speak to, even though he felt he had more to say. Was he really not proud of the greatest Animals' records? Perhaps it is better to be heard and misunderstood than not to be heard at all.

PAUL
SIMON

If an artist is someone who keeps working at his craft regardless of the commercial reaction, Paul Simon must be a true artist. They say if at first you don't succeed, try, try again, and Paul Simon didn't succeed at first as part of a duo or as a soloist – nor again as part of a duo nor one more time as a soloist. Then he did succeed, as half of the most successful duo in pop music history, and he decided to try again anyway as a soloist. He keeps working. He's an artist.

Almost every pop star who wins popular attention turns out to have had an apprenticeship away from the public eye. In the case of Paul Simon and Art Garfunkel, the warming-up period was nearly a decade long. They grew up together in Forest Hills in the New York borough of Queens, though Simon had actually been born in Newark, New Jersey. In 1957 the teenage pals entered a local recording studio and emerged with a track that climbed to number fifty-nine on the Billboard Hot 100. They even won an appearance on 'American Bandstand' the daily afternoon rock and roll show that was a must-see for US teenagers in the late fifties. Years later Dick Clark, the perennially youthful-looking host of the series, went through old editions of the programme to assemble an anniversary show, and was dismayed to discover that one of the very few appearances that hadn't been kept was that of Tom and Jerry. Posterity has no chance of seeing Tom and Jerry perform – Tom Graph and Jerry Landis, to be exact, since they even gave themselves false surnames. 'Hey! Schoolgirl' was one of the scores of one-off chart entries by teenage hopefuls during the heyday of rock and roll. When no further success was forthcoming, Simon and Garfunkel anticipated Mick Jagger's question 'What can a poor boy do 'cept sing in a rock and roll band?' and provided an answer. They went back to school.

For Simon, who was sixteen, it was the logical thing to do. But he didn't stop making music. While at Queens College he met Carole Klein, later better known as Carole King. They started making demonstration

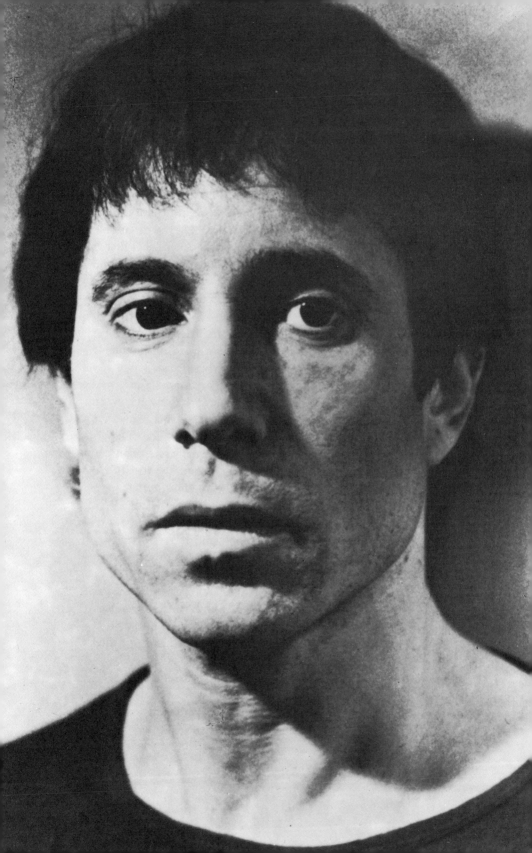

records for publishers. Simon was paid fifteen dollars per song, but more importantly learned how to sing into a microphone and how to overdub tracks in a studio.

He started but didn't finish law school. In 1963 he got to number ninety-seven with 'The Lone Teen Ranger', released under the old name Jerry Landis. He came to England in 1964 to sing on the folk club circuit. While in the country another Landis single was released, the songs written under yet another alias, Paul Kane. The A-side was called 'Carlos Dominquez'.

'Carlos Dominquez' is now an extremely rare piece of Paul Simon memorabilia. In 1964 it was nothing, but at least the artist interested Columbia Records in New York into releasing an album of his songs and some folk standards in partnership with Art Garfunkel. The folk music boom of the early sixties had just hit its peak – the Beatles and their offspring in the British Invasion of America were about to give pop music a very different focus. But Columbia had registered great success with Bob Dylan, so they were willing to give a couple of other folkies a shot. They even gave Simon and Garfunkel Dylan's producer, Tom Wilson. The resulting LP was *Wednesday Morning, 3 a.m.* which got a reception as quiet as the time of day itself, though after the duo became international stars a few years later it sold hundreds of thousands of copies. Once again Paul and Arthur parted, the tall blonde one to graduate school at Columbia University in New York City and the short stocky one back to Britain to try it again as a soloist. He recorded a twelve-song programme called *The Paul Simon Songbook*. It would be difficult to find now, since in the late seventies the artist succeeded in his wishes to have it withdrawn from the CBS catalogue, but were one to find a copy one would be stunned to see how many subsequent Simon and Garfunkel favourites first appeared on a solo album by a foreign folk singer earning £10 per performance. 'April Come She Will', 'Kathy's Song', 'A Most Peculiar Man' – they're all on *The Paul Simon Songbook*, as was 'I Am A Rock'.

The package was produced by the no doubt respectable but nonetheless odd-sounding team of Reginald Warburton and Stanley West. The singer might not be a star, but at least he was making a living. He didn't realise that events had occurred that would make him a very comfortable living.

A Boston disc jockey had begun playing a track on *Wednesday Morning, 3 a.m.* called 'The Sound Of Silence'. The cut became a favourite on area college campuses. CBS executives suspected that with a harder instrumental track the number could be a hit single. They spoke to Tom

Wilson, producer of the original recording. After making 'Like A Rolling Stone' with Bob Dylan, Wilson used the backing band to add electric guitar, bass and drums to 'The Sound Of Silence'. The resulting 45 quickly went to number one in Boston and spread across America, becoming the nation's first chart-topper of 1966. Simon and Garfunkel were back in the charts after eight years, with the third version of the same song. Ironically, the single didn't even chart in Britain, where The Bachelors took the song to the top three. Garfunkel was in graduate school when he got the news about the record's success. Simon was in London. According to *The New Musical Express Book Of Rock*, which is good on details, he was producing an album for Jackson C. Frank. He returned to New York where the boyhood pals made an album featuring many of the songs which had previously appeared on *Songbook*. It was a very good thing the success of 'Sound Of Silence' came after he had accumulated a body of songs in England. These were recorded directly and satisfied the quick demand for what was thought was new material.

'Homeward Bound', a song written while waiting for a train in Widnes, Lancashire, was the next single, and gave the duo their UK top ten debut. 'I Am A Rock', a remake of the first track on *Songbook*, was the next hit. 1966 was a very good year for Simon and Garfunkel, with three top ten hit singles and two hit albums, the second being *Parsley, Sage, Rosemary And Thyme*. 1967 was not so good. Three minor hit 45s and no new albums showed Simon's natural productive pace.

The partnership came back to public attention courtesy of film director Mike Nichols, who used four cuts from existing albums in the soundtrack of his film *The Graduate*. He also used a one-minute fragment of a new song: 'Mrs Robinson'. The full version gave Simon and Garfunkel their second American number one, their first Grammy Award, and their first number one LP, *Bookends*.

Criticising the foibles of society without uttering revolutionary threats, rocking gently without making a heavy noise, Simon and Garfunkel captured the concerns of the campuses and presented them in a palatable package. Simon's literate lyrics and Garfunkel's heavenly harmonies made the pair's platters distinctive discs. They virtually invented the 'soft rock' style that came to be predominant in America in the seventies.

It reached a peak in 1970 with *Bridge Over Troubled Water*. Ironically, the album itself was made under troubled conditions. Garfunkel was in Mexico appearing in Mike Nichols' film of Joseph Heller's novel *Catch-22*. As Paul explained to Jon Landau in a lengthy *Rolling Stone* interview, songs would be written, partially recorded, or mixed in Artie's absence. One number was presented to him for a vocal solo and he decided he didn't want to sing it, that Paul should do it. Paul often wished he had. Paul stood at the side of the stage while Art got the ovations for a masterful performance on a song Paul wrote. 'Bridge Over Troubled Water' was Simon and Garfunkel's greatest hit, but Simon wasn't even on it. He came to resent the recognition Garfunkel got for that number, and realised it was a sign he was growing dissatisfied with the partnership. *Bridge Over Troubled Water* wasn't just the duo's biggest success. At the time it was the best-selling album ever, going over nine million copies in only a few years. It was Britain's number one LP of the seventies. There were four hit singles in the set: the title track, 'El Condor Pasa', 'Cecelia', and the song that boasts two-man harmony at its best: 'The Boxer'.

'The Boxer' had a long fade suggested to Simon by Garfunkel and co-producer Roy Halee. The partnership had a long fade, too. There was no single argument or planning meeting; Art went off to do another movie, *Carnal Knowledge*, and Simon started a solo album. By the time both were finished, it was obvious the two careers were no longer one.

Strictly speaking, *Paul Simon* wasn't a debut album. *The Paul Simon Songbook* had been the artist's first solo outing. But now he had financial resources and studio technique to use, and he produced a set of songs that were separate entities musically and thematically, although a mood of despondency did seem to affect a few tracks. 'Duncan', about a Canadian boy's odyssey to manhood, was a minor classic, with a series of basic experiences poetically phrased and beautifully backed by the South American group, Los Incas. 'Run That Body Down' was a whimsical warning not to let a never-too-fit frame go to absolute rot, while 'Me And Julio Down By The Schoolyard' was enough fun to make a novelty single. The most fondly remembered number was one inspired by a chicken-and-egg dish on a Chinese menu, 'Mother And Child Reunion'.

Despite the amusing origin of its title, 'Mother And Child Reunion' did have a serious content. After his dog was run over and killed, Simon had been upset, and he wondered how he would have felt if a person close to him perished. These considerations directly inspired some of the lines in the song.

Paul Simon was a very well-received album, both critically and commercially. It even reached number one in the UK chart. But its sales total was just about a million: wonderful for most artists, modest for

Simon and Garfunkel.

It can be argued that lyrically and musically Paul Simon's solo work has been more precise, more telling, and more accomplished than the duo days. But without Garfunkel's sweetening harmonies, and the angelic quality he lent the twosome's appearance, many of Simon's sentiments seemed starker and sadder, and those record buyers on the look-out for something 'nice' did not buy Paul Simon like they had bought Simon and Garfunkel.

The artist had to earn his hits, and earn them he did. His next LP, *There Goes Rhymin' Simon*, was consistently illuminating *and* entertaining in a set that was lyrically brilliant and musically diverse, ranging from the light New Orleans jazz of 'Take Me To The Mardi Gras' to the good-time gospel of 'Loves Me Like A Rock' and the irreverent rock of the first American single from the package, 'Kodachrome'.

'Kodachrome' reached number two in the American singles chart, but because its obvious reference to a commercial trademark conflicted with the BBC's advertising policy it received restricted air-play on the Beeb. The damage done wasn't great, because the other side, 'Take Me To The Mardi Gras', made the top ten itself. The second choice from the LP, 'Loves Me Like A Rock', was an international hit, absolutely uplifting in its joyous affirmation of devoted and almost unquestioning love.

It would have been the high point of almost any album, but not *There Goes Rhymin' Simon*. Simon managed the nearly impossible feat of writing a song about Watergate and Vietnam without getting bogged down in rhetoric and revolution. He did so by speaking from the point of view of an American far from home – he was, in fact, in London. Every line of 'American Tune' is packed with power, made subtle but even more effective through understatement and symbolism. It was the best song Paul Simon had written and, accordingly, *Rolling Stone* chose it 1973's Song Of The Year.

There Goes Rhymin' Simon has been the high spot of the artist's career. Every song was meticulously planned and executed, with different players according to the musical style of the track. Quincy Jones, The Dixie Hummingbirds, two of The Roches and The Muscle Shoals Sound Rhythm Section were just some of the other talents represented.

This eclecticism was reflected again on the next studio album, *Still Crazy After All These Years*. But it didn't appear until 1975, two years after *Rhymin' Simon*. It took longer for Paul to write songs in the seventies than it had in the sixties. 'I was a beginning writer then,' he told

Jon Landau, 'so I wrote anything I saw. Now I sift. Now I say, "Well, that's not really a subject that I want to write a song about".'

Two of the subjects that recurred on *Still Crazy* were interrelated: death and the disintegration of relationships. Both were consequences of aging. 'Still crazy . . . after all these years.' 'Nothing but the dead and dying back in my little town.' 'There must be fifty ways to leave your lover.' 'The pitcher died.' Simon's own once-happy marriage had soured, and having said an artist does his most creative work in his mid-thirties, he found himself at that relatively advanced age. At least a jury of his peers agreed that he was doing his best work: they awarded him The Album Of The Year Grammy.

Still Crazy After All These Years was rapturously received by fellow artists, who recognised the fine music and the skilfully utilised contributions of Phoebe Snow, Patti Austin, Toots Thielman, David Sanborn and even Art Garfunkel in a one-off reunion, 'My Little Town'. But Simon was disturbed that rock critics gave most of their praise to his lyrics. Many pop journalists, particularly in America, are English majors and/or frustrated writers, and they concentrate on the words. Simon's lyrics are case studies in word economy and effectiveness, and he reproduced them on all his solo albums. They were rightly celebrated, but at the expense of his musical ideas, which were equally exciting. There was an extended descending phrase on 'I Do It For Your Love' which seemed a rare example of making a musical exercise a moving composition. And then there was the military drumbeat on '50 Ways To Leave Your Lover', which stated as clearly as the lyric that one can literally march out of an unsatisfying affair.

'50 Ways To Leave Your Lover' was an American number one, the only US chart topping single by Simon or Garfunkel alone. Ironically, in Britain, Paul didn't manage the feat, but Art made it twice, with 'I Only Have Eyes For You' and the number one of the entire year 1979, 'Bright Eyes'.

There followed an almost unbelievable five-year gap between studio albums. Simon was concentrating on a movie about the problems of an ageing folk-rocker, though he called the character Jonah and not Paul. As early as 1966, he had told Robert Shelton of the *New York Times* 'Pop music is catching up with film as the leading medium in which to make some comment about the world for a large audience.' Having mastered pop, it now seemed logical to try film. His outings at scoring other people's movies hadn't been completely satisfactory, since Mike Nichols had used predominantly old rather than new material for *The Graduate* and Warren Beatty hadn't used much of Paul's work at all in *Shampoo*. Simon decided to co-write, act and sing himself in a production he called *One Trick Pony*. Indeed, it is assumed that one reason he left CBS for Warner Brothers Records was because of the easy association his new label had with the motion picture division of Warners.

Unfortunately, Simon was an occasionally amusing but not attention-grabbing actor. There wasn't enough meat in the plot, and too many shots of being on the road – literally the road, motorways, backroads, city streets. For once the introspection of Paul's lyrics infiltrated the music, which was almost relentlessly downbeat and ultimately uninteresting. The two bright moments were a cameo appearance by Lou Reed as a record producer and the upbeat reminiscence of neighbourhood a cappella street corner symphonies: 'Late In The Evening'.

It is deeply disturbing to think that the talent of Paul Simon was lost for a few years making a flop film. There is a scene in the movie where Jonah, the aging sixties star, is offstage listening to the act he's just finished supporting, the B-52s. He admits to his backing group – which happened to consist of superlative session musicians – that he doesn't understand current trends in pop music and cannot relate to them. It is almost unthinkable that that should happen to Paul Simon, who has always been in touch with the best of folk, rock, soul and light jazz. Yet one has to admit, it is a possibility.

He did, after all, recently turn forty, and there is no requirement that he take any more interest in the always changing chart scene. But the mere fact that 400,000 people turned out in September of 1981 to hear Simon And Garfunkel give a reunion concert in Central Park suggests that Paul's extremely big audience is always there waiting for him. They feel that even if he is now past his mid-thirties, he has good creative work ahead, and that, after the noble but failed experiment of *One Trick Pony*, he may yet be homeward bound.

THE TEMPTATIONS

'There are three things that improve with time,' the comedian Bill Cosby wrote in 1966, 'a good tobacco, a woman, and The Temptations' performance.' We can't speak for his smoke nor his wife, but it is certainly true that a decade and a half later his observation about the Temptations has proved correct. Their more than two dozen top forty hits sound as good as ever . . . and in the absence of any comparable current group, they sound even better.

The Temptations were Motown's most successful sixties male vocal group. Smokey Robinson of the Miracles wrote the best songs and Levi Stubbs of the Four Tops had the most distinctive voice, but it was the Tempts who had more frequent and bigger hits. The evolution of their sound reflected the basic changes in black music itself.

Eddie Kendricks and Paul Williams grew up in Birmingham, Alabama. While in high school in the late fifties they sang in several groups, including the Primes who, as Kendricks put it, 'used to do "shooby shooby doo" kinda things'. The two teenagers wanted to make music a career, but their friends didn't, so Eddie and Paul went to Detroit in search of new partners for the Primes.

They met Otis Miles and David English, who used the stage names Otis Williams and Melvin Franklin and who sang in a series of groups fronted by Otis – the Questions, the Distants, the Elegants. The four youngsters added a handsome singer called Elbridge Bryant and once again Eddie Kendricks had his Primes. They sang locally around Detroit and enlisted a female vocal group to open the show for them. They were the Primettes, who later became the Supremes.

The Primes paid a visit to Jackie Wilson, the great fifties soul star who had a home in Detroit. For some reason unknown to this day, Wilson left the house when the Primes arrived, but returned five hours later to listen to them perform. Impressed, he called the man who had written and produced many of his big records, Berry Gordy, Jr.

The Primes briefly became the Elgins, until they discovered another group already had that name, and then the Temptations, perhaps not realising that a white group had used that monicker on a minor 1960 hit, 'Barbara'. The Temptations were placed on the Miracle label. Their first single was 'Oh Mother Of Mine'. Almost bizarrely, the slogan of Miracle Records was 'If it's a hit, it's a Miracle'. Apt words for 'Oh Mother Of Mine' – the only Miracles in Detroit were singing with Smokey.

In 1962, Berry Gordy started a record company named after himself, Gordy Records. The Temptations had the label's first entry on the rhythm and blues chart: 'Dream Come True'. Written by Berry Gordy, it climbed to number twenty-two in the *Billboard* rhythm and blues chart. It seemed the Temptations' dream of a musical career was going to come true. But the next release, 'Paradise', only left them in limbo. They still had a lot to learn.

The quintet suffered a bad blow when Elbridge Bryant was drafted. He was replaced by David Ruffin, who was hardly as handsome but could at least sing well. They'd met him at the Miracle label, where he was a struggling solo artist. This unnatural substitution turned out to be one of the best things that ever happened to the Temptations. So was their partnership with their next producer – Smokey Robinson.

'I'd always liked them,' the Motown vice-president recalled. 'They always had that churchy kind of feeling, the soulful sound, from the high tenor to the low bass.' Robinson decided not only to produce the group, but provide the material, beginning with 'I Want A Love I Can See', and continuing with 'The Way You Do The Things You Do'.

It was this second effort with Smokey that gave the Temptations their break-through. It's a kind of record that isn't made any more: a rhythm number with light jazz overtones. Over it all floated the top tenor voice of Eddie Kendricks.

'The Way You Do The Things You Do' made it to number eleven in the Hot 100 in the spring of 1964. It was co-written by Smokey Robinson and his fellow Miracle, Robert Rogers. The next Robinson–Temptations release, 'I'll Be In Trouble', was only a minor hit, and when the flip side, 'The Girl's Alright With Me', got some action, the novice who had produced it got his chance to make an A-side, 'Girl Why You Wanna Make Me Blue'. That newcomer was Norman Whitfield, who lost the assignment when his record didn't make the top twenty.

Not everything was lost. The Temptations heard a song Smokey and Ronnie White had written, presumably for The Miracles. They begged

Robinson to let them have a try at it. Sweet soul that he was and still is, he gave them a number one.

'The song was a romantic song, a sweet song,' Smokey explained. 'I thought a counterbalance to that would be to use David on lead. He had a rough kinda voice.' The tension created by a gruff voice singing a beautiful ballad was one reason for the historic success of The Temptations' first chart-topper, 'My Girl'.

'My Girl' was the first of the Temptations' four American number ones. It also provided their debut in the British charts, though Otis Redding would later do better in the UK with the song.

Like 'The Way You Do The Things You Do', 'My Girl' showcased Smokey Robinson's unequalled skill at using simile and metaphor in pop lyrics. So did 'It's Growing', the not so successful but still splendid successor to 'My Girl'. These three songs, all contained on the classic album *The Temptations Sing Smokey*, are case studies in craftsmanship.

David Ruffin didn't get to take all the lead vocals just because he'd sung on a number one. The Temptations were known as a group with five lead singers, though it most often suited the sound to go with Ruffin or Kendricks. On the 1965 hit 'Since I Lost My Baby', Paul Williams fronted the five, and Melvin Franklin supplied a prominent bass line. On this tune better than any other we hear the Temptations' harmonies applied to the call-and-response technique rhythm and blues borrowed from gospel, in which, for dramatic effect, the group answers the soloist, in this case by restating his previous line. This style was a major feature of fifties and sixties r & b.

'Since I Lost My Baby' gave the Temptations who weren't singing the lead line an important role regardless, and it perfectly suited their stage style. When they were starting out, they had been overwhelmed by the live act of Gladys Knight And The Pips. That family foursome moved around the stage in an orderly arranged fashion the Tempts had not considered. The men were further startled by the professionalism of the Flamingos in concert, and the double dose convinced them to design their own choreography. By the time they themselves were consistent hit-makers, the Temptations had mastered movements that became their trademark. Four men would make identical motions around the lead singer, or all five would move together like a chorus line. Dressed in the same suits, they seemed a race unto themselves, a smooth-singing, smart stepping species. The style was copied by scores of groups. As Berry Gordy's sister, Esther Edwards, said when Paul Williams died in 1973,

'All over the world, young men sing in groups in a fashion created by the Tempts. They dance with choreography that so closely matches the Tempts that one might think Paul had personally tutored them.'

The Temptations' success survived a producer change. After more hits with 'My Baby' and 'Get Ready', Smokey Robinson left the group in the now-experienced hands of Norman Whitfield. The first single he cut with them in 1966, 'Ain't Too Proud To Beg', became a soul standard.

'I suppose Norman took time to find himself,' Melvin Franklin remarked in retrospect. No one could have predicted from his brief early efforts that Whitfield would be capable of getting such a tough, tight sound with the Tempts. 'Ain't Too Proud To Beg' was the second of four consecutive number ones on the r & b list, spending the group's personal best of eight weeks at the top. Norman Whitfield's production gave the Tempts new potency in the pop chart, too. His next effort, 'Beauty Is Only Skin Deep', went to number three, the best placing since 'My Girl'.

'Beauty Is Only Skin Deep' artificially ended the first portion of the Temptations' career. Here Motown issued a Greatest Hits album that passed the sales required for a gold disc, but since the company was not then accepting auditing by the Record Industry Association of America the LP was never properly certified. The collection stayed on the album chart for over a year and became the definitive party platter of the late sixties just as Johnny Mathis' hits set had been the make-out music of the late fifties and early sixties.

Two B-sides were included in the anthology, not as filler but because both had been minor hits, 'The Girl's Alright With Me' and 'Don't Look Back'. The latter was a tender tune that set the pattern for Temptations' B-sides. The best flips of the sixties were on Tempts' records. 'Fading Away', 'You'll Lose A Precious Love', 'I Truly, Truly Believe', 'Just One Last Look' – these and others were superb slowies. When it was announced the group would release an album called *In A Mellow Mood*, some fans assumed it would be a collection of best ballads. It turned out to be a programme of show tunes and standards, one of Berry Gordy's attempts to expand his artists' audience.

Norman Whitfield picked up where he had left off before *The Greatest Hits* album by co-writing and producing another smash, '(I Know) I'm Losing You'. This is still one of the great records in all soul music. David Ruffin's urgent delivery of a dramatic lyric conveys both hopelessness and horror at the prospect of love lost. The song has invited cover versions by acts including Rare Earth and Rod Stewart, but the original remains definitive.

It was strange that after such a solid success The Temptations issued two very different singles, on the first of which Norman Whitfield was not even involved. 'All I Need' and 'You're My Everything' were production numbers making extensive use of the Detroit Symphony Orchestra members who moonlit at Motown. But both were exciting, and the duet between Kendricks and Ruffin on 'You're My Everything' was exquisite.

Norman Whitfield used David Ruffin as the lead singer on Temptations singles, changing the pattern of alternation Smokey Robinson had used. 'It's You That I Need', 'I Wish It Would Rain', 'I Could Never Love Another' – Ruffin fronted them all.

The trend affected David. He began to think the group should be billed as David Ruffin and The Temptations, just as other Motown stars like Smokey Robinson, Martha Reeves and Diana Ross were getting top ranking over the Miracles, Vandellas and Supremes. Ruffin had once said the group always travelled together and, because they were all at least six feet tall, were frequently mistaken for a basketball team. Now he used his own luxurious transport; now he stayed in his own hotel. He was setting himself up for promotion. Instead, he got relegated. He was told that the four friends had voted him out. The last Temptation in, before their success, David Ruffin was now the first one out.

He didn't take the decision well. For a time he even followed the group around and, concertgoers claimed, he would sing from the audience and leap on stage on occasion. Finally he accepted that his was to be a solo career; he had one big hit, 'My Whole World Ended', and then went into the wilderness until Van McCoy rescued him in the mid-70s.

The Temptations' new lead singer was Dennis Edwards, formerly of the Contours. He made his debut in the autumn of 1968. Norman Whitfield chose the occasion to give the group a completely new sound. He mixed r & b with rock for the landmark single 'Cloud Nine'. 'Cloud Nine' was authored by Whitfield and Barrett Strong, who had previously penned 'I Heard It Through The Grapevine' and now became a regular writing team. It was lyrically bold, dealing with a retreat to a dream world which most listeners assumed was marijuana-induced. Musically, Whitfield was trying to make the Temptations as contemporary as Sly And The Family Stone or Jimi Hendrix, singing songs of black consciousness against a rock-influenced backing track. 'Cloud Nine' was a success; it won Motown's first Grammy Award. The follow-up

'Runaway Child Running Wild' was another hit.

It was also nine minutes and thirty-eight seconds long, though shortened to a still-long 4:47 for single release. There were long instrumental passages and the cries of a hysterical lost boy. It was, in short, a production number, and Whitfield was the boss.

'Working with Norman was always a strain,' Dennis Edwards recalled. 'He had such a definite idea of how things should be done. There was very little freedom.'

For the 1969 album *The Temptations Puzzle People*, Whitfield had Edwards sing the key phrase 'I'm black and I'm proud' in the black power anthem 'Message From A Black Man'. But the mentor did always keep one eye on the charts, and manufactured a pop piece that gave the quintet their second number one, 'I Can't Get Next To You'. Not only did the Temptations have a number one with the song but Al Green borrowed it to begin his string of historic hits in the seventies.

While Norman Whitfield was giving the Tempts a heavier, socially-conscious image, a short-lived parallel career was presenting a completely different picture. The Temptations and Supremes were booked on the same Ed Sullivan Show and got the idea to record together. The octet had five singles that became hits in America, Britain, or both in less than a year and a half, billed under the mouthful 'Diana Ross And The Supremes And The Temptations'. Ross characterised the sessions as opportunities to out-do the other group, particularly on ad libs. The best-selling of these friendly battles was the international hit 'I'm Gonna Make You Love Me'. The composition had originally been a US hit for Madeline Bell in 1968. It did even better and went around the world the following year in the duet version that marked an unofficial reunion of The Primes And Primettes. But any chance the partnership might become commercially viable in the long term were dashed when Diana Ross left the Supremes at the turn of the decade.

It was Norman Whitfield or nothing for the Temptations. 'We are still number one,' Melvin Franklin said in 1970, 'and we are grateful to Norman for helping to keep us there.' He helped keep them there in 1970 with 'Ball Of Confusion'.

Norman Whitfield had made the Temptations over. With 'Ball Of Confusion' and its clearly derivative follow-up, 'Ungena Za Ulimwenga', the group were the ultimate social commentators. Not just on smoking dope to escape from everyday pressures, not only on runaway children or identity-seeking blacks, but on everything worth saying anything about.

Eddie Kendricks thought the change wrong. He had wanted to leave the group for two years, but he hadn't saved his money and couldn't afford to exit. In 1971, the right moment came. He got his first A-side in three years with 'Just My Imagination', and he made the most of it. This is one of the most beautifully controlled and conveyed lead vocals on vinyl. When Kendricks sings 'she doesn't even know me', the effect is ethereal.

'Just My Imagination' was the Temptations' third American number one, and the perfect launch point for Eddie Kendricks' solo career. His Birmingham buddy Paul Williams also left the group in 1971, but for less happy reasons. Depression compounded by drink had occasionally left Paul unable to perform. Two years later Williams took his life.

Two new Temptations were inducted, but their identities really didn't matter. The Tempts were now not just Norman Whitfield's act, but one of his acts. He switched songs amongst his various charges. 'War', from the Temptations' *Psychedelic Shack* album, became a number one for Edwin Starr. *His* 'Funky Music Sho Nuff Turns Me On' was used again with the Tempts. *Their* album track 'Smiling Faces Sometimes' became a smash for the Undisputed Truth, whose LP marathon 'Papa Was A Rolling Stone' was given to the Temptations.

The music really was going round and round, but in this case to good effect. 'Papa Was A Rolling Stone' on the LP *All Directions* was the most successful of Norman Whitfield's production epics. They'd begun with the nearly ten-minute 'Runaway Child Running Wild', so it was only appropriate the finest of the form should also be with the Temptations. Edited to just over a third of its length for a single release, 'Papa Was A Rolling Stone' was a 1972 number one.

'Papa Was A Rolling Stone' won a Grammy Award for the best rhythm and blues group vocal performance. It also won a Grammy for the best rhythm and blues instrumental performance. 'Papa Was A Rolling Stone' was so long it had been considered both a vocal and an instrumental. The Temptations had been guests on their own record!

It could only get worse. Norman Whitfield succumbed to excess on the 1973 album *Masterpiece*. Despite the moderate success of the title track and 'Law Of The Land', it was clear that he'd already cut his masterpiece with the Temptations. Now he needed new directions, and in the mid-seventies he found them working with the group Rose Royce on music for the film *Car Wash*.

The Temptations were stranded, and they floundered. They left Motown for Atlantic Records. Then, in 1980, they came back to Motown, when Berry Gordy told them he had written a song only they could perform properly. 'Power' brought them back to the top ten of the soul charts.

Of course, they're not really back. Recurring reunion rumours have to date proved overly optimistic. Until a full-scale reunion occurs, Otis Williams and Melvin Franklin are the last of the original Temptations. 'We have both put the group first always,' Otis once said, 'because we believe that if we allow egos to come into the group, we won't prosper.' On the sleeve of the first album back in the Motown fold, they wrote 'We hope once again that fate is a little kind, for we are wiser men this time'. They were humble words. They were no doubt sincere. But humility doesn't make hit records. At Motown, the best producers and writers do that. If the Temptations get their help, and only if they get their help, they might not yet be lost.

CAROLE KING

I used to know a girl named Carole Klein. She was the daughter of the local stationer – red hair, loud voice, nice personality. I lost touch with her after high school.

Then there was a Carole Klein I didn't know. I do know what happened to her. She changed her name to Carole King, wrote more hit songs than any women ever, and recorded the world's best-selling album by a female vocalist.

I think I knew the wrong Carole Klein.

Carole Klein – the musical one – was born in Brooklyn on 9 February 1942. She started to take piano lessons at the age of four. She later confessed 'I was a terrible pupil.' Her mother, who taught her, wanted Carole to learn her lessons in sequence. But the daughter, who almost from the start was more interested in writing than playing, wanted to know advanced techniques related to composing.

While in high school Carole got together with three fellow geometry students to form the Co-Sines, an all-girl group that foreshadowed some of the ensembles she would write for a few years later. That was recreation. Teaching chemistry – that was a living, and Carole went to Queens College, New York, to get her qualifications. She got more than she bargained for. She was drawn into the music business while still at college, befriending, among others, Paul Simon, who had enjoyed a minor one-off hit with his buddy Art Garfunkel under the aliases Tom and Jerry. Paul and Carole made demos together, but nothing as successful as the song fellow young writer Neil Sedaka came up with to proclaim his love for the lady. Sedaka immortalised her in 'Oh Carol', an international top ten hit in 1959. Carole returned the compliment with 'Oh Neil', but it didn't have quite the same effect. She was primarily a music writer. She couldn't write good lyrics yet, so it was a blessing when she met fellow chemistry student Gerry Goffin. He had lyrics, but hadn't mastered melodies. They made a perfect partnership, and not just in music. They fell in love and married; their chemistry was really right.

Gerry and Carole wrote under the names 'Goffin and King'. They needed to write and, in Carole's case, do session work because she'd had a baby shortly after their marriage. One of the songs Carole and Gerry came up with was suitable for one of the girl groups whose material came from Tin Pan Alley. They were the Shirelles; the song was 'Will You Love Me Tomorrow?'

So much for teaching chemistry. Carole never did get her degree. 'Will You Love Me Tomorrow' became number one in America in January of 1961 and made the British top five soon thereafter. Carole King and Gerry Goffin joined the stable of songwriters at The Brill Building on Broadway. Neil Sedaka was there with his friend Howard Greenfield, and Barry Mann and Cynthia Weil were also on board. They and their colleagues all composed on the piano, which meant they all had to have separate if small rooms. In *The Rolling Stone Illustrated History of Rock & Roll*, Barry Mann recounted the chaos: 'It was insane. Cynthia and I would be in this tiny cubicle, about the size of a closet, with just a piano and a chair; no window or anything. We'd go in every morning and write songs all day. In the next room Carole and Gerry would be doing the same thing, and in the next room after that Neil or somebody else. Sometimes when we all got to banging on our piano you couldn't tell who was playing what.'

King called the place a 'musical chicken coop', but somehow they kept laying golden eggs. 'Take Good Care Of My Baby' was the second 1961 number one written by Goffin and King. The artist was Bobby Vee, the biggest rock star ever to emerge from North Dakota. The collaboration had other successes, too, including 'How Many Tears', 'Sharing You' and 'Walkin' With My Angel'.

Carole was absolutely enthusiastic about the effect her husband had on her work. 'Until I met Gerry I was just a musician who wrote bad lyrics,' she said. 'Now we do everything together, and it's impossible to tell where his work begins and mine leaves off.'

The duo had another hit enter the Hot 100 the same week as 'Take Good Care Of My Baby'. 'Every Breath I Take' was performed by Gene Pitney and produced by Phil Spector, with both young men showing evidence of the talents that would make them top forty regulars. Pitney was in thrilling command of his high voice, while Spector offered one of the debut appearances of his 'wall of sound'. That was a one-off. Some of the artists Goffin and King wrote for got more than one song. The middle-of-the-road singing sweethearts Steve Lawrence and Eydie Gorme were personal favourites of Carole's music publisher, Don Kirshner, so they got numbers including 'Go Away Little Girl', which Lawrence took to number one in America, and 'I Want To Stay Here', with which the duo reached number three in Britain. Then there was Tony Orlando, a fellow New Yorker who worked on demos with Carole and then got to sing on the final products. In 1961 Goffin and King gave him two hit tunes, 'Halfway To Paradise' and 'Bless You'. In Britain, he hit the top five with 'Bless You', but was eclipsed on 'Halfway To Paradise' by Billy Fury, who kept the song in the charts for five months.

The latter was one of the rare pre-Beatle cases when the British cover version of an American rock song could be considered superior. Almost all of Carole King's great hits during the years 1961–3 were with American artists. The fact that there were so many stars involved was due to the Brill Building philosophy: it was the song, not the singer, who was most important. Indeed, ninety per cent of the time, not only Carole's composition but the arrangement she had used on the demo were accepted, and almost any young artist being promoted at the time might be blessed with a King number.

1962–3 top ten hits with Carole King songs included 'One Fine Day' by the Chiffons, 'Her Royal Majesty' by James Darren, 'Don't Say Nothin' Bad About My Baby' by Carole's former session singers, the Cookies, 'Hey Girl', a soul standard by Freddie Scott, 'I Can't Stay Mad At You' by Skeeter Davis, and the Everly Brothers' 'Cryin' In the Rain'. (The last was co-written by Howard Greenfield, not Gerry Goffin.) It seemed that Carole could write a hit song for anybody, and one day she and Gerry proved it. They came home from a movie and heard their babysitter singing. They looked at each other and thought, why not? Without even knowing it, the seventeen-year-old girl had passed her audition with rock and roll's hottest songwriters. Within weeks, Little Eva had America's number one single, 'The Loco-Motion'.

A decade later, a prominent rock critic pointed out that the singing style was very much like Carole King's, as if Carole had taught the song to Eva note by note. It's the kind of observation that could only be made years later because, by the summer of 1962, Carole still hadn't released a record of her own. There was certainly no rush – she was still only twenty.

Then Don Kirshner heard her latest demo for Bobby Vee. He'd toyed with the idea of launching Carole as an artist. This performance seemed so good that it was decided to feature the writer as the vocalist, and in August of 1962 Carole King issued her first 45, 'It Might As Well Rain Until September'. It was a worldwide winner. Ironically, its number three placing remains Carole's best showing in the UK singles chart. Certainly there was no contender in the near future: the follow-ups failed, and King simply stopped singing solo.

In 1963, she turned twenty-one. On her birthday, there was real reason to celebrate: one of Goffin and King's greatest songs, 'Up On The Roof', was in the top ten courtesy of the Drifters. Perhaps because she was reaching adulthood, Carole King's songs suddenly assumed a new maturity. 'Go Away Little Girl', the number one for Steve Lawrence, was a ballad, not a rocker, covering exactly the same delicate subject broached years later by Gary Puckett And The Union Gap in 'Young Girl'. 'Up On The Roof' was decidedly philosophical, even if naïvely so. It could only have been written by a New Yorker: when the cares and pressures of urban life get too great to take, there is one way of escape, one place with space to go to and relax, where there are stars instead of skyscrapers: 'Up On The Roof'.

With songs this good it seemed that Gerry and Carole could go on dominating the charts for years. But there's always something unforeseen just around the corner in pop music. In 1963, that something was the Beatles.

The Fab Four took the UK by storm that year, and dominated the US scene the following year. The British groups who rushed into the American charts in their wake constituted an invasion that was all too real to artists like Neil Sedaka and Bobby Vee. Suddenly they were unfashionable, and early sixties stalwarts vanished from the top forty.

Goffin and King managed to cope by getting British artists to record their songs. They were still supplying the hits, but to clients of different nationality. British Goffin and King successes included 'Chains', a Cookies title cut by the Beatles for their first album, 'Oh No Not My Baby', a Maxine Brown original covered by Manfred Mann and years later by Rod Stewart, 'Don't Bring Me Down', an international hit for the Animals, 'I'm Into Something Good', the introductory smash from Herman's Hermits, 'He's In Town' by the Rockin' Berries, 'Some Of Your Lovin'' by Dusty Springfield and 'When My Little Girl Is Smiling', an early number written for the Drifters and taken to the UK top ten by Jimmy Justice.

Many top songwriters have identifiable styles. Smokey Robinson has made heavy use of simile and metaphor, Rod Stewart has written love songs with plots, Harry Chapin was known for his 'story songs'. Goffin and King were able to write almost anything, from the sublime ('Up On The Roof') to the ridiculous ('Let's Turkey Trot'), from the romantic ('Will You Love Me Tomorrow') to the danceable ('The Loco-Motion'). They could write for teenage lovers, as they did many times, or they could write realistically about the emotional dilemmas of adults. 'Hey Girl, I want you to know / I'm gonna miss you so much if you go', Freddie Scott confessed. 'Just once in my life/Let me get what I want', the Righteous Brothers pleaded, adding with their next release 'Why did I have to get so hung on you?'

But suffering isn't the only experience in love; there is the joy of romance that allows lovers to realise their full personal potential. Aretha Franklin rejoiced, '(You Make Me Feel Like) A Natural Woman'.

A three-way songwriting collaboration with Jerry Wexler, 'A Natural Woman' was a success in 1967, the same year the Monkees scored with the Goffin–King number 'Pleasant Valley Sunday'. But the ace cleffers had to face facts: the Beatles had changed the music business beyond recognition, affecting them as much as anyone else. It was now expected that most major artists would write their own material. They didn't need, or for reasons of ego and image, didn't want, people behind the scenes supplying songs.

Carole King, who was beginning to fall out with Goffin personally anyway, decided that she had to make a new effort. 'I never wanted to be an artist,' she claimed, 'but after a while it became the most efficient way to get songs to people.' She made an album called *The City* with a trio including Dan Kortchmar and Charles Larkey, who later became her husband. The album only sold five thousand copies and is today a genuine collector's item, but at least it was a start. Carole took the next step and accepted the billing of a solo artist. After managing to get through the sixties without issuing an album on her own, she put one out in 1970. *Writer* was the simple title of Carole King's first solo LP, although the backing band did include both Kortchmar and Larkey.

Writer also featured a guest appearance by Kortchmar's friend James Taylor who persuaded King to join him on tour. The supporting musicians were the players on the album plus another vocalist, now collectively known as Jo Mama.

Perhaps it was the playing together live that made the band jell, that gave Carole confidence in her vocals. Whatever it was, it was right . . . but then everything seemed right about Carole King's next album. The first single released from the set suggested something special. 'It's Too Late' and the album it came from were released in the summer of 1971. They dominated American radio that season. The single was number one for six weeks. The album was in the charts for five years.

Tapestry was the best-selling LP ever made by a woman. For a time, it might have been the number one, period, but precise sales figures are not released and *Saturday Night Fever* has long since surpassed it anyway. But thirteen million units, the current estimated total, is still a lot of albums. Just over ten years later, the figure is no easier to achieve.

Even allowing for the facts that the songs were excellent, that Lou Adler provided clean production to solve the problem that had cursed the wretchedly-mixed *Writer*, that the players and soloist came over as one voice, there has to be a further explanation. Thirteen million albums is, after all, of fad proportions. Perhaps the reason is this: America and consequently the world were in the throes of the seemingly never-ending Vietnam War. Bad news just wouldn't go away.

The psychedelic life style and rock music that had started with such good intentions had not achieved its goals, and now seemed a parody of themselves. *Tapestry* offered simple emotional feelings, clearly stated and directly expressed. *Tapestry* seemed relevant and reassuring to millions. In times of trauma, it was comforting to hear someone sing 'It would be so fine to see your face at my door'. 'So Far Away' was the second top ten single from *Tapestry*. 'I Feel The Earth Move' was another radio favourite. The old hits 'Will You Love Me Tomorrow' and 'Natural Woman' were done so well that, even if the originals did remain the best-loved versions, it became clear that someone else could sing the song with effect. That someone else just happened to be the co-writer.

Of course, it was inevitable that some of Carole King's compositions would be used by other artists, and this was done most fruitfully by Quincy Jones and James Taylor. Quincy won a Best Instrumental Grammy with his version of 'Smackwater Jack'. Carole won some Grammy Awards, too – Album Of The Year for *Tapestry*, Single Of The Year for 'It's Too Late', Female Vocal Performance Of The Year for *Tapestry*. There was one other major Grammy Award, one which must have meant a great deal to a woman who had grown up a writer. The 1971 Song Of The Year was 'You've Got A Friend', appropriately a number one hit for her friend, James Taylor.

His single was the most successful cover version from *Tapestry*, but it wasn't the only number one version of a Carole King composition during those years. In one of the oddest coincidences in all pop music, Donny Osmond went to the very top of the Hot 100 with a remake of 'Go Away Little Girl' just one month after 'You've Got a Friend', and in 1974 Grand Funk scaled the summit with a heavy version of 'The Loco-Motion'. These occasions were the first two times in which a song had become number one in America by two different artists. Both numbers were by Gerry Goffin and Carole King.

Their break-up had not ended Carole's writing career. She'd worked successfully with Toni Stern on two of the *Tapestry* tracks; others she'd written alone. But, in the long term, neither arrangement was as consistently fulfilling as sharing the job with Goffin had been. She only used a few of his numbers on *Tapestry* and the follow-up, *Music*, and by the second album the shortage of first-rate material began to show. After *Music*, the only real moment of exhilaration came in 1974. It wasn't so much the contribution of her co-writer, David Palmer, as of the instrumental soloist, Tom Scott.

'Jazzman', an American number two, was Carole King's last major success. She's had the occasional minor hit since, but minor hits do not become a legend. The future is not particularly promising, since Carole, forty in February 1982, is a grown woman who has nothing to prove and perhaps, one says it with all affection, nothing left to say.

But in the case of Carole King's career, who needs a future when you've got the past? Having written more hits than anyone other than John Lennon and Paul McCartney is as good a credential as any. Having done that and made *Tapestry* is twice as good as any.

THE BEATLES

I think of the Beatles whenever I hear John Lennon's song 'Number Nine Dream'. I think of the Beatles many times, but always when I hear John sing 'So long ago/Was it in a dream? Was it just a dream? . . . Seemed so real to me.'

That's how anyone who lived through the Beatle era must feel facing the distant but still vivid memory of a Liverpudlian quartet who revolutionised popular music and popular culture so profoundly it now seems impossible. But the wonderful thing about this dream is that it was genuinely real.

The Beatles were the most important and best musical entertainers of the twentieth century. That is quite a claim, but if we're going to consider a historical subject we might as well take the long view and look at our era as academics of the far future will. The five massively popular singers of this century, each associated with a breakthrough in style, have been Al Jolson, Bing Crosby, Frank Sinatra, Elvis Presley and the Beatles. The Fab Four have the edge over the other four because they wrote their own material, and several of their compositions seem certain to survive as has the music which is now called classical.

Of course, this judgment is possible through hindsight. No one would have predicted it just over twenty-five years ago, when John Lennon first played in the Quarrymen, named after the Quarry Bank High School he attended. Nor was the young rowdy's initial meeting with Paul McCartney particularly auspicious. Brought to see the Quarrymen by mutual friend Ivan Vaughan in 1957, McCartney thought 'He's good. That's a good band there.' Taken backstage, Paul thought the sixteen-year-old John smelled a bit drunk . . . but they got along fine. The Eddie Cochran number that brought them together was 'Twenty Flight Rock'. Paul was impressed that John also liked it, and Lennon was knocked out that McCartney could write out all the words. A week later, Paul joined the Quarrymen. He soon introduced them to his friend, George Harrison, a guitar buff who liked rock-and-roll so much that he drew on a false moustache so he could look old enough to get in to see *The Blackboard Jungle*, the film that featured Bill Haley's 'Rock Around The Clock'. The evolution of the Quarrymen into Johnny And the Moondogs, the Silver Beatles, and finally the Beatles, complete with several personnel changes, is best told in Philip Norman's book *Shout!* It's a goldmine for Beatle buffs – their first hit doesn't make the top fifty until page 159!

'Love Me Do' entered the British charts in October, 1962, and ultimately reached number seventeen. Two versions were recorded, one with the recently acquired drummer Ringo Starr and the other with safe session man Andy White. When White drummed, Ringo shook a tambourine. 'Love Me Do' also featured a harmonica solo by John Lennon that had been directly inspired by the playing of Delbert McClinton on Bruce Channel's 'Hey Baby'. They'd been on a concert bill together earlier in the year. The song chosen for the next single had also been inspired by a current hitmaker. 'Please Please Me' had been written in the slow dramatic style of Roy Orbison, but producer George Martin had suggested the group speed it up. When they did play the faster version, Martin agreed to scrap the Mitch Murray composition 'How Do You Do It' which he and publisher Dick James had wanted the Beatles to release. They lengthened the song by repeating the first verse. The producer was so pleased he accepted the first take, saying 'Gentlemen, you have just made your first number one'.

He was right – or almost right, depending on which chart you went by in those days before the British Market Research Bureau. 'Please Please Me' got to either one or two, certainly well enough to call for an album, which was named after the single.

Please Please Me showed the Beatles in transition, beginning to write their own material but still doing American rock and roll favourites. They were not copyists: the original versions hadn't charted in Britain, and the Beatles had needed material to fill the hours of playing they had to do in The Cavern in Liverpool and in German club residencies. They were not revivalists: the Quarrymen had started at the beginning of the rock and roll era, and the voice of John Lennon singing 'Twist And Shout' or 'Money' or the voice of Paul McCartney singing à la Little Richard is the voice of authentic rock and roll at its best.

Not many singers of any kind could vocalise with the commitment and frightening energy John Lennon gave 'Twist And Shout'. Rock historians won't find the track in books of hit singles because it came out on an EP, and EPs had their own lists in 1963. On that table, 'Twist And Shout' did extremely well, and even more importantly, the album it came from, *Please Please Me*, dominated the LP chart that year, spending thirty weeks at number one, eventually eclipsed only by the next Beatles' set.

Here was the revolution of a form of entertainment. Before the Beatles, the best-selling albums were predominantly film soundtracks or original Broadway cast recordings. True, Elvis Presley did break through occasionally, and so did Ricky Nelson in the States and Cliff Richard and the Shadows in Britain. But it was the Beatle blockbusters that brought money to the album share of the market as no rock records had before. Almost overnight, young people bought LPs as they had previously purchased singles. To this day, rock music still rules the LP roost.

The Beatles achieved their massive album sales without hurting their singles figures. Indeed, every piece of plastic fed what quickly became a phenomenon. They began 1963 with 'Please Please Me' and then had a seven-week run at number one with 'From Me To You', the first single to sell a million and a half copies in Britain ('She Loves You'), and the Christmas number one ('I Want To Hold Your Hand'). No artist has dominated British popular music in a single year as the Beatles did in 1963. Yet they were more than pop stars. They were news, regularly appearing in newspapers, magazines and newsreels.

They were a mass cult, subjects of hysterical carryings-on by young women that earned the phrase 'Beatlemania'. And they were cutters of class and age barriers, genuinely appealing to both sexes and all age groups and within the first three years of their success being named Members Of The British Empire and lunching with the Prime Minister, Harold Wilson. In a class-conscious society like Britain's, this was a precedent-setting penetration of the Establishment.

The Beatles feared that they might not succeed in the United States. No British rock singer had. They were also scared that if one act of the Beat Boom they led was going to cross the Atlantic, it might be fellow Liverpudlians Gerry and the Pacemakers, who had also scored three number ones in 1963, indeed, with their first three releases. The Beatles needn't have worried.

Everything they had released in the United States had been dismissed before 'I Want To Hold Your Hand'. A couple of singles actually had received an odd play on radio and the televised *American Bandstand* but none had sold. The only chart version of a Beatle tune had been Del Shannon's cover of 'From Me To You' and that had only crept to number seventy-seven.

The American breakthrough was probably inevitable strictly on the merits of the music. But the form it took was undoubtedly shaped in part by the assassination of President John Kennedy on 22 November 1963. This traumatic tragedy, a constant possibility for world leaders today, was unthinkable then, and the nation's grief was genuine. As if by a gesture of repentance, the Singing Nun became number one for a month. Come the New Year, it was time to shake off the sadness. It is said that one extreme feeling can only be replaced by another. America substituted for its deep sense of loss a passion for the Beatles. 'I Want To Hold Your Hand' made its chart debut in January. Within the month it was number one. Their first February appearance on *The Ed Sullivan Show* drew record viewing figures. What had happened in the UK in 1963 took place in the US in 1964: the Beatles became a national obsession.

Not just a chart craze – although re-releases of their previous discs did give them the top five singles in the United States one week in April, a feat which has never been duplicated. There was merchandising on a scale hitherto unknown, with a range of products never before associated with any show business sensation. Manager Brian Epstein has since been criticised for not winning better deals than he did, but the simple truth is that he could not have foreseen the unforeseeable, and was lucky to get the piece of the action he got.

There were more fundamental changes affected by the Beatles. Men had previously worn their hair short, perhaps in a crew cut. Now the male sex of the Western world let their hair grow, influenced by or in direct emulation of the Beatle haircut that came over the forehead.

There was another major move in 1964. The Beatles became the first rock stars to appear in a critically acclaimed motion picture.

'The new film with those incredible chaps, the Beatles, is a whale of a comedy,' the movie critic of *The New York Times* wrote. 'I wouldn't believe it either if I hadn't seen it with my own astonished eyes.' *A Hard Day's Night*, a black-and-white film made on a limited budget, was an international critical and commercial success less than two years after 'Love Me Do' had crawled into the British chart. The Beatle phenomenon was far-reaching and fast-moving.

One talent they had kept them going when other performers might have been stymied: they wrote their own material, so at least they knew from where the next song was coming. The Beatles were the first fully self-contained rock group: they wrote, sang and played their own material.

Other rock and rollers had required writers, as in the case of Elvis Presley, or a backing band, as with Chuck Berry. The Beatles provided the complete package. But the writing: that was crucial. After the Beatles, the power of Tin Pan Alley was drastically diminished, as it became assumed top artists would compose as well as sing. The solo singer, previously the norm in pop, had to make room for the group, as legions of rockers joined together in guitar-bass and drum ensembles modelled on the Beatles. Even the most contemporary of pop bands are working on a variation of the Beatles' line-up, allowing for the keyboards which Lennon, McCartney or even Billy Preston would sometimes play.

Lennon and McCartney were the outstanding songwriters of the sixties, providing themselves with a flow of first-rate material. 'The greatest composers since Beethoven,' the *Sunday Times* enthused. 'The best songwriters since Schubert,' said another critic.

Those were opinions; this is a statistic: 'Yesterday', penned by McCartney, is the most recorded song in history. The melody of 'Yesterday' occurred to Paul McCartney first thing one morning. He got out of bed and worked out the melody, using the temporary words 'Scrambled egg, how I love a scrambled egg'. It's now had well over a thousand versions, though none under the title 'Scrambled egg'. It originally appeared as an album cut to fill out the soundtrack to the second film, *Help!* Only the Beatles had enough quality material to use a song like 'Yesterday' as an album track. Almost every Beatle track received radio exposure in its time, especially in America. Artists queued to record Lennon and McCartney songs, both when they were writing together and, later, separately. To this day John Lennon has written more British number one hits than anyone else, Paul McCartney the most American number ones. But it must never be assumed that John and Paul were the Beatles, regardless of their great individual talents. George and Ringo added elements of personality which helped give the Beatles all aspects of young manhood in one group.

The Beatles – the unit – was greater than the sum of its parts. They were John, Paul, George *and* Ringo – not *or* – the first and, to this day, the only rock group whose Christian names were all known to all society.

There were other names important in the Beatles story, too, especially Brian Epstein and George Martin. Epstein was the Liverpool record store owner who made several brilliant strokes as their manager, particularly putting them in matching suits and haircuts, to tone down the rebellious streak that might have alienated part of the mass audience. The Rolling

Stones, Bob Dylan, the Who – they all had their audience, but the Beatles belonged to everybody, thanks in no small measure to Brian Epstein. George Martin made his contributions in the studio, embellishing the Beatle compositions with the sounds they told him they wanted to hear but couldn't make themselves. Consider the haunting backing on 'Eleanor Rigby', which remains one of the most astonishing tracks in all of pop, establishing an intense mood and telling a full story in just over two minutes. McCartney had originally called the woman 'Daisy McKenzie', but changed it when he saw a clothing shop named 'Rigby's' in Bristol. McKenzie became the name of the priest.

'Eleanor Rigby' first appeared on the 1966 album *Revolver*, one of the two consecutive masterpieces of the Beatles' so-called 'middle period'. The other was *Rubber Soul*, issued the previous year. They are both showcases for the possibilities of pop: John's reflective memoir, 'In My Life', Paul's beautiful ballad, 'Here There And Everywhere', the universally appealing children's song 'Yellow Submarine', John's anticipation of psychedelia, 'Tomorrow Never Knows', and Paul's ultra-commercial 'Michelle'. It is certainly impossible to single out one Beatles' album by chart position reached, since every studio LP they ever made was a number one. No other major act that made more than one record can make that claim. But these two packages are certainly peerless celebrations of rock music, the Beatles' greatness indicated by their seemingly effortless mastery of several styles.

In 1967 the Beatles released what are generally considered the finest single and the best album of all-time. The 45 was issued in February to placate the fans who were waiting for the next LP. There had not been a gap between Beatle albums as long as the ten months that separated *Revolver* and its successor.

By now McCartney and Lennon were writing many of their songs alone. On the single they each sang about Liverpool in a vastly different but equally brilliant way. Paul remembered 'Penny Lane'; John longed for 'Strawberry Fields Forever'.

The two numbers each made perfectly ordinary parts of Liverpool seem to be magical places of wonder, proof that the feeling that goes into a song is more vital to its impact than its actual subject. Both tracks gave evidence of the experimentation the two men favoured. McCartney tended to go for new musical sounds, as he had with 'Yesterday', 'Eleanor Rigby', and 'For No One'. Lennon went for studio effects – the feedback at the start of 'I Feel Fine', the first use of guitar feedback by a major artist, the reversed tape that served as the end of 'Rain', the varispeed vocal on 'Strawberry Fields Forever', which came courtesy of George Martin. Then there was George Harrison's idea of ending 'She Loves You' on a sixth chord, and the unusual intervals used in the highly segmented 'Paperback Writer'. The Beatles made some radically experimental music, but people weren't conscious of it at the time because it was also incredibly commercial. They made the studio an instrument, inspiring countless others to try to make the most of its possibilities.

They certainly did so with their 1967 magnum opus, *Sgt Pepper's Lonely Hearts Club Band*. As befitted the Beatles, it was the ultimate offering of the summer of love. The title tune began and almost ended the work and because much of the subject matter seemed inspired by music hall and carnival characters, *Sgt Pepper* became known as the first 'concept album'. Many followed, quite a few lacking their model's wit and variety, and all without the dramatic power of 'A Day In The Life', *Sgt Pepper's* last track. It wasn't a coda or an afterthought, it was simply too daring and distinct to put anywhere but the end.

Ten years after it was issued, *Sgt Pepper* was voted the best rock album of all-time by an international panel of critics. In another sense, too, it was the Beatles' peak. *Sgt Pepper* and the single that followed it, 'All You Need Is Love', marked the last occasions the Beatles took the world with them as a unit. Millions hopped on the psychedelic bandwagon the Fab Four were simultaneously riding and leading.

The advocacy of peace and love, the rather obvious use of drugs, the donning of colourful costumes, the incorporation of Indian music meditation – young people around the world sampled them all. Some reined themselves in, some delved further into the fields. So it was with the Beatles. Without the restraining influence of Brian Epstein, who died that summer, the now grown men led their own lives.

John concentrated on his highly publicised personal and musical partnership with Yoko Ono. George won attention for his student–teacher relationship with Ravi Shankar, and praise for his work with Eric Clapton. It wasn't easy for him to revert to being the young one in a group dominated by Paul, who more than anyone else was desperately trying to save the world's most popular attraction.

The Beatles' 1968 work is clearly divisible into the efforts of individual members. The eponymous double LP, which became known as *The White Album*, had many marvellous moments, but they were obviously

John's or Paul's or George's. Similarly, that autumn's single, which launched the group's Apple Label, is in retrospect one side John's 'Revolution', and the A-side Paul's, 'Hey Jude', originally conceived as a song for Julian Lennon, John's son, with the 'Hey Jules' changed to 'Hey Jude'. The gesture showed that even though working separately the men were still friends, and Paul was pleased that John and Yoko considered the song wonderfully avant garde. At the time, it was: the words are often opaque or nonsensical, the song ends on a chant, and it was the longest number one ever. 'Hey Jude' was number one in America for nine weeks, the Beatles' longest chart-topping run. It was one of the group's seventeen UK and twenty US number ones (more tracks were released as singles in the States). No act has ever had more number ones in either country.

The lasting memory of 'Hey Jude' is the promotional clip, shown on *The David Frost Show* in Britain and *The Smothers Brothers* in America. The group are surrounded by a motley group of everyday Britons, almost a cross-section of society, all of them singing along. That image sums up the Beatles better than any other film or photograph.

Certainly better than this next feature film. *Get Back* was to be the title of an album that would return the Beatles to their roots. Instead, it was a half-hearted effort filmed for a documentary that turned out to be the record of their disintegration. The album and motion picture were called *Let It Be*; 'Get Back' survived as a single which revealed that even in their death throes the Beatles could still cut it. *Let It Be* was the last album put out by the Beatles. Between its recording and release, held up to await editing of the movie, *Abbey Road* was made and issued.

It was a glorious goodbye. They pretty much knew it: the last song listed on the label was 'The End'. But John Lennon agreed not to speak of his decision to leave the group, and it wasn't until the spring of 1970 that Paul McCartney told the world press the Beatles had disbanded.

Those who have maintained a vigil ever since waiting patiently for 'the next Beatles' are probably looking in the wrong direction. There will certainly again be consistently excellent songwriters and perhaps even an artist who will have seventeen number ones to match the Beatles and Elvis Presley. But that act will not be a rock group. It won't be because it can't be. The Beatles drew the boundaries they worked within; no one staying inside those boundaries can possibly duplicate their impact. The next 'big thing' will have to be inventive in a new area, perhaps video.

It is only someone working in the most popular field of the moment turning out quality work quickly who can affect society as the Beatles did. The work of any major artist has a context. The Beatles' context was the sixties, not the seventies. They were part of a time when youth had just discovered a voice in rock and roll. A whole culture shaped by economic affluence and political circumstances built up around that voice, which the Beatles spoke with the greatest clarity. They came to stand for the very world they were part of, and thus became personally vital to millions.

The Beatles were creatures of the sixties, four men together, not part of the seventies, a decade of self-analysis and self-fulfilment. The Beatles flourished in good economic times, not depression. They were part of an era where it was thought music and love could make anything possible, not a decade with a punk philosophy. The Beatles could not have been part of a world that said 'no'. The Beatles said 'yeah yeah yeah'.

ELVIS PRESLEY

His first nickname was the Hillbilly Cat. He was the hippest cat country music had ever known. His second nickname was The Pelvis, the mass media's reference to his then-scandalous stage movements. I like his third nickname best – The King. After all, he was the single most important figure in rock and roll, and even after his death, Elvis Presley is still The King.

Without ever giving evidence of a commitment to culture, popular or classical, and without ever showing he truly understood the nature of his gifts, Elvis Presley affected mass audience art more than any other individual since World War II. It is this near contradiction that has so infuriated both those who hate rock and roll and those who love it so intensely they resent those who squander their talent. How dare a hick from East Tupelo, Mississippi, be the walking synthesis of country and western and rhythm and blues, make the best series of records ever made in the new rock and roll style, then leave the world stuck with second-rate imitators while he himself went off to make an appalling series of films and more than a few discs that weren't much better?

It was easy for Elvis. He just did what he naturally wanted to do. Some of that was brilliant, some banal. Until he started recording in 1954, his life had been completely undistinguished. Born on 8 January 1935, to a man Elvis himself later described as a 'common labourer', the young Presley grew up devoted to his mother and inhabited by the curious thought that he might have incorporated the qualities of his twin brother Jesse, who died at birth.

When Elvis was thirteen, the family moved to Memphis. The three worshipped together, and Elvis later said 'Since I was two years old all I knew was gospel music. We borrowed the style of our psalm singing from Negroes.' The boy heard black music from another source. He would sit in the cab of the truck his father drove and listen to the blues on the radio. Station WDIA was pumping out Negro music to metropolitan Memphis.

Two of the DJs, B.B. King and Rufus Thomas, became recording stars, making early discs at Sam Philips' Sun Studios. It was there that Elvis Presley went in 1953. For four dollars he made a record of two Inkspots songs to give to his mother. One shudders to think what it would be worth now if it still exists.

The following year Presley returned to Sun. This time Sam Philips remembered him, and subsequently called him back to the studio. He got nowhere trying ballads, the first of which was 'I Love You Because'. Then during a break he started singing a favourite of his by another hero, blues singer Arthur Crudup. Philips was like a dog hearing a high frequency whistle. This was what he had been looking for. He had often told his secretary, 'If I could find a white boy who could sing like a Negro, I could make a million dollars.' He had found him.

'That's Alright Mama' was the first example of the sound which would revolutionise popular music. It was recorded by Elvis Presley with western swing guitarist Scotty Moore and string bassist Bill Black, who discovered they had a similar sense of rhythm. This was crucial to Presley's success, for rhythm was one of the main elements he intuitively gave a song. The other was, to be blunt, sex, and to be polite, a sense of physical presence. Elvis took an existing composition (he did not write his own) and breathed urgency into it. His early records all seemed vital, no matter how trite the lyrics.

Albert Goldman, who authored a debunking biography of Elvis, nonetheless gave full marks to the initial Sun efforts, and credited Sam Philips with a vital contribution to Presley's success, not just in steering him towards r & b material, but by enhancing his voice with an echo that made it sound even more extraordinary. Philips was also shrewd in guiding the boys to put a country number, 'Blue Moon of Kentucky', on the B-side. This way the nineteen-year-old Presley was offering the gamut of southern American music.

Memphis DJ Dewey Philips played both sides immediately, to enthusiastic response. But becoming a local star was a far cry from making it nationally. Presley toured the Southland for a year before he earned his first American number one, and that was on the country and western chart. His 1955 c & w chart-topper was 'I Forgot To Remember To Forget'.

Elvis Presley was winning airplay on southern stations, but not cracking the Mason-Dixon Line that separates the North from Dixie. Some programmers said he sounded too black to broadcast, others that he was too white to sing r & b. His greatest success was in live performance, where his originally unconscious leg movements wowed the women and where his tough image got the guys. It was all derivative: he got the hair-do from a Tony Curtis movie, the sideburns from Rudolph Valentino, and the hard look because he had originally idolised truck drivers, even briefly becoming one. He thought truck drivers were, as he put it, 'real wild'. But although all the elements came from other sources, their compound, like his musical fusion, was distinctly Presley's.

For all his impact in concert, the Hillbilly Cat still hadn't registered an entry in the pop chart, and when RCA offered Sam Philips 35,000 dollars for Elvis' contract, plus 5,000 in back royalties for the artist himself, the Sun Records boss let his protégé go. It sounds like peanuts now, but in those days it was a lot of money. Atlantic Records, which just failed to match the bid, has always said their decision was reasonable at the time. Philips has always defended selling Elvis' contract because he needed the funds to launch his other artists, who ultimately included Johnny Cash, Jerry Lee Lewis, Carl Perkins, Charlie Rich and Roy Orbison. Even without Elvis, Sam Philips' contribution to rock and roll would be enormous. RCA struck gold. Even they could not have known how well Elvis was about to do. His very first single for them was number one in America for seven weeks in the spring of 1956.

'Heartbreak Hotel' had been co-written by publicist Mae Axton, mother of Hoyt Axton, and Tommy Durden, who had been haunted by an anonymous suicide's farewell note, 'I walk a lonely street'. They offered it to Presley, with the inducement that they'd credit him as the third writer if he'd record it on RCA. According to Albert Goldman, Presley copied the demo version by Glen Reeves, who himself had been duplicating Elvis' style.

'Heartbreak Hotel' was already one step removed from Presley's Sun recordings, which had seemed to flow naturally from him. This single was consciously hysterical, but that didn't lessen its impact on the public. Ever since Bill Haley had gone to number one with 'Rock Around The Clock' nearly a year before, it was obvious that some good-looking white youth who could sing rock and roll was going to be a teenage idol. It had all been set up: by DJs like Alan Freed, who had played the new music to white kids, by black rock and roll artists like Chuck Berry, Fats Domino and Little Richard, who had already charted in 1955, and by Haley, who had shown a white man could succeed with black rhythmic influence.

When Bill Randle, who had been the first Northern DJ to push Presley, introduced Presley to television on the Dorsey Brothers' *Stage Show*, he compared the reaction of his Cleveland radio listeners to the mania that had surrounded Johnny Ray five years earlier. Ray, who had borne the bizarre nickname The Nabob of Sob, had been popular music's last great heart-throb, sending women into fits by weeping on stage while singing 'Cry' and 'The Little White Cloud That Cried'. His act was remarkably tame compared to that of the openly sensual Presley, but at the time it was the best analogy Bill Randle could make. The point was that, as with Johnny Ray and Frank Sinatra before him, there was something about Elvis Presley that deeply affected his audience.

Seventeen Presley titles charted in 1956. He had not arrived on the scene, he had exploded, and not just at home in the States, but internationally. To have Elvis record one of your songs was a writer's dream. Mike Stoller recalled how when he arrived safely in New York City, having been rescued from the sinking Italian liner *Andrea Doria*, his partner Jerry Leiber greeted him at dockside not with a remark about the tragedy but with the news 'Elvis Presley's recorded "Hound Dog"! Elvis Presley's recorded "Hound Dog"!'

He had indeed, having heard the song as performed by Freddy Bell and the Bellhops, hence the different lyrics from the original r & b hit by 'Big Mama' Thornton. When Elvis sang the number on the *Steve Allen* show, he was forced to do so dressed in formal wear singing to the bust of a dog. It was typical of the entertainment establishment that it didn't take Presley seriously. Why should it? Popular culture had previously been white and monolithic, with the same heroes for all age groups. Now suddenly teenagers generated their own sub-culture, with heroes like Marlon Brando and James Dean, and their focal figure was Elvis Presley. The adult world did take this phenomenon seriously when it recognised the economic consequences – that teenagers would spend fortunes on their own favourite fashions, records, and motor vehicles.

Elvis Presley dominated the music business so thoroughly that 'Hound Dog', a number two, wasn't the biggest hit on RCA 6604. The other side, 'Don't Be Cruel', was number one for seven weeks.

'Don't Be Cruel' was written by Otis Blackwell, a black man who penned several rock and roll classics, including 'Great Balls Of Fire', a British number one for Jerry Lee Lewis, and 'All Shook Up', Presley's first UK chart-topper. But though Blackwell did all the work on 'Don't Be Cruel', Elvis again got a co-writer credit, the price Otis paid to have his song recorded. Presley's manager, the self-styled 'Colonel' Tom

Parker, usually made the extra profit more subtly, requiring that numbers Elvis cut had publishing rights assigned to his company. Mike Stoller shrugged when asked about this, saying that the bonus sales one got from having a tune recorded by Elvis Presley more than made up for any loss in publishing.

While 'Don't Be Cruel' and 'Hound Dog' were in the charts, Presley made his first appearance on the *Ed Sullivan Show*. The legendary variety show host had been furious when Steve Allen, his rival on another network, had won a higher viewing figure with the rock and roller. Sullivan had banned the new music when Bo Diddley had refused to sing all of 'Some Enchanted Evening', the respectable song he'd been ordered to perform, and instead broke into his hit 'Bo Diddley', completely confusing the orchestra and causing chaos on live coast-to-coast television. Now that he'd been caught out by Steve Allen, Sullivan plotted revenge, signed Presley for three appearances at a record sum, and, according to biographer Jerry Bowles, ordered his cameraman to shoot the hip-shaking star from the waist up. He then informed the press he would be presenting America's hottest musical star and protecting the nation's morals. It was front page news, and the 9 September programme won what was then an unprecedented rating. Sullivan's stroke of public relations genius was so effective that many people think that Elvis made his TV debut on the show, and that all Presley's early appearances were censored.

The renegade rocker sang a ballad on the Sullivan Show that provoked such an extraordinary viewer response that RCA rush-released a single and Twentieth Century Fox changed the name of Elvis' forthcoming first film, *The Reno Brothers*, to the title of the tune, 'Love Me Tender'.

The record was number one during the autumn of 1956. The backing vocalists were the Mello Men, who this one time replaced the Jordannaires, who sang on most of Elvis' sessions for fourteen years.

It had been a historic twelve months. Unknown at the beginning of the year, Elvis Presley had scored the number one single in eighteen of its last thirty-eight weeks. He returned home to Memphis that December a hero, and when visiting Sam Philips' studio got into a jam session with Carl Perkins, whose 'Blue Suede Shoes' he had successfully covered, and Jerry Lee Lewis, who had just made his first 45. Johnny Cash joined them around the piano for a photograph, but then went shopping. For years, fans wondered what the so-called Million Dollar Quartet (or Trio) had sung. The answer came at last in 1981: they'd worked on informal versions of predominantly religious material, including 'Just A Little Talk With Jesus', 'I Shall Not Be Moved', and 'Peace In The Valley'.

The Sun super-session was all for fun and recorded by Sam Philips merely for interest and posterity. It wasn't of professional recording quality. But it does seem to have affected Elvis' career. Up to that point he had not cut any gospel material. The next month he sang 'Peace In The Valley' on the Sullivan Show and recorded the song as the lead track on a religious EP. That made the top forty of the Hot 100 and began an occasional series of inspirational platters. Elvis was devoutly religious; his sincerity of feeling came across on these recordings long after his rock material acquired an air of self-parody.

Nonetheless, 'Peace In The Valley' was part of the process of taming Elvis Presley. He had been the most outrageous major star of the century. By presenting him as a young freak instead of an important artist, television diluted his image. Elvis himself softened his impact by broadening his blues base with conventional pop, like 'Don't Be Cruel', and ballads, like 'Love Me Tender'. Both he and manager Parker completed the humanising of the demon by starring him in over thirty simple-minded motion pictures. Elvis longed to be a film star, at least as much as he wanted to make hit records, and in this way he shared the misconception of Barbra Streisand, failing to make the most of a great vocal gift and devoting a major share of energy to a never-ending Hollywood ego trip. The best moments in his movies came early on, when he still embodied qualities of animal magnetism. No one who has seen *Loving You* can forget the breathtaking moment when he leaps from the stage into a live audience and makes a series of movements rivalling the best ballet. To this day this type of whirling, thrusting, dipping action remains the model for rock and roll singers, including, of course, Shakin' Stevens. Ironically, after his mother died in 1958, Elvis himself never watched the scene, for both his parents had been seated in the audience as extras, and he could not bear the sight.

Two other films which respected Presley's abilities were *King Creole* and *Jailhouse Rock*. The greatest factor in their success was that they contained songs by Leiber and Stoller. 'Jailhouse Rock' was a massive international number one, and the dance sequence accompanying the title tune Elvis' best-remembered movie scene. He did his own choreography on the number, which stands as a bittersweet reminder of what his films could have achieved. Jerry Leiber didn't think it was as fully-realised as the other Leiber–Stoller prison piece, 'Riot In Cell Block Number Nine' by the Robins. 'Not surprisingly,' he told Charlie Gillett for the book *Making Tracks*, 'since in the film we had to deal with the contradiction of having a fifty-piece orchestra playing offstage. It's harder to capture a prison atmosphere in those conditions.'

'Jailhouse Rock' was the last of the great Presley singles released before he was inducted into the United States Army in 1958. There were more hits, including the touching 'Don't' and the frantic 'Wear My Ring Around Your Neck', but they weren't quite of the same standard. When Elvis emerged from the forces in 1960, he was a totally different artist. 'Elvis died the day he went into the Army,' John Lennon remarked in retrospect, and in terms of relevance to rock and roll he was right. The great rebel was tamed to become a lasting family entertainer.

'It's Now Or Never' was based on the well-known Italian song 'O Sole Mio'. The American writers Wally Gold and Aaron Schroeder gave the standard a new lyric and Elvis Presley had the biggest hit of his career, with total sales well in excess of ten million. It spent eight weeks at number one in the UK, his longest run at the top, and began an amazing sequence of nine number ones in ten tries. Elvis accumulated seventeen British chart-toppers in all, a total equalled only by the Beatles. Musically, 'It's Now Or Never' was drastically different from the artist's earlier sound. Manager Parker was steering him towards the middle of the road, a trend dramatically demonstrated by having his client make his comeback television appearance on a Frank Sinatra television special. The next single was even further proof that the sixties Elvis, in contrast to his fifties counterpart, would be a man for all audiences. 'Are You Lonesome Tonight' didn't match the phenomenal sales of 'It's Now Or Never', but still sold a remarkable four million copies. The narration in the middle was a successful use of the spoken technique that had not worked on 'I Love You Because' in the Sun Studio in 1954.

The next British number one, 'Wooden Heart', was a curiosity. It came from the film *G.I. Blues* and because of its partly German lyric was not issued as a single in the United States. It nonetheless sold a million in Europe alone. It was co-written by Bert Kaemphert, who by also being the first record company executive to sign the Beatles and by co-writing 'Strangers In The Night', the number one by Frank Sinatra, could claim to be the only man intimately involved with the three most important recording acts of the last half century.

Just because Elvis' version of 'Wooden Heart' wasn't released in the States didn't mean the song wasn't a hit. An eighteen-year-old American named Joe Dowell covered it and went to number one, but Elvis had little to regret. The week it was on top, one of Presley's best sixties singles entered the Hot 100. 'Little Sister' and its flip side, 'His Latest Flame', were both top five hits in the United States. Though Elvis Presley was no longer innovating, he was making good records and remaining the world's top recording artist.

Even this reputation was to fade. The Beatles swept Britain in 1963 and America in '64, and almost everything that had happened before them seemed ancient history. Presley hastened his own decline by making his worst records and worst movies, discs like 'Do The Clam' and films like *Tickle Me*. Between 1964 and 1968, his only great hit was 'Crying In The Chapel', and that had been recorded in 1960. Just when he had been written off as an embarrassing relic of another era, tolerated only because his historic contributions could never be diminished, Elvis Presley made something of a return to form. Perhaps it was pride. Just as likely it was the realisation that the money wasn't coming in quite like it once did. He appeared before a live audience for the first time in a dozen years for a network television special, dressing in leathers to perform some of his greatest hits. 'If I Can Dream', the show's finale, was a plea for racial tolerance that brought him back to prominence. The ballad 'In The Ghetto' restored him to the top three in both America and Britain, and 'Suspicious Minds', one of his very finest efforts, was deservedly his first US number one in seven years.

'Suspicious Minds' was one of a string of fine singles cut in Memphis. Elvis hadn't recorded there in nearly fourteen years. The recovery was short-lived. Barring the occasional strong song like 'Burning Love', Elvis' output in the seventies was mediocre. He became so uncaring about his craft that he sang cover versions of records he liked, such as Dusty Springfield's 'You Don't Have To Say You Love Me' and B.J. Thomas' 'I Just Can't Help Believing'. His versions were usually inferior to the originals. That Elvis Presley, the first and greatest hero of rock and roll, should be reduced to second-rate re-readings of his successor's successes bothered him not one bit. It certainly did not bother 'Colonel' Parker, actually a Dutchman who kept his background a secret and a businessman who never showed interest in stretching Elvis to the limits he might have reached as an artist.

The King of Rock and Roll's sad physical decline in the seventies has been well-documented. Drugs, junk food and bad habits all contributed to his deterioration. He died early but wrecked at the age of forty-two. At the time of his death he had a record in the charts. At least it was a good one.

'Way Down' soared to number one in Britain and eight former hits re-entered the top fifty. Mourners pilgrimaged to the gates of Graceland, his Memphis residence. Souvenir vendors and tasteless merchandisers turned a tragic occasion into a tacky one.

Stories came out of Presley's personal inadequacies, of his misuse of the personal power and social responsibility with which he had been entrusted. They were no doubt true. It is sad that Elvis was not a paragon of virtue.

But this is not what record buyers care about. As Berry Gordy Jr said about his record company, it's what's in the grooves that counts. Elvis Presley records, specifically those of his first few years, had it where it counted, in the grooves that capture performance – in his case, the most exciting performances of a generation. Though he was in many ways derivative, he was an original, moulding existing forms into a new product and forcing an entire generation to follow him.

I could have started this series with the King, but I have chosen to end it with him. When it comes to rock and roll, Elvis Presley had the first word, and he is the last word.

Picture credits

Page 18 Bob Sorce LFI; Page 50, 58, 66, 74, 90, 170, 194, 212, Rex Features; Page 100 CBS; Page 108 LFI; Page 124 SKR Photos/LFI; Page 143 Atlantic Records; Page 152 Columbia Records; Page 160 LFI; Page 178 Warner Brothers.